LSAT®
THE OFFICIAL TRIPLE·PREP PLUS
With Explanations

From the producers of the LSAT

"The most noted authority in legal publications." — *Choice*

A   P U B L I C A T I O N   O F

LAW SCHOOL ADMISSION COUNCIL

Contains three complete *Official PrepTests*—XI (June 1994 LSAT), XII (October 1994 LSAT), XIII (December 1994 LSAT)

The Law School Admission Council

The Law School Admission Council (LSAC or Law Services) is a nonprofit corporation whose members are 192 law schools in the United States and Canada. It was founded in 1947 to coordinate, facilitate, and enhance the law school admission process. All law schools approved by the American Bar Association (ABA) are LSAC members. Canadian law schools recognized by a provincial or territorial law society or government agency also are included in the voting membership of the Council.

This book contains information about all of the services provided by Law Services including:

- Law School Admission Test (LSAT);

- Law School Data Assembly Service (LSDAS);

- Candidate Referral Service (CRS); and

- Publications related to legal education.

The LSAT, LSDAS, and CRS are provided to assist law schools in serving and evaluating applicants. Law Services does not engage in assessing an applicant's chances for admission to any law school; all admission decisions are made by individual schools.

The Law School Admission Council provides services for both the law schools and their candidates for admission. Last year, Law Services administered 132,000 LSATs, processed 186,600 transcripts and 449,000 law school report requests resulting in the production of 547,900 law school reports.

■ The Law School Admission Test (LSAT)

The Law School Admission Test is a half-day standardized test required for admission to all 192 LSAC-member law schools. It consists of five 35-minute sections of multiple-choice questions. Four of the five sections contribute to the test taker's score. These sections include one reading comprehension section, one analytical reasoning section, and two logical reasoning sections. The fifth section typically is used to pretest new test items and to preequate new test forms. A 30-minute writing sample is administered at the end of the test. The writing sample is not scored by Law Services; however, copies of the writing sample are sent to all law schools to which you apply. Explanations of the three LSAT question types are found beginning on page 3. The score scale for the LSAT is 120 to 180, with 120 being the lowest possible score and 180 the highest possible score.

The LSAT is designed to measure skills that are considered essential for success in law school: the reading and comprehension of complex texts with accuracy and insight; the organization and management of information and the ability to draw reasonable inferences from it; the ability to reason critically; and the analysis and evaluation of the reasoning and argument of others.

The LSAT provides a standard measure of acquired reading and verbal reasoning skills that law schools can use as one of several factors in assessing applicants.

■ Scoring

Your LSAT score is based on the number of questions you answer correctly (the raw score). There is no deduction for incorrect answers, and all questions count equally. In other words, there is no penalty for guessing.

LSAT Scores as Predictors of Law School Performance

Over the years, the vast majority of law schools have participated in Law School Admission Council validity studies that compare students' LSAT scores with their first-year grades in law school. Although the correlations between test scores and grades are not perfect, the studies show that LSAT scores help to predict which students will do well in law school. Moreover, a combination of students' scores and undergraduate grade-point averages (GPAs) gives a better prediction than either the LSAT or the GPA alone.

Correlation is stated as a coefficient for which 1.00 indicates an exact correspondence between candidates' test scores and subsequent law school performance. A coefficient of zero would indicate nothing more than a coincidental relationship between test scores and subsequent performance. The closer to 1.00 the correlation coefficient is, the greater the test's predictive validity. In other words, the closer to 1.00 the correlation coefficient is, the less chance there will be of candidates with high LSAT scores failing in their studies or candidates with low test scores performing at the top of their law school class.

The correlation between LSAT scores and first-year law school grades varies from one law school to another (as does the correlation between GPA and first-year law school grades). During 1992, validity studies were conducted for 180 LSAC-member law schools. Correlations between LSAT scores and first-year law school grades ranged from .13 to .63 (median is .42). Correlations between LSAT scores combined with undergraduate grade-point averages and first-year law school grades ranged from .25 to .68 (median is .50).

The LSAT, like any aptitude test, is not a perfect predictor of law school performance. The predictive power of an admission test is ultimately limited by many factors, such as the complexity of the skills the test is designed to measure, the imperfections in the variable the test tries to predict (i.e., law schools using different measures to assess law school performance), and the unmeasurable factors that can affect students' performances (i.e., motivation, physical and mental health, or work and family responsibilities). In spite of these factors, the LSAT compares very favorably with admission tests used in other graduate and professional fields of study.

■ Test Score Accuracy—Reliability and Standard Error of Measurement

Reliability is a measure of how consistently a test measures the skills under investigation. The higher the reliability coefficient for a test, the more certain we can be that test takers would get very similar scores if they took the test again.

LSAC reports an internal consistency measure of reliability for every test form which can vary from 0.00 to 1.00. A test with no measurement error would have a reliability coefficient of 1.00 (never attained in practice). Reliability coefficients for past LSAT forms have ranged from .90 to .95, indicating a high degree of consistency for these tests. LSAC expects the reliability to continue to fall within the same range.

The LSAT, like any standardized test, is not a perfect measuring instrument. One way to quantify measurement error is through calculation of the **standard error of measurement**. The standard error of measurement provides an estimate of the error that is present in a test score because of the imperfect nature of the tests.

The standard error of measurement for the LSAT is reported to score users following each administration of the test. The chances are approximately two out of three that a score obtained by a test taker will lie within a range from one standard error of measurement below to one standard error of measurement above his or her true score. The true score is the score that a test taker would have obtained if the

test contained no measurement error. About 95 percent of the test takers will have test scores that fall within two standard errors of measurement of their true scores. The standard error of measurement for LSAT forms tends to be approximately 2.6.

Measurement error also must be taken into account when comparing LSAT scores of two test takers. It is likely that small differences in scores are due to measurement error rather than to meaningful differences in ability. The standard error of score differences provides some guidance as to the importance of differences between two scores. The standard error of score differences is approximately 1.4 times as large as the standard error of measurement for the individual scores.

Thus, a test score should be regarded as a useful but approximate measure of a candidate's abilities as measured by the test, not as an exact determination of his or her standing. LSAC encourages law schools to examine the range of scores within the interval that probably contains the examinee's true score rather than solely interpret the reported score alone.

■ Adjustments for Variation in Test Difficulty

All test forms of the LSAT reported on the same score scale are designed to measure the same abilities, but one test form may be slightly easier or more difficult than another. The scores from different test forms are made comparable through a statistical procedure known as equating. As a result of equating, a given scaled score earned on different test forms reflects the same level of ability.

■ Research on the LSAT

Summaries of LSAT validity studies and other LSAT research can be found in member law school libraries.

Preparing for the LSAT

In preparing to take the LSAT, you should familiarize yourself with test directions, test mechanics, and question types. Law Services believes that one valuable form of preparation is taking a sample test under timed conditions. Although it is impossible to say when you are sufficiently prepared for the LSAT, very few people achieve their full potential without preparing at all.

The five sections of the test contain three different question types. The following materials presents a general discussion of the nature of each question type and some strategies that can be used in answering them. It also includes the directions for each question type and selected questions from PrepTest XI with a discussion of the answers.

When possible, explanations of the selected questions indicate their comparative level of difficulty.

The following descriptive materials reflect the general nature of the test. It is not possible or practical to cover the full range of variation that may be found in questions on the LSAT. Be aware that material may appear in the test that is not described in the discussion of question type found here. For additional practice, you can purchase *The Official LSAT PrepTests*, and *LSAT: The Official TriplePrep—Volume 1, 2, or 3,* listed on the publications order form at the end of this book.

The Three LSAT Question Types

■ Reading Comprehension Questions

The purpose of reading comprehension questions is to measure your ability to read, with understanding and insight, examples of lengthy and complex materials similar to those commonly encountered in law school work. The reading comprehension section of the test consists of four passages, each approximately 450 words long, followed by five to eight questions that test the candidate's reading and reasoning abilities. Passages for reading comprehension items draw from a variety of subjects—including the humanities, the social sciences, the physical sciences, ethics, philosophy, and the law.

Reading comprehension questions require test takers to read carefully and accurately, to determine the relationships among the various parts of the passage, and to draw reasonable inferences from the material in the passage. The questions may ask about:

- the main idea or primary purpose of the passage;

- the meaning or purpose of words or phrases used in the passage;

- information explicitly stated in the passage;

- information or ideas that can be inferred from the passage;

- the organization of the passage;

- the application of information in the passage to a new context; and

- the tone of the passage or the author's attitude as it is revealed in the language used.

Suggested Approach

Since passages are drawn from many different disciplines and sources, you should not be discouraged if you encounter material with which you are not familiar. It is important to remember that questions are to be answered on the basis of the information provided in the passage. There is no particular knowledge that you are expected to bring to the test, and you should not make inferences based on any prior knowledge of a subject that you may have. You may, however, wish to defer working on a passage that seems particularly difficult or unfamiliar until after you have dealt with passages you find easier.

Strategies. In preparing for the test, you should experiment with different strategies, and decide which work most effectively for you. These include:

- reading the passage very closely and then answering the questions;

- reading the questions first, reading the passage closely, and then returning to the questions; and

- skimming the passage and questions very quickly, then rereading the passage closely and answering the questions.

Remember that your strategy must be effective under timed conditions.

Reading the passage. Whatever strategy you choose, you should give the passage at least one careful reading before answering the questions. Separate main ideas from supporting ideas and the author's own ideas or attitudes from factual, objective information. Note transitions from one idea to the next and examine the relationships among the different ideas or parts of the passage. For example, are they contrasting or complementary? Consider how and why the author makes points and draws conclusions. Be sensitive to the implications of what the passage says.

You may find it helpful to mark key parts of the passage. For example, you might underline main ideas or important arguments, and you might circle transitional words— 'although,' 'nevertheless,' 'correspondingly,' and the like—that will help you map the structure of the passage. Moreover, you might note descriptive words that will help you identify the author's attitude toward a particular idea or person.

Answering the Questions

- Always read all the answer choices before selecting the best answer. The best answer choice is the one that most accurately and completely answers the question being posed.

- Respond to the specific question being asked. Do not pick an answer choice simply because it is a true statement. For example, picking a true statement might yield an incorrect answer to a question in which you are asked to identify the author's position on an issue, since here you are not being asked to evaluate the truth of the author's position, but only to identify correctly what that position is.

- Answer the questions only on the basis of the information provided in the passage. Your own views, interpretations, or opinions, and those you have heard from others, may sometimes conflict with those expressed in the passage; however, you are expected to work within the context provided by the passage. You should not expect to agree with everything you encounter in reading comprehension passages.

Ten Reading Comprehension Questions from PrepTest XI and Explanations

The questions on the following pages have been selected from the Reading Comprehension section of PrepTest XI (Section 3, pages 50-57). While each passage here is followed by only three or four questions, each passage in PrepTest XI is followed by five to eight questions. **If you wish to answer these questions before reading explanations for them, you should skip this section and return to it after you have completed your practice on Section 3 of PrepTest XI.**

Directions: Each passage in this section is followed by a group of questions to be answered on the basis of what is stated or implied in the passage. For some questions, more than one of the choices could conceivably answer the question. However, you are to choose the best answer; that is, the response that most accurately and completely answers the question, and blacken the corresponding space on your answer sheet.

In *Democracy and its Critics*, Robert Dahl defends both democratic values and pluralist democracies, or polyarchies (a rough shorthand term for Western political systems). Dahl argues
(5) convincingly that the idea of democracy rests on political equality—the equal capacity of all citizens to determine or influence collective decisions. Of course, as Dahl recognizes, if hierarchical ordering is inevitable in any structure of government, and if
(10) no society can guarantee perfect equality in the resources that may give rise to political influence, the democratic principle of political equality is incapable of full realization. So actual systems can be deemed democratic only as approximations to
(15) the ideal. It is on these grounds that Dahl defends polyarchy.

As a representative system in which elected officials both determine government policy and are accountable to a broad-based electorate, polyarchy
(20) reinforces a diffusion of power away from any single center and toward a variety of individuals, groups, and organizations. It is this centrifugal characteristic, Dahl argues, that makes polyarchy the nearest possible approximation to the democratic
(25) ideal. Polyarchy achieves this diffusion of power through party competition and the operation of pressure groups. Competing for votes, parties seek to offer different sections of the electorate what they most want; they do not ask what the majority
(30) thinks of an issue, but what policy commitments will sway the electoral decisions of particular groups. Equally, groups that have strong feelings about an issue can organize in pressure groups to influence public policy.
(35) During the 1960s and 1970s, criticism of the theory of pluralist democracy was vigorous. Many critics pointed to a gap between the model and the reality of Western political systems. They argued that the distribution of power resources other than
(40) the vote was so uneven that the political order systematically gave added weight to those who were already richer or organizationally more powerful. So the power of some groups to exclude issues altogether from the political agenda effectively
(45) countered any diffusion of influence on decision-making.

Although such criticism became subdued during the 1980s, Dahl himself seems to support some of the earlier criticism. Although he regrets that some
(50) Western intellectuals demand more democracy from polyarchies than is possible, and is cautious about the possibility of further democratization, he nevertheless ends his book by asking what changes in structures and consciousness might make political
(55) life more democratic in present polyarchies. One answer, he suggests, is to look at the economic order of polyarchies from the point of view of the citizen as well as from that of producers and consumers. This would require a critical examination
(60) of both the distribution of those economic resources that are at the same time political resources, and the relationship between political structures and economic enterprises.

Question 9, Section 3, page 52

9.   In the third paragraph, the author of the passage refers to criticism of the theory of pluralist democracy primarily in order to

(A)   refute Dahl's statement that Western intellectuals expect more democracy from polyarchies than is possible

(B)   advocate the need for rethinking the basic principles on which the theory of democracy rests

(C)   suggest that the structure of government within pluralist democracies should be changed

(D)   point out a flaw in Dahl's argument that the principle of political equality cannot be fully realized

(E)   point out an objection to Dahl's defense of polyarchy

Explanation for Question 9

This question requires the examinee to understand and analyze the criticism that the author mentions in the third paragraph of the passage and how that criticism is related to what the author does in the rest of the passage, in order to determine why the author refers to this criticism.

The best answer is (E) because it correctly identifies the author's purpose in referring to the criticism of pluralist democracy. The criticism in the third paragraph is, in brief, that there is a gap between the model of pluralist democracy (polyarchy) and the reality of the political systems it purports to describe. This gap is the result of an imbalance in the distribution of "power resources" so extreme that some groups have the power to "exclude issues altogether from the political agenda." Moreover, this power is said to "effectively counter" any diffusion of influence on decision making (lines 34-46).

In the first paragraph of the passage the author states "Dahl argues convincingly that the idea of democracy rests on political equality—the equal capacity of all citizens to determine or influence collective decisions" (lines 4-7). The passage goes on to state that Dahl recognizes that this principle may be incapable of full realization and that those systems that best approximate this ideal can be deemed democratic (lines 7-15). The second paragraph of the passage describes Dahl as defending polyarchy as being "the nearest possible approximation of the democratic ideal" (lines 24-25) because it "reinforces a diffusion of power ... toward a variety of individuals, groups, and organizations" (lines 20-23) "through party competition and the operation of pressure groups" (lines 26-27). It is an approximation because instead of all individual citizens having the direct ability to determine or influence policies, as the ideal would have it, in a polyarchy this capacity resides with elected representatives who compete for votes by appealing to the interests of various individuals, groups, and organizations. Presumably, as members of interest groups, individuals can overcome inevitable inequalities in individual resources that give rise to political influence, thus compensating for a feature of the world that prevents the ideal of democracy from ever being realized.

The criticism of the theory of pluralist democracy in the third paragraph—that "the power of some groups to exclude issues altogether from the political agenda" (lines 43-44)—constitutes a telling objection to Dahl's defense of polyarchy. It suggests that inequalities of power are so extreme that the diffusion of power to a variety of individuals and organizations cannot be effectively accomplished. This is because the extremes of power allow some groups to set the political agenda, thus, effectively denying a voice to other groups.

The fact that the criticism in the third paragraph is mentioned immediately following the author's account of Dahl's defense of polyarchy suggests that it is offered as an objection to that defense. This is reinforced by the discussion of the criticism in the fourth paragraph. There the author discusses Dahl's response to the criticism, pointing out that despite the fact that this criticism is not made as vigorously as it once was, Dahl seems to accept its force as a criticism because he ends his book by asking "what changes in structures and consciousness might make political life more democratic in present polyarchies." The author does not support or rebut the criticism in the fourth paragraph, but merely discusses Dahl's response to it. Therefore, both the content of the criticism and its context in the passage show that the criticism of the theory of pluralist democracy in the third paragraph is referred to primarily in order to "point out an objection to Dahl's defense of polyarchy."

Response (A) is incorrect for several reasons. First, Dahl's statement that Western intellectuals expect more democracy from polyarchies than is possible appears in the fourth paragraph where it is part of Dahl's response to the criticism of the theory of pluralist democracy referred to in the third paragraph of the passage. It is implausible that the criticism in the third paragraph would be made to refute a claim made only after and in response to that criticism. Secondly, to refute Dahl's claim that Western intellectuals expect more democracy from polyarchies than is possible one would have to present evidence contrary to that claim. But, rather than offering such evidence, those making the criticism in the third paragraph would seem to be open to Dahl's criticism that they demanded more democracy of polyarchies than is possible. This is further supported by the fact that Dahl's response to the criticism is to speculate how to make polyarchies even more democratic. Had he been responding to critics who expected less democracy of polyarchies, he would have taken a different tack. Given this, the criticism in the third paragraph is not referred to in order to refute Dahl's statement that Western intellectuals expect more democracy than is possible, but, if any thing, it tends to support that statement.

Response (B) is incorrect because nowhere in the passage does the author suggest the need for rethinking the *basic principles* on which the theory of democracy rests. Though the criticism referred to in the third paragraph of the passage and the avenues of further democratization explored by Dahl in the fourth paragraph may be said implicitly to advocate a rethinking of Western political structures, it is a rethinking only of political, social, and economic structures that prevent us from realizing a closer approximation of the ideal democracy, not the basic principles on which the *theory* of democracy rests. Lines 37-38 of the passage indicate that the critics "pointed to a gap between the model and the reality of Western political systems." This would suggest that the critics concurred with the basic principles of democracy, but were critical of the extent to which polyarchies truly reflected these principles.

Response (C) is incorrect because, though the criticism in the third paragraph can be read as implicitly criticizing the political structures within pluralist democracies, it is not the "structure of government" that is criticized, but the "distribution of power resources." Thus, Dahl's response to the objection, as discussed in the fourth paragraph, is not to suggest the critical examination of structures of government, but of "the economic order of polyarchies," of the "distribution of those economic resources that are at the same time political resources, and the relationship between political structures and economic enterprises." The criticism in the third paragraph has nothing to do with the structure of government. Indeed, the author does not offer in the passage any view whatsoever on what the structure of government in pluralist democracies should be.

Response (D) is incorrect. It is wrong in two respects. The criticism in the third paragraph is directed against the idea that polyarchy is the closest approximation possible to the democratic ideal. So, it is not a criticism of the argument that the ideal of democracy cannot be *fully realized*. Rather, the criticism could be used to *support* the claim that the ideal democracy can never be fully realized. According to the passage, "polyarchy reinforces a diffusion of power away from any single center and toward a variety of individuals, groups, and organizations, … [making it] the nearest possible approximation to the democratic ideal" (lines 19-25). The critics' view that the "power of some groups, already richer or organizationally more powerful, to exclude issues altogether from the political agenda countering any diffusion of influence on decision-making," lends support to Dahl's general claim that the principle of political equality cannot be fully realized. The criticism in effect shows that the democratic ideal is not even closely approximated by polyarchy.

This question was answered correctly by 44 percent of test takers. It is classified as a "difficult" item.

Question 10, Section 3, page 52

10. According to the passage, the aim of a political party in a polyarchy is to do which one of the following?

   (A)   determine what the position of the majority of voters is on a particular issue

   (B)   determine what position on an issue will earn the support of particular groups of voters

   (C)   organize voters into pressure groups in order to influence public policy on a particular issue

   (D)   ensure that elected officials accurately represent the position of the party on specific issues

   (E)   ensure that elected officials accurately represent the position of the electorate on specific issues

Explanation for Question 10

This question requires the examinee to identify and understand the facts, ideas, and arguments presented in the passage and to determine precisely what is and what is not stated by the author.

The credited response is (B) because it most accurately paraphrases information from the passage. According to lines 25-29 of the passage, "[p]olyarchy achieves this diffusion of power through party competition and the operation of pressure groups. Competing for votes, parties seek to offer different sections of the electorate what they most want."

In lines 30-32, the passage goes on to state that parties must determine "what policy commitments will sway the electoral decisions of particular groups."

Response (A) is incorrect because it contradicts information in the passage. Lines 29-30 of the passage explicitly state that "… [political parties in a polyarchy] do not ask what the majority [of voters] thinks of an issue." Rather, in competing for votes, political parties concern themselves with where particular groups stand on issues.

Response (C) is incorrect because it ascribes to political parties a role in the democratic process that is not supported by the passage. Though the passage does indicate that in a polyarchy groups of voters can organize into pressure groups in order to influence public policy on a certain issue (lines 32-34), the passage does not describe this organization of voters into pressure groups as an aim of political parties. Lines 32-34 describe pressure groups as forming "equally" with political parties. Pressure groups are formed in addition to political parties to address particular issues, not as a result of actions taken by political parties.

Response (D) is incorrect because the passage simply doesn't describe the party as a mechanism for ensuring that elected officials follow a "party line," even if that party line represents the will of the electorate. Its role is to diffuse power through competition between other parties that try to determine what various groups in the electorate want.

Response (E) is incorrect because it overstates information from the passage. Though elected officials are accountable to a broad-based electorate, the passage does not support the idea that these elected officials *accurately represent* the position of the electorate as a whole on specific issues. Rather, a political party, in competing for votes, determines "what policy commitments will sway the electoral decisions of particular groups" (lines 30-32).

This question was answered correctly by 58 percent of test takers, making it a question of "middle difficulty."

Question 11, Section 3, page 53

11. It can be inferred from the passage that Dahl assumes which one of the following in his defense of polyarchies?

   (A)   Polyarchies are limited in the extent to which they can embody the idea of democracy.

   (B)   The structure of polyarchical governments is free of hierarchical ordering.

   (C)   The citizens of a polyarchy have equal access to the resources that provide political influence.

   (D)   Polyarchy is the best political system to foster the growth of political parties.

   (E)   Polyarchy is a form of government that is not influenced by the interests of economic enterprises.

Explanation for Question 11

This question requires the examinee to go beyond what is explicitly stated in the passage and to draw an inference from the passage regarding an assumption involved in Dahl's defense of polyarchy.

The credited response is (A) because it is a reasonable inference supported by information from lines 8-16 of the passage. Dahl argues that the idea of democracy rests on political equality. But the passage goes on to say that "as Dahl recognizes, if hierarchical ordering is inevitable in any structure of government, and if no society can guarantee perfect equality in the resources that may give rise to political influence, the democratic principle of political equality is incapable of full realization." Since the passage then concludes from this that "actual systems can be deemed democratic only as approximations to the ideal," we can reasonably infer that the author accepts that hierarchical ordering is inevitable in any structure of government and that no society can guarantee perfect equality, with the result that "the democratic principle of political equality is incapable of full realization." So we can then further infer that Dahl assumes this in his defense of polyarchies, since the passage goes on to say "[i]t is on these grounds that Dahl defends polyarchy."

Response (B) is incorrect because it contradicts information in the passage. Lines 8-9 explicitly state that "Dahl recognizes [that] hierarchical ordering is inevitable in any structure of government." The only inference to be drawn from this is that, because polyarchies are a type of government, Dahl believes that hierarchical ordering is indeed present in polyarchies.

Response (C) is incorrect because it is incompatible with Dahl's view as it can be reasonably inferred from the first paragraph of the passage. As demonstrated in the discussion above of response (A), the passage supports a reasonable inference that Dahl believes that no society can guarantee perfect equality in the resources that give rise to political influence. But this is incompatible with (C), that "[t]he citizens of a polyarchy have equal access to the resources that provide political influence," since if *no society* can guarantee perfect equality, there is no basis for saying that the citizens of a polyarchy have such equal access.

Response (D) is incorrect because there is simply no evidence from the passage to support it. Though it may be inferred that various political parties may exist under polyarchy, in no way does the passage suggest that polyarchy is the best political system to foster the growth of political parties.

Response (E) is incorrect because the passage never rules out the interests of economic enterprises as having influence in a polyarchy. While "party competition" and "the operation of pressure groups" are mentioned as mechanisms by which a polyarchy functions, the passage does not rule out the interests of economic enterprises having influence

within these mechanisms. The fourth paragraph of the passage discusses Dahl's response to the criticism in the third paragraph that in a polyarchy unequal distributions of power can counter any diffusion influence on decision-making. In discussing what changes might make political life in polyarchies more democratic, the passage mentions that "[t]his would require a critical examination of ...the relationship between political structures and economic enterprises." This strongly implies that one of the factors that might make polyarchies less democratic is the influence of economic enterprises. So, rather than (E), it is more reasonable to infer from the passage the opposite of (E), that government in polyarchies is influenced by the interests of economic enterprises.

This question was answered correctly by 47 percent of test takers, making it a question of "middle difficulty."

Question 13, Section 3, page 53

13. Which one of the following, if true, would most strengthen Dahl's defense of polyarchy?

  (A) The political agenda in a polyarchy is strongly influenced by how power resources other than the vote are distributed.
  (B) The outcome of elections is more often determined by the financial resources candidates are able to spend during campaigns than by their stands on political issues.
  (C) Public policy in a polyarchy is primarily determined by decision-makers who are not accountable to elected officials.
  (D) Political parties in a polyarchy help concentrate political power in the central government.
  (E) Small and diverse pressure groups are able to exert as much influence on public policy in a polyarchy as are large and powerful groups.

Explanation for Question 13

This question requires the examinee to evaluate the effect of additional evidence on material contained in the passage, determining which response gives additional evidence that, if true, would most strengthen Dahl's defense of polyarchy.

The credited response is (E). Dahl's defense of polyarchy is essentially that it is "the nearest possible approximation to the democratic ideal" (lines 23-25). This means that it comes closer to the ideal of political equality than any other system. That ideal holds that each individual's capacity to influence or determine collective decisions is equal to any other citizen's (lines 5-7). However, things being as they are, in actual political systems not every individual's political influence is equal. Polyarchies, he argues, approximate the democratic ideal by diffusing the ability to influence political decisions among a variety of individuals and interest groups. This argument is strengthened if it is true that in a polyarchy small and diverse pressure groups are able to exert as much influence on public policy as large and powerful groups, for that would be evidence for such diffusion of power. If (E) is true, in a polyarchy the power of a variety of individuals is relatively equal because the power of various groups of individuals is relatively equal, thus making polyarchy a close approximation of the democratic ideal.

Responses (A)–(D) are all incorrect basically because they weaken rather than strengthen Dahl's defense of polyarchy. If, as (A) asserts, the political agenda in a polyarchy is strongly influenced by how power resources other than the vote are distributed, this reinforces the criticism made in paragraph three of Dahl's defense of polyarchy. This criticism casts doubt on the argument that polyarchies are the nearest approximation of the democratic ideal, for if (A) were true, the mechanism Dahl describes in lines 25-29 for dispersing power through competition for votes would not work to diffuse power among a variety of individuals and interest groups. So, if true, (A) actually weakens rather than strengthens Dahl's defense of polyarchy.

Response (B) is incorrect for very similar reasons. Dahl's defense of polyarchy describes polyarchy as diffusing power among various individuals and interest groups through political parties competing for votes by offering different sections of the electorate what they most want (lines 25-29). If (B) were true, then political parties would not compete for votes by offering different interest groups what they want, but individuals would compete for votes by applying their financial resources. So, if true, (B) weakens Dahl's defense of polyarchy, since, like (A), it would undermine the mechanism Dahl describes as the means by which polyarchy comes to approximate closely the democratic idea.

Response (C) is also incorrect because it weakens rather than strengthens Dahl's defense of polyarchy. Dahl describes polyarchy as "a representative system in which elected officials both determine government policy and are accountable to a broader based electorate" and his defense of polyarchy as an approximation of the democratic ideal because it diffuses influence on policy decisions among a variety of individuals and groups is based on that description. (C), if true, contradicts that description. So, if (C) is true, Dahl's defense of polyarchy is without foundation and must fail.

Response (D) also weakens Dahl's argument. In his defense of polyarchy Dahl argues that it approximates the democratic ideal of equal distribution of the ability to influence public policy by diffusing power "away from any single center and toward a variety of individuals, groups, and organizations." If (D) were true and political parties in a polyarchy concentrated power in the central government, this would undermine the reason that Dahl offers for why polyarchy approximates the democratic

ideal—the root of his defense of polyarchy as the nearest approximation of the democratic ideal.

This is classified as an "easy" item, as 72 percent of test takers answered it correctly.

Passage for Questions 18, 20, and 21

The old belief that climatic stability accounts for the high level of species diversity in the Amazon River basin of South America emerged, strangely enough, from observations of the deep sea. Sanders
(5) discovered high diversity among the mud-dwelling animals of the deep ocean. He argued that such diversity could be attributed to the absence of significant fluctuations in climate and physical conditions, without which the extinction of species
(10) should be rare. In the course of time new species would continue to evolve, and so the rate of speciation would be greater than the rate of extinction, resulting in the accumulation of great diversity. Sanders argued that the Amazon tropical
(15) rain forest is analogous to the deep sea: because the rain forest has a stable climate, extinction should be rare. Evidence that some species of rain-forest trees have persisted for some 30 million years in the Amazon basin, added to the absence of
(20) winter and glaciation, supports this view.

Recently, however, several observations have cast doubt on the validity of the stability hypothesis and suggest that the climate of the Amazon basin has fluctuated significantly in the past. Haffer
(25) noted that different species of birds inhabit different corners of the basin in spite of the fact that essentially unbroken green forest spreads from the western edge to the eastern edge of the region. This pattern presented a puzzle to biologists
(30) studying the distributions of plants and animals: why would different species inhabit different parts of the forest if the habitat in which they lived had a stable climate?

Haffer proposed a compelling explanation for
(35) the distribution of species. Observing that species found on high ground are different from those on low ground, and knowing that in the Amazon lowlands are drier than uplands, he proposed that during the ice ages the Amazon lowlands became a
(40) near-desert arid plain; meanwhile, the more elevated regions became islands of moisture and hence served as refuges for the fauna and flora of the rain forest. Populations that were once continuous diverged and became permanently
(45) separated. Haffer's hypothesis appears to explain the distribution of species as well as the unusual species diversity. The ice-age refuges would have protected existing species from extinction. But the periodic geographic isolation of related populations

(50) (there have been an estimated 13 ice ages to date) would have facilitated the development of new species as existing species on the lowlands adapted to changing climates.

Although no conclusive proof has yet been
(55) found to support Haffer's hypothesis, it has led other researchers to gauge the effects of climatic changes, such as storms and flooding, on species diversity in the Amazon basin. Their research suggests that climatic disturbances help account for
(60) the splendid diversity of the Amazon rain forest today.

Question 18, Section 3, page 55

18. Which one of the following best describes the organization of the passage?

   (A)   A hypothesis is discussed, evidence that undercuts that hypothesis is presented, and a new hypothesis that may account for the evidence is described.
   (B)   A recently observed phenomenon is described, an explanation for that phenomenon is discussed, and the explanation is evaluated in light of previous research findings.
   (C)   Several hypotheses that may account for a puzzling phenomenon are described and discounted, and a more promising hypothesis is presented.
   (D)   A hypothesis and the assumptions on which it is based are described, and evidence is provided to suggest that the hypothesis is only partially correct.
   (E)   Two alternative explanations for a phenomenon are presented and compared, and experiments designed to test each theory are described.

Explanation for Question 18

This question requires the examinee to analyze the passage to determine the organization of the information it contains and then recognize the structure of the passage described abstractly.

The credited response is (A). In the opening paragraph of the passage, the author discusses Sanders' hypothesis, i.e., that species diversity in the Amazon River basin of South America is due to climactic stability (lines 1-3). After discussing this hypothesis, the author then presents evidence that undercuts this hypothesis, namely that different species of Amazon River basin birds were found to inhabit different parts of the basin, something that should not be the case if their habitat had remained stable (lines 21-33). Finally, the author describes Haffer's alternate hypothesis, which posits a relationship between species diversity and distribution

and various climactic disturbances and changes, and which may account for this evidence regarding the birds of the Amazon basin, as well as the evidence of species diversity (lines 34-53).

Response (B) is incorrect because it does not describe all the elements discussed in the passage. Response (B) excludes the information discussed in the first paragraph— the "old belief that climactic stability accounts for the high level of species diversity in the Amazon River basin of South America" (lines 1-3). The "recently observed phenomenon" to which this response refers would most reasonably be the different species of the Amazon River basin birds that were found to inhabit different parts of the basin— a recently observed phenomenon that the author of the passage does not describe until the second paragraph. Further, even without this neglect of information in the first paragraph, response (B) is still incorrect. While an explanation of the recent phenomenon is discussed (Haffer's hypothesis), there is no mention of previous research findings in the passage, except perhaps for evidence that some tree species have survived for 30 million years, and that is not mentioned in connection with the exposition of Haffer's hypothesis.

Response (C) is incorrect in the number of hypotheses it attributes to the passage. The mention of "several hypotheses" and then in addition "a more promising hypothesis" indicates the presence of at least three hypotheses in the passage. But the author of the passage discusses only two, one being Sanders' hypothesis that climactic stability accounts for species diversity in the Amazon River basin of South America and the second being Haffer's hypothesis that climactic disturbances and changes account for species diversity and distribution.

Response (D) is incorrect because it can give, at best, only a partial account of the passage. Sanders' hypothesis and the assumption upon which it is based (namely, that all the regions of the Amazon rain forest have always had the same tropical climate) is indeed described. Evidence from the distribution of species is then given to show that Sanders' hypothesis does not account for recently observed species distribution. While the evidence cited could be used to argue that Sanders' view is completely wrong, one could also argue that since some climactic stability somewhere in the basin would have been necessary for species to exist for millions of years (an implication of Haffer's view is that the uplands' climate would have been fairly stable), Sanders' hypothesis is at least partially correct. Nevertheless, even granting this, (D) makes no mention of the discussion of an alternative hypothesis (Haffer's), a discussion that takes up half the passage. It cannot, therefore, be the best answer.

Response (E) is incorrect because, although the two hypotheses discussed in the passage—Sanders' hypothesis and Haffer's hypothesis—are alternative explanations for species diversity and distribution in the Amazon River basin of South America, there is no subsequent discussion of experiments designed to test each theory. Mere observation of that which is naturally occurring does *not* constitute an experiment. An experiment involves observations *under controlled conditions*. The observation of the natural existence of "some species of rain-forest trees [that] have persisted for some 30 million years in the Amazon basin [without] winter and glaciation" (lines 17-20), and the observation of "different species of [Amazon basin] birds [that] inhabit different corners of the basin" (lines 20-21), are observations of natural phenomena without an attempt to control conditions. Hence they do not describe experiments.

Approximately 70 percent of test takers answered this question correctly, making it an "easy" question.

Question 20, Section 3, page 55

20. The passage suggests that which one of the following is true of Sanders' hypothesis?

    (A)   He underestimated the effects of winter and glaciation in the Amazon basin on the tropical rain forest.
    (B)   He failed to recognize the similarity in physical conditions of the Amazon lowlands and the Amazon uplands.
    (C)   He failed to take into account the relatively high rate of extinction during the ice ages in the Amazon basin.
    (D)   He overestimated the length of time that species have survived in the Amazon basin.
    (E)   He failed to account for the distribution of species in the Amazon basin.

Explanation for Question 20

This question requires the examinee to go beyond what is explicitly stated in the passage and identify from among the responses an inference regarding Sanders' hypothesis that is supported by information in the passage.

The credited response is (E) because, though Sanders' hypothesis concerns itself with explaining the high level of species diversity in the Amazon basin, his hypothesis, as it is presented in the passage, does not address, let alone account for, the observed distribution of species in the Amazon basin. It is not clear if Sanders was even cognizant of the peculiarities of species distribution in the basin. The second paragraph begins by telling us that the observations in species distribution that have cast doubt on Sanders' hypothesis have only recently been made, suggesting that this particular information about species distribution in the basin was not available to Sanders when he formulated his hypothesis. Since these observations of species distribution cast doubt on Sander's hypothesis, it can be inferred that this is because his hypothesis fails to account for these observations.

Response (A) is incorrect. While it is true that winter and glaciation in other parts of the world and at different periods of history might have had effects upon the tropical rain forest (as Haffer's hypothesis in the third paragraph indicates), the passage explicitly states that winter and glaciation do not occur *in* the Amazon basin itself (lines 17-20). Therefore, Sanders, in formulating his hypothesis, would not have made any estimations regarding the effects of winter and glaciation in the Amazon basin on the tropical rain forest.

Response (B) is incorrect. The passage makes it clear that Sanders recognizes the similarity in the present physical conditions of the Amazon lowlands and uplands. In arguing that "the Amazon tropical rain forest is analogous to the deep sea" (lines 14-15), Sanders clearly treats the Amazon basin as one relatively homogeneous area. It is "the absence of significant fluctuations in climate and physical conditions" (lines 7-9) that, in his view, accounts for the high levels of species diversity in the Amazon basin. Not only does his hypothesis recognize the similarity in physical conditions of all regions of the Amazon basin (including the lowlands and uplands), but part of the hypothesis' inadequacy can be traced to Sanders' apparent assumption that this homogeneity has always existed. If Sanders failed to recognize anything, it was not the *similarity* in current physical conditions between lowlands and uplands, but rather the *differences* in physical conditions between the uplands and lowlands during the ice ages.

Response (C) is incorrect because it presumes that the rate of extinction in the Amazon basin during the ice ages was in fact relatively high. However, nothing in the passage suggests that this is true. Both Haffer's and Sanders' hypotheses accept that some extinction took place, but nowhere do they, or the author of the passage, talk about the specific rate of extinction during the ice ages.

Response (D) is incorrect. There is only one place in the passage that the length of time a species has survived in the Amazon basin is brought up. Lines 17-20 point out that there is evidence that some species of trees have survived in the basin for 30 million years. This information is said by the author of the passage to support Sanders' view that in the Amazon basin extinction should be rare. In other words, the author seems to agree with Sanders' point about the rate of extinction. There is nothing in the passage that questions, let alone contradicts, Sanders' estimations about length of time species have survived in the Amazon basin. In fact, though we can infer that Sanders must believe that some species have survived a very long time, we are never told anything about how long he has estimated some species to have survived.

This question was answered correctly by 60 percent of test takers, making it a question of "middle difficulty."

Question 21, Section 3, page 55

21. Which one of the following is evidence that would contribute to the "proof" mentioned in line 54?

   (A) Accurately dated sediment cores from a freshwater lake in the Amazon indicate that the lake's water level rose significantly during the last ice age.

   (B) Data based on radiocarbon dating of fossils suggest that the Amazon uplands were too cold to support rain forests during the last ice age.

   (C) Computer models of climate during global ice ages predict only insignificant reductions of monsoon rains in tropical areas such as the Amazon.

   (D) Fossils preserved in the Amazon uplands during the last ice age are found together with minerals that are the products of an arid landscape.

   (E) Fossilized pollen from the Amazon lowlands indicates that during the last ice age the Amazon lowlands supported vegetation that needs little water rather than the rain forests they support today.

Explanation for Question 21

This question requires the examinee to determine what additional evidence would support Haffer's hypothesis.

The credited response is (E) because among all the response choices, it supports an essential part of Haffer's explanation for the distribution of species, viz., that "during the ice ages the Amazon lowlands became a near-desert arid plain…" (lines 39-40). This part of Haffer's hypothesis implies that any vegetation the lowlands then supported would have to have survived on little water. The discovery of fossilized pollen that indicates the lowlands once supported vegetation that needed little water rather than the rain forests they support today provides evidence that at one time the climate of the lowlands was such that vegetation needed to be able to survive on little water, that is, that at one time the climate of the lowlands was "near-desert arid."

Response (A) is incorrect because, in the absence of further details such as the lake's location, it is not clear how it is relevant to Haffer's claim. (A)'s truth could even be construed as evidence against Haffer's hypothesis—if the freshwater lake referred to in (A) were in the lowlands, then its flooding during the last ice age would seem to contradict Haffer's claim that the lowlands were arid then. Even if the lake were in the uplands, the flooding of the lake would at best suggest that the moisture content of the uplands *increased* during the last ice age (which is not part of Haffer's contention), but remain silent about

the climate of the lowlands. While other researchers suggest that climactic changes, such as flooding, help account for the species diversity of the Amazon rain forest (suggestions that might be supported by the truth of (A)), it is specifically Haffer's hypothesis that this questions asks about.

Response (B) is incorrect because it actually provides evidence against Haffer's hypothesis. We are told in lines 40-43 that Haffer hypothesizes that "the more elevated regions became islands of moisture and hence served as refuges for the fauna and flora of the rain forest." If, as (B) would have it, the elevated regions were too cold to support rain forests during the last ice age, then it is not clear how the uplands could serve as refuges for species that were adapted for life in a rain forest.

Response (C) is incorrect because it makes less likely Haffer's contention that the Amazon lowlands became desert-like arid plains during the ice ages. The occurrence of monsoon rains in the Amazon during the ice ages would be inconsistent with Haffer's hypothesis that "during the ice ages the Amazon lowlands became a near-desert arid plain" and would probably have produced similar conditions for the lowlands as the uplands, i.e., areas of moisture. Therefore, only insignificant reductions of monsoon rains during the ice ages would tend to disprove Haffer's hypothesis.

Response (D) is incorrect because it does not support Haffer's explanation that the Amazon River basin can be divided into two separate and distinct areas—uplands and lowlands—with differing ice-age climates. Haffer's hypothesis depends on this ice-age climatic division of the basin. Minerals that are the products of an arid landscape being found in the basin together with fossils preserved in the uplands during the last ice age would strongly suggest that the uplands were also arid (as were, by hypothesis, the lowlands). (D) would instead support the claim that the basin would be one continuous area of consistent climatic conditions throughout. At the very least, (D) would clearly contradict Haffer's proposal that the uplands were "islands of moisture" (line 41) during the ice ages.

This question was answered correctly by 46 percent of test takers. It is classified as an item of "middle difficulty."

Passage for Questions 22, 23, and 27

     Although surveys of medieval legislation, guild organization, and terminology used to designate different medical practitioners have demonstrated that numerous medical specialities were recognized
(5) in Europe during the Middle Ages, most historians continue to equate the term "woman medical practitioner," wherever they encounter it in medieval records, with "midwife." This common practice obscures the fact that, although women
(10) were not represented on all levels of medicine equally, they were represented in a variety of

specialties throughout the broad medical community. A reliable study by Wickersheimer and Jacquart documents that, of 7,647 medical practitioners in
(15) France during the twelfth through fifteenth centuries, 121 were women; of these, only 44 were identified as midwives, while the rest practiced as physicians, surgeons, apothecaries, barbers, and other healers.

While preserving terminological distinctions
(20) somewhat increases the quality of the information extracted from medieval documents concerning women medical practitioners, scholars must also reopen the whole question of why documentary evidence for women medical practitioners
(25) comprises such a tiny fraction of the evidence historians of medieval medicine usually present. Is this due to the limitations of the historical record, as has been claimed, or does it also result from the methods historians use? Granted, apart from
(30) medical licenses, the principal sources of information regarding medical practitioners available to researchers are wills, property transfers, court records, and similar documents, all of which typically underrepresent women because of
(35) restrictive medieval legal traditions. Nonetheless, the parameters researchers choose when they define their investigations may contribute to the problem. Studies focusing on the upper echelons of "learned" medicine, for example, tend to exclude healers on
(40) the legal and social fringes of medical practice, where most women would have been found.

The advantages of broadening the scope of such studies is immediately apparent in Pelling and Webster's study of sixteenth-century London.
(45) Instead of focusing solely on officially recognized and licensed practitioners, the researchers defined a medical practitioner as "any individual whose occupation is basically concerned with the care of the sick." Using this definition, they found primary
(50) source information suggesting that there were 60 women medical practitioners in the city of London in 1560. Although this figure may be slightly exaggerated, the evidence contrasts strikingly with that of Gottfried, whose earlier survey identified
(55) only 28 women medical practitioners in all of England between 1330 and 1530.

Finally, such studies provide only statistical information about the variety and prevalence of women's medical practice in medieval Europe.
(60) Future studies might also make profitable use of analyses developed in other areas of women's history as a basis for exploring the social context of women's medical practice. Information about economic rivalry in medicine, women's literacy, and
(65) the control of medical knowledge could add much to our growing understanding of women medical practitioners' role in medieval society.

Question 22, Section 3, page 56

22. Which one of the following best expresses the main point of the passage?

(A) Recent studies demonstrate that women medical practitioners were more common in England than in the rest of Western Europe during the Middle Ages.

(B) The quantity and quality of the information historians uncover concerning women's medical practice in medieval Europe would be improved if they changed their methods of study.

(C) The sparse evidence for women medical practitioners in studies dealing with the Middle Ages is due primarily to the limitations of the historical record.

(D) Knowledge about the social issues that influenced the role women medical practitioners played in medieval society has been enhanced by several recent studies.

(E) Analyses developed in other areas of women's history could probably be used to provide more information about the social context of women's medical practice during the Middle Ages.

Explanation for Question 22

This question requires the examinee have a comprehensive understanding of the passage in order to identify the main point that the passage as a whole is making, as opposed to subsidiary points or points that the passage does not make at all.

The credited response is (B) because it most fully and accurately describes the main point of the passage. The quantity and quality of the information historians uncover concerning women's medical practice in medieval Europe that this response refers to is the author's discussion of the discrepancies in the reported number of women medical practitioners, the inaccuracy regarding the many terminological distinctions of the phrase "women medical practitioners," and the possible problems of researchers' methods. After a discussion in the second paragraph about whether earlier studies were limited by the historical record, or if their findings were limited instead by their methods, the author goes on, in the fourth paragraph, to give an example of how changing one's methodology can result in richer information about women medical practitioners. Then, in the last paragraph, the author goes on to suggest that instead of using traditional methods, which give "only statistical information about the variety and prevalence of women's medical practice in medieval Europe" (lines 57-59), historians should use "analyses developed in other areas of women's history as a basis for exploring the social context of women's medical practice" (lines 61-63), arguing that these analyses "could add much to our ... understanding of women medical practitioners' role in medieval society" (lines 65-67).

Response (A) is incorrect for several reasons. First of all, the passage does not even cite a recent study which demonstrates that women medical practitioners were more common in England than in the rest of Western Europe during the Middle Ages. The author of the passage does cite the Wickersheimer and Jacquart study that documents 121 women medical practitioners in France during the twelfth through fifteenth centuries—but there is no indication that this study had anything to say about the situation in England. The Pelling and Webster study cited in the third paragraph gives statistics for sixteenth-century England alone, and while this study is contrasted with the Gottfried study that identifies a smaller number than that of Pelling and Webster, no mention is made of the situation in Europe. More importantly, the passage does not concern itself at all with a comparative analysis or discussion of women medical practitioners in England versus the whole of Europe during the Middle Ages.

Response (C) is incorrect because it conveys at best only a partial account of the passage. Though the author of the passage does speculate that the sparse evidence for women medical practitioners in studies dealing with the Middle Ages may be due partly to limitations of the historical record, the author does not conclude that the sparse evidence is due primarily to such limitations. Rather, the author speculates that the sparse evidence may also be the result of historians' faulty research methods (lines 26-29). Moreover, response (C) is also incorrect because it leaves out the subsequent discussion that historians should improve their methods of study in order to achieve a higher quantity and better quality of information regarding women medical practitioners in medieval Europe.

Response (D) is incorrect primarily because it contradicts information from the final paragraph of the passage. According to lines 57-63, recent studies have succeeded in providing "only statistical information about the variety and prevalence of women's medical practice in medieval Europe." The idea that social issues affected the role women medical practitioners played in medieval society is an idea that the author expressly feels *future* studies might make use of, which suggests that no previous studies have explored any relationship between social issues and the role of women medical practitioners.

Response (E) is incorrect because while it expresses a supporting idea, it is not the main point of the passage. Though the author ends the passage with the idea that "analyses developed in other areas of women's history [could be used] as a basis for exploring the social context of women's medical practice" (lines 61-63), such analyses are presented as one way to improve the quantity and quality of the information historians' uncover concerning women medical practitioners in medieval Europe. Response

(E) functions as an example of an advantage that could result if historians would change their methods of study, but it is not the main point of the passage to establish the benefits of this particular example. The passage discusses other examples in the context of making a general point about methods of studying women's medical practice in medieval Europe.

This question is classified as a question of "middle difficulty," as 55 percent of test takers answered it correctly.

Question 23, Section 3, page 56

23. Which one of the following is most closely analogous to the error the author believes historians make when they equate the term "women medical practitioners" with "midwives"?

   (A) equating pear with apple
   (B) equating science with biology
   (C) equating supervisor with subordinate
   (D) equating member with nonmember
   (E) equating instructor with trainee

Explanation for Question 23

This question requires the examinee to move outside the passage and to select a response stating a relationship most closely analogous to the equating of the phrase "women medical practitioners" with "midwives" in the passage.

The credited response is (B) because "science" and "biology" stand in the same relationship to each other as do "women medical practitioners" and "midwives." According to lines 16-18 of the passage, midwives, as well as "physicians, surgeons, apothecaries, barbers, and other healers" constitute the class of women medical practitioners. Therefore, midwives constitute a subset of women medical practitioners. Similarly, the equating of science with biology in response (B) is guilty of the same error of equating—biology is a particular type of science, but not all types of science are biology.

Response (A) is incorrect because both pear and apple are separate and distinct categories. Neither is a subdivision of the other. An apple is not a type of pear, nor is a pear a type of apple. This response would be analogous to the equating of women medical practitioners with midwives if it had said "equating fruit with pear" or "equating fruit with apple."

Response (C) is incorrect because it confuses the relationship between the set of women medical practitioners and the set of midwives. Since all midwives are women medical practitioners, but not all women medical practitioners are midwives, the set of midwives can be said to be a part of, i.e., a subset of the larger set of women medical practitioners. In this sense, midwives *fall under the category of* women medical practitioners. Whereas quite differently in response (C), "subordinate"denotes one who *falls under the authority of* a supervisor. The passage does not suggest that midwives fall under the authority of women medical practitioners.

Response (D) is incorrect. "Member" and "nonmember" are contradictories of each other. On the contrary, the equating of women medical practitioners with midwives in the passage does not involve mistaking something for its contradictory. It involves mistaking a part for the whole. Wholes contain the parts, but contradictories do not overlap. To be a woman medical practitioner *may* mean to be a midwife and to be a midwife *is* to be a woman medical practitioner.

Response (E) is incorrect because it mistakenly takes the passage to be describing a teacher-student relationship between a woman medical practitioner and a midwife. So while a woman medical practitioner who practices a particular specialty may train another who aspires to practice the same specialty, there is no evidence in the passage to suggest that all women medical practitioners train or teach midwives.

Slightly more than 50 percent of test takers answered this question correctly, making it a question of "middle difficulty."

Question 27, Section 3, page 57

27. In the passage, the author is primarily concerned with doing which one of the following?

 (A)   describing new methodological approaches
 (B)   revising the definitions of certain concepts
 (C)   comparing two different analyses
 (D)   arguing in favor of changes in method
 (E)   chronicling certain historical developments

Explanation for Question 27

This question requires the examinee to look at the passage as a whole and determine its primary purpose.

The credited response is (D) because it accurately expresses the overall purpose of the passage. The author's introduction of the error researchers make in equating the phrase "women medical practitioners" with the term "midwives," the subsequent discussion of discrepancies in information these researchers report about women medical practitioners, and probable causes for the discrepancies, followed by an example of one such discrepancy, together function as supporting the author's argument that researchers should change their methods of study. When the author speculates that it may be "the parameters researchers choose when they define their investigations" (lines 36-37) that contribute to the problem of historical inaccuracies in records regarding women medical practitioners, it is to emphasize "the advantages of broadening the scope of such studies" (lines 42-43). By referring to the major differences in data reported by the Pelling and Webster study as compared to that of an earlier study by Gottfried, the author gives a specific

example of how a change in method, broadly speaking, makes for a change in resulting findings. Because Pelling and Webster, unlike Gottfried, expanded the definition of the phrase "women medical practitioners" to make it more inclusive, they identified substantially more women medical practitioners than had been reported by Gottfried. For these reasons, the author feels that there should be changes in researchers' methods and ends the passage with an entire paragraph suggesting directions such changes can take.

Response (A) is incorrect because it confuses the express purpose of the passage—that the methods researchers use in studying women medical practitioners in Medieval Europe should be changed—with the author's *proposals* for broadening the scope of studies. Simply put, this response confuses the end (a change in method) with the means to that end. Only with the final paragraph of the passage does the author introduce ideas on the general direction such studies should take. While these ideas anticipate possible future studies, they do not describe new methodologies actually being used by historians. This response completely ignores the directive aspect of the passage and focuses only on a portion of its descriptive aspect.

Response (B) is incorrect because, though the author is concerned in the first paragraph with researchers' arbitrary definition of the phrase "women medical practitioners" as "midwives," it is a concern that stems *not* from a desire merely to "revise the definitions of certain concepts" as this response strongly suggests. Rather, the author uses this practice as supporting evidence for researchers' broadening their methods of study, the author is attentive to the (mis)use of this *one* term to show how "this common practice [of equating the phrase 'women medical practitioners' with the term 'midwives'] obscures the fact that ... [women] were represented in a variety of specialties throughout the broad medical community" (lines 8-12). In other words, this response is too narrow, focusing on only one aspect of the author's concerns. The response ignores the other sorts of changes the author advocates (e.g., "analyses developed in other areas of women's history" (lines 61-62)). It is not merely a revision of definitions that the author advocates, but rather a general rethinking of researchers' methods (revision of definitions would only play a small, though perhaps necessary part of that rethinking).

Response (C) is incorrect because, of the three studies regarding women medical practitioners in Europe during the Middle Ages mentioned in the passage, the author of the passage compares the study of Pelling and Webster with that of Gottfried only to illustrate the discrepancies in data that result from potentially faulty research methods. That is, the comparison between the two studies is intended as a supporting example in the author's argument for new methods of studying the instances of women medical practitioners in Europe during the Middle Ages. The author is more concerned with how future studies might make more than just statistical information about these women available; that is, with how to increase the quality of information about women medical practitioners.

Response (E) is incorrect because it misrepresents the structure and intent of the passage. The author of the passage spends far too much time comparing different analyses, and far too little time detailing the facts about women medical practitioners in middle age Europe for this passage to be simply a chronicling of developments in middle age Europe. A passage that, say, chronicled the growing numbers of women medical practitioners and their medical specialties would have begun by identifying and discussing some of the first known women medical practitioners and then, perhaps progressing to a discussion of the social context of their practice. Such a passage would only briefly touch on the reliability of the available information if its primary purpose were merely to chronicle historical developments. Nor can the passage be read as a chronicling of the development of historiography in this area, since to read it as such would be to ignore the argumentative structure of the passage and the author's advocacy of change in future research. Since the passage does not present a chronology of sorts, but rather is preoccupied with arguing in favor of expanding the scope of research concerning women medical practitioners during the Middle Ages, the passage cannot be read as "chronicling certain historical developments" as this response states.

This is classified as an item of "middle difficulty," as 55 percent of test takers answered it correctly.

■ Analytical Reasoning Questions

Analytical reasoning items are designed to measure the ability to understand a structure of relationships and to draw conclusions about the structure. The examinee is asked to make deductions from a set of statements, rules, or conditions that describes relationships among entities such as persons, places, things, or events. They simulate the kinds of detailed analyses of relationships that a law student must perform in solving legal problems. For example, a passage might describe four diplomats sitting around a table, following certain rules of protocol as to who can sit where. The test taker must answer questions about the implications of the given information, for example, who is sitting between diplomats X and Y.

The passage used for each group of questions describes a common relationship such as the following:

- Assignment: Two parents, P and O, and their children, R and S, must go to the dentist on four consecutive days, designated 1, 2, 3, and 4 …;

- Ordering: X arrived before Y but after Z;

- Grouping: A basketball coach is trying to form a lineup from seven players— R,S,T,U,V,W, and X … and each player has a particular strength—shooting, jumping, or guarding;

- Spatial: Country X contains six cities and each city is connected to at least one other city by a system of roads, some of which are one-way.

Careful reading and analysis are necessary to determine the *exact nature of the relationships involved.* Some relationships are fixed (e.g., P and R always sit at the same table). Other relationships are variable (e.g., Q must be assigned to either table 1 or table 3). Some relationships that are not stated in the conditions are implied by and can be deduced from those that are stated. (e.g., If one condition about books on a shelf specifies that Book L is to the left of Book Y, and another specifies that Book P is to the left of Book L, then it can be deduced that Book P is to the left of Book Y.)

No formal training in logic is required to answer these questions correctly. Analytical reasoning questions are intended to be answered using knowledge, skills, and reasoning ability generally expected of college students and graduates.

Suggested Approach

Some people may prefer to answer first those questions about a passage that seem less difficult and then those that seem more difficult. In general, it is best not to start another passage before finishing one begun earlier, because much time can be lost in returning to a passage and reestablishing familiarity with its relationships. Do not assume that, because the conditions for a set of questions look long or complicated, the questions based on those conditions will necessarily be especially difficult.

Reading the passage. In reading the conditions, do not introduce unwarranted assumptions. For instance, in a set establishing relationships of height and weight among the members of a team, do not assume that a person who is taller than another person must weigh more than that person. All the information needed to answer each question is provided in the passage and the question itself.

The conditions are designed to be as clear as possible; do not interpret them as if they were intended to trick you. For example, if a question asks how many people could be eligible to serve on a committee, consider only those people named in the passage unless directed otherwise. When in doubt, read the conditions in their most obvious sense. Remember, however, that the language in the conditions is intended to be read for precise meaning. It is essential to pay particular attention to words that describe or limit relationships, such as 'only,' 'exactly,' 'never,' 'always,' 'must be,' 'cannot be,' and the like.

The result of this careful reading will be a clear picture of the structure of the relationships involved, including the kinds of relationships permitted, the participants in the relationships, and the range of actions or attributes allowed by the relationships for these participants.

Questions are independent. Each question should be considered separately from the other questions in its group;

no information, except what is given in the original conditions, should be carried over from one question to another. In some cases a question will simply ask for conclusions to be drawn from the conditions as originally given. Some questions may, however, add information to the original conditions or temporarily suspend one of the original conditions for the purpose of that question only. For example, if Question 1 adds the information "if P is sitting at table 2 ...," this information should NOT be carried over to any other question in the group.

Highlighting the text; using diagrams. Many people find it useful to underline key points in the passage and in each question. In addition, it may prove very helpful to draw a diagram to assist you in finding the solution to the problem.

In preparing for the test, you may wish to experiment with different types of diagrams. For a scheduling problem, a calendar-like diagram may be helpful. For a spatial relationship problem, a simple map can be a useful device.

Even though some people find diagrams to be very helpful, other people seldom use them. And among those who do regularly use diagrams in solving these problems, there is by no means universal agreement on which kind of diagram is best for which problem or in which cases a diagram is most useful. Do not be concerned if a particular problem in the test seems to be best approached without the use of a diagram.

Ten Analytical Reasoning Questions from PrepTest XI and Explanations

The questions on the following pages have been selected from the Analytical Reasoning section of PrepTest XI (Section 1, pages 38-41). While each passage here is followed by only two or four questions, each passage in PrepTest XI is followed by five to eight questions. **If you wish to answer these questions before reading explanations for them, you should skip this section and return to it after you have completed your practice on Section 1 of PrepTest XI.**

Directions: Each group of questions in this section is based on a set of conditions. In answering some of the questions, it may be useful to draw a rough diagram. Choose the response that most accurately and completely answers the question and blacken the corresponding space on your answer sheet.

Passage for Questions 4 and 6

Eight camp counselors—Fran, George, Henry, Joan, Kathy, Lewis, Nathan, and Olga—must each be assigned to supervise exactly one of three activities—swimming, tennis, and volleyball. The assignment of counselors must conform to the following conditions:

> Each activity is supervised by at least two, but not more than three, of the eight counselors.
> Henry supervises swimming.
> Neither Kathy nor Olga supervises tennis.
> Neither Kathy nor Nathan supervises the same activity as Joan.
> If George supervises swimming, both Nathan and Olga supervise volleyball.

Question 4, Section 1, page 38

4.   If George and Kathy are two of three counselors assigned to supervise swimming, which one of the following could be true of the assignment?

(A)   Fran supervises swimming.
(B)   Henry supervises tennis.
(C)   Joan supervises volleyball.
(D)   Lewis supervises volleyball.
(E)   Nathan supervises tennis.

Explanation for Question 4

This question provides additional information for the test taker to consider in addition to the information given in the passage. The test taker is asked to consider which one of the response options could be true if, in addition to what is given in the passage, it is true that George and Kathy are two of three counselors assigned to supervise swimming.

There are a variety of ways to solve this question. By a direct appeal to certain conditions several of the response options can be eliminated. A simple diagram will then suffice to display which of the responses could be true. In the following diagrams, "S," "T," and "V" stand for "swimming," "tennis," and "volleyball" respectively, and to indicate that a particular counselor is assigned to supervise one of the activities, the initial of that counselor's name appears beside the appropriate activity's abbreviation.

From the initial conditions we know that Henry supervises swimming, which eliminates (B), since counselors supervise exactly one activity. From the information given in the question, we know that George and Kathy also supervise swimming. The diagram below reflects these facts:

S: G, H, K
T:
V:

Since the original conditions state that no more than three can supervise any particular activity, we infer that Fran cannot also supervise swimming, which allows us to eliminate (A). Since George supervises swimming, we infer from the last condition given in the passage that both Nathan and Olga supervise volleyball. Adding this information to our diagram, we have the following:

S: G, H, K
T:
V: N, O

Nathan cannot supervise tennis as well as volleyball, eliminating (E), and since neither Kathy nor Nathan supervises the same activity as Joan (condition 4), Joan must supervise tennis, eliminating (C). This leaves only option (D), and under testing conditions one could choose it as the correct answer at this point. To verify the answer, however, complete the diagram and see that it is indeed possible for Lewis to supervise volleyball:

S: G, H, K
T: F, J
V: L, N, O

Even though Lewis could have supervised tennis, it is clearly possible for him to supervise volleyball. (D) is therefore the credited response.

This was classified as an "easy" question. Roughly 70 percent of those taking the test on which this item appeared answered it correctly.

Question 6, Section 1, page 38

6.   If Joan is assigned to supervise the same activity as Olga, which one of the following CANNOT be true of the assignment?

(A)   Fran supervises swimming.
(B)   George supervises swimming.
(C)   Kathy supervises volleyball.
(D)   Lewis supervises volleyball.
(E)   Nathan supervises tennis.

Explanation for Question 6

This item gives the test taker additional information with which to determine which of the responses cannot be true. An effective way to determine the answer to this question is to see if each particular response can be true. If the response does not cause a contradiction with the passage or the new information given in the question, then that response can be eliminated. If a particular response yields a contradiction, then it is the correct answer.

Let us see what effect the supposition that Joan and Olga supervise the same activity as each other has on each of the

options. Option (A) has Fran supervising swimming. Joan and Olga thus supervise volleyball, since condition 3 specifies that Olga cannot supervise tennis and condition 1 requires that at most three counselors supervise any activity (so if Joan and Olga supervised swimming, in addition to Henry and Fran, four counselors would be supervising swimming). This in turn entails Kathy's supervising swimming, since she can neither supervise tennis (condition 3) nor supervise volleyball with Olga (condition 4). This leaves us with several possible complete assignments, of which the diagram below is one:

S: F, H, K
T: G, N
V: J, L, O

Since option (A) is possible, it is not the credited response.
Option (B) has George supervising swimming. If George supervised swimming, both Nathan and Olga would have to supervise volleyball (condition 5), which would mean that Joan also would have to supervise volleyball. However, we know from condition 4 that this cannot be the case because Nathan cannot supervise the same activity as Joan. Therefore, George cannot supervise swimming. Option (B) cannot be true, and so it is the credited response.

If there is time, one should verify that the remaining options can be true. Options (C) through (E) can all be shown to be possible by the following single assignment:

S: H, J, O
T: G, N
V: F, K, L

This assignment is consistent with all the given information. This illustrates a strategy that sometimes helps: when eliminating response options, try to find a permissible scenario that rules out as many of the options as possible. Of course, this strategy will not always work as effectively as it did for this particular question.

Another point of strategy, one about determining which options to concentrate on first, is worth noting. Since options (A) and (D) involve Fran and Lewis, respectively, people to whom no specific conditions apply, they are less likely to be restricted, and thus are less likely to be the correct response in this case. The test taker would do well to ignore them in his or her initial pass through the item. In this particular question (B) would be the first option examined, which, as luck would have it, is the correct response.

Fifty-two percent of test takers answered this item correctly, making it an item of "middle difficulty."

Passage for Questions 10 and 11

A fire chief is determining the work schedules of five firefighters: Fuentes, Graber, Howell, Iman, and Jackson. The schedule must meet the following conditions:

Except for Saturday and Sunday, when none of them works, exactly one of the firefighters works each day.

None of the firefighters can work more than two days per week.

No firefighter works on two consecutive days.

Fuentes never works later in the week than Jackson.

If Howell works, then Graber must work on the following day.

Question 10, Section 1, page 39

10. If Fuentes works two days during the week and Jackson works on Thursday, which one of the following statements could be true?

(A) Fuentes works on Tuesday.
(B) Graber works on Tuesday.
(C) Howell works on Tuesday.
(D) Graber works on Wednesday.
(E) Howell works on Wednesday.

Explanation for Question 10

This question asks the test taker to determine which of the options could be true if, in addition to what is given in the passage, Fuentes works two days during the week and Jackson works on Thursday. As with many passages that deal with ordering relations, a chart or table is useful to keep track of possibilities. The information that Jackson works on Thursday may be represented as follows (letters under the days of the week are the initials of the firefighters):

Monday	Tuesday	Wednesday	Thursday	Friday
			J	

Fuentes works two days a week, and from conditions 3 and 4 it follows that Fuentes must work on Monday and Wednesday (since Fuentes has to work only on days before the day Jackson works, and since working on either Monday and Tuesday or on Tuesday and Wednesday would violate the condition that no one works on consecutive days). This is represented below:

Monday	Tuesday	Wednesday	Thursday	Friday
F		F	J	

From this we can immediately eliminate options (A), (D), and (E). Fuentes does not work on Tuesday for the reasons given earlier, which eliminates (A). Fuentes works on Wednesday and since the first condition tells us that exactly one firefighter works on each day, no one else can work on Wednesday, eliminating options (D) and (E). This leaves only options (B) and (C) as viable selections.

(C) is incorrect. To see this suppose Howell works on Tuesday. According to the last condition, if Howell works Graber must work on the following day, in this case on Wednesday. Using the same reasoning by which we eliminated (D) and (E) above, Graber cannot work on Wednesday, and thus Howell cannot work on Tuesday.

(B) is the correct response, as the acceptable table below verifies:

Monday	Tuesday	Wednesday	Thursday	Friday
F	G	F	J	I

This is considered an item of "middle difficulty"— 57 percent of test takers answered it correctly.

Question 11, Section 1, page 39

11. If Graber does not work during the week, which one of the following statements must be true?

(A) Fuentes works exactly one day during the week.
(B) Fuentes works exactly two days during the week.
(C) Iman works exactly one day during the week.
(D) Iman works exactly two days during the week.
(E) Jackson works exactly one day during the week.

Explanation for Question 11

The test taker is asked to choose the response which must be true if Graber does not work during the week. Frequently, it is best to handle such questions by seeing if each option can be falsified within the parameters set by the passage and any additional information given by the question. If an option can be falsified then it need not be true and it can be eliminated from contention. Pragmatically, one selects the remaining response if all the others have been successfully falsified. Actually proving that the option must be true directly can be difficult and time consuming, though it is quite instructive and technically correct to do so.

To falsify (A), it is necessary to show that there is a schedule that either has Fuentes working more than one day, or that has Fuentes not working at all. Since Graber does not work, the last condition tells us that Howell does not work either, so only Fuentes, Jackson, and Iman can work that week. Fuentes must work, since at least three firefighters are required to meet the condition that no one works more than two days per week (two firefighters can cover at most four days due to this condition). We need to show that Fuentes can work two days a week. The possible schedule below, which meets all the conditions, does exactly that:

Monday	Tuesday	Wednesday	Thursday	Friday
F	I	I	F	J

This schedule falsifies not only (A), but option (C) as well—as it shows, Iman does not have to work exactly one day a week.

To falsify option (B), we need to prove that it is possible that Fuentes works exactly one day a week. We have established that Fuentes must work at least one day, now we need to show that Fuentes does not need to work more than that. The schedule below demonstrates this possibility:

Monday	Tuesday	Wednesday	Thursday	Friday
F	J	I	J	I

Like the earlier schedule this one also falsifies two options. In addition to (B), it also eliminates option (E) by showing that Jackson can work on more than one day. This leaves (D) as the only viable choice, and indeed it is the correct response.

To prove that (D) must be true it is necessary to show that if Iman worked only one day during the week, at least one of the conditions would be violated. One way to do this is to assume that Iman works exactly one day and consider which day that would be. If Iman worked on Monday then Fuentes would have to work on Tuesday and Jackson on Wednesday (since Fuentes never works later in the week than Jackson). But now who would work on Thursday? It can't be Iman, nor can it be Fuentes, and since no one works on consecutive days it can't be Jackson. Since every day has to be covered, we can infer that Iman cannot work on Monday. In fact no matter what day of the week Iman works, if Iman works exactly one day, some condition—that no one works on consecutive days, that no one works more than two days, or that Fuentes never works later in the week than Jackson—would have to be violated. Since Iman works at least one day a week and no more than two (as do Fuentes and Jackson), and cannot work just one day a week, Iman must work exactly two days a week.

As with most questions, this one can be approached in a different way. The test taker can draw some general inferences from the information given in the question to see if groups of responses can be eliminated without having to create schedules for each individual response. Since the week is to be divided among three firefighters, two of the firefighters must be working two days and the other only one. Moreover, if any of them is required to work exactly one day, then the other two are required to work two. So, if (A), (C), or (E) were true then either (B) or

(D) would also have to be true. Since there is only one correct answer for each question, none of (A), (C), and (E) can be correct. The only viable options are (B) and (D). While one still has to construct a schedule for both to verify that (D) is the correct answer, one does not have to construct schedules for the other three options. Again, while this strategy works for this item, there is no guarantee that it will work for others.

This question was answered correctly by 36 percent of test takers, making it a "difficult" item.

Passage for Questions 13, 16, 18, and 19

A housing committee will consist of exactly five representatives, one of whom will be its chairperson. The representatives will be selected from among a group of five tenants—F, G, J, K, and M—and a group of four homeowners—P, Q, R, and S. The following conditions must be met:

> The committee must include at least two representatives from each group.
> The chairperson must be a representative belonging to the group from which exactly two representatives are selected.
> If F is selected, Q must be selected.
> If G is selected, K must be selected.
> If either J or M is selected, the other must also be selected.
> M and P cannot both be selected.

Question 13, Section 1, page 40

13. Which one of the following lists three representatives who could be selected together for the committee?

   (A) F, G, J
   (B) F, G, M
   (C) F, J, M
   (D) G, J, K
   (E) G, J, M

Explanation for Question 13

This question deals with possible assignments of representatives to a five-person committee. Notice that each response lists only tenants.

Of the responses, (C) gives the only list of three tenants that could be selected together. If F, J, and M are selected from the tenants, along with (for example) Q and R from the homeowners, this selection violates none of the listed conditions.

Responses (A), (B), and (E) are all incorrect for the same reason. In each response, G is selected and consequently K also needs to be selected (by the fourth condition). Since K is a tenant, there would be four tenants on the committee, violating the first condition.

Likewise for response (D), the tenants listed could not all three be on the committee. Since J is selected, M would also have to be selected (by the fifth condition). If M is selected, there are four tenants on the committee, once again contradicting the first condition.

Sixty-five percent of examinees answered this question correctly, making it an "easy" question.

Question 16, Section 1, page 40

16. If F is selected, any one of the following people could be the chairperson of the committee EXCEPT:

    (A)   G
    (B)   K
    (C)   P
    (D)   Q
    (E)   S

Explanation for Question 16

In essence the test taker must determine which of the representatives cannot be chairperson if F is selected.

The second condition states that the chairperson must be a representative belonging to the group from which exactly two representatives are selected. If F is selected, Q must also be selected (by the third condition). If G chaired the committee, as response (A) would have it, K would also have to be a member of the committee (condition 4), but that would mean that the committee had three tenants (F, G, and K), so none of them could be the chairperson. Thus G cannot be the chairperson, making (A) the correct response.

K could be the chairperson if the committee were composed of F, K, P, Q, and S, since F and K are the only tenants on the committee. Since the conditions allow the committee to be composed of these individuals, (B) is incorrect.

Either P or Q could be chairperson of a committee composed of F, G, K, P, and Q, since P and Q would be the only homeowners on the committee. A quick look at the conditions will verify that the committee could be so composed. Thus both (C) and (D) are incorrect.

Finally, S could chair the committee if it were composed of F, G, K, Q, and S, again, because S would belong to the group with exactly two representatives. Since the committee can be so composed, option (E) is also incorrect.

With 54 percent of test takers answering this question correctly when it appeared on the LSAT, this is classified as an item of "middle difficulty."

Question 18, Section 1, page 40

18. If the chairperson of the committee is to be a homeowner, which one of the following must be true?

    (A)   If G is selected, Q is also selected.
    (B)   If G is selected, R is also selected.
    (C)   If J is selected, F is also selected.
    (D)   If J is selected, Q is also selected.
    (E)   If J is selected, R is also selected.

Explanation for item 18

The test taker is asked to determine which response option must be true if the chairperson is a homeowner. Each response option is a conditional statement, that is, an "if … then …" statement. To show that a conditional statement must be true, we need to show that if the antecedent of the conditional (that which immediately follows the "if") is true, the consequent (that which immediately follows the "then") must also be true. To show that a conditional need not be true, one has to show that it is possible for the antecedent to be true while the consequent is false.

(A) is the credited response. To see this, assume that G is selected to the committee. Since the chairperson is to be a homeowner, and since the chairperson must come from that group with only two representatives, there can only be two homeowners. G's selection requires K's selection (condition 4). Since both G and K are tenants, there is exactly one other tenant. Neither J nor M can be on the committee, since by condition 5, J and M are either both on, or both off of the committee. This means F must be on the committee and so, by condition 3, must Q. Therefore, if G is on the committee, Q must be on the committee.

From the above, it is not hard to see why (B) is incorrect. Essentially, if G is selected then F, K, and Q are on the committee, leaving room for exactly one other homeowner and no one else. There are no restrictions as to who that remaining homeowner can be, so S could be the remaining representative selected. In particular, it is possible for G to be selected while R is not.

To show that options (C), (D), and (E) are incorrect, we need to first note what is implied by J's selection. Condition 5 guarantees that M is also selected and this means that P cannot be selected (by the final condition). Thus, two of Q, R, and S must be selected, and one of F, G, and K as well. G cannot be selected (because K would then have to be selected and would be a fourth tenant). Either F or K can be selected. Selecting K allows us to select, as the two homeowners on the committee, Q and R (showing that (C) is not correct), or R and S (showing that (D) is not correct), or Q and S (showing that (E) is not correct). This eliminates options (C) through (E).

This question was classified as "very difficult." Only 24 percent of test takers answered the item correctly when it appeared on the LSAT.

Question 19, Section 1, page 40

19. The committee must include at least one representative from which one of the following pairs?

(A)   F, P
(B)   G, J
(C)   K, Q
(D)   M, P
(E)   R, S

Explanation for Question 19

An effective way to deal with this question is to consider each response and try to form a committee without either of the people listed in the pair. If you are able to do this, then neither member of the pair must be included, and the response is an incorrect one. (If it is possible to form the committee with neither person in a pair being on the committee, then it is false that the committee must include at least one representative from that pair.) If there is no committee that fails to include at least one member of the pair in a response, then that response is correct.

We can see that (A) is an incorrect response since the committee could be made up of J, K, M, R, and S. This shows that neither F nor P must be included on the committee. Similarly we can see that (B) is incorrect: F, K, P, Q, and R can make up a committee, so neither G nor J need to be included.

Considering response (C), when we try to form a committee that does not include K, we note that it also cannot include G (by the fourth condition). Since this committee also would not include Q, it follows that it would not include F (by the third condition). The committee would have to be made up of the five representatives who have not been thus far ruled out—J, M, P, R, and S. But by the final condition M and P cannot both be selected, so even this is not a legitimate committee. Since it is not possible to form a committee without either K or Q, (C) is the correct response.

(D) and (E) are each incorrect responses. F, G, K, Q, and S are a possible committee, so neither M nor P need to be included, eliminating (D). F, G, K, P, and Q could make up the committee, hence neither R nor S need to be included, eliminating (E).

Thirty-one percent of examinees answered this question correctly, making it a "difficult" question.

Passage for Questions 22 and 24

Four apprentices—Louis, Madelyn, Nora, and Oliver—are initially assigned to projects Q, R, S, and T, respectively. During the year in which they are apprentices, two reassignments of apprentices to projects will be made, each time according to a different one of the following plans, which can be used in any order:

Plan 1. The apprentice assigned to project Q switches projects with the apprentice assigned to project S and the apprentice assigned to project R switches projects with the apprentice assigned to project T.

Plan 2. The apprentice assigned to project S switches projects with the apprentice assigned to project T.

Plan 3. Louis and Madelyn switch projects with each other.

Question 22, Section 1, page 41

22. If at some time during the year, Louis is reassigned to project R, which one of the following could have been the assignment of apprentices to the projects immediately before the reassignment?

(A)   Q: Louis; R: Madelyn; S: Oliver; T: Nora
(B)   Q: Louis; R: Nora; S: Oliver; T: Madelyn
(C)   Q: Nora; R: Madelyn; S: Louis; T: Oliver
(D)   Q: Nora; R: Oliver; S: Louis; T: Madelyn
(E)   Q: Oliver; R: Nora; S: Louis; T: Madelyn

Explanation for Question 22

Basically, this question asks the examinee to identify an assignment of apprentices to projects which can be attained from the original assignment and from which Louis could be directly reassigned to project R. Looking at the three plans, we notice that only two of those plans could possibly reassign Louis to project R in one step. If Louis is assigned to project T, he can be reassigned to project R by plan 1. Alternatively, if Madelyn is assigned to project R, Louis can be reassigned to project R by plan 3.

Louis is not assigned to project T in any of the five responses to this question: this rules out his reassignment by plan 1. The only way that Louis could be reassigned to project R is by plan 3, and only in those cases where Madelyn is assigned to project R. Thus (A) and (C) are the only viable responses. (B), (D), and (E) can be ruled out because, given those assignments, there is no plan by which Louis can be reassigned to project R in one step.

Because only two reassignments of apprentices to projects will be made, and reassigning Louis to project R uses one of those reassignments, the correct assignment needs to be attainable from the original assignment with at most one reassignment. Response (A) gives such an assignment. (A) can be obtained from the original assignment by using plan 2. Thus (A) is the correct response. On the other hand, none of the plans allows you to obtain the assignment in (C) from the original assignment in one step, so (C) is an incorrect response.

Thirty-two percent of examinees answered this question correctly, making it a "difficult" question.

Question 24, Section 1, page 41

24. If the first reassignment is made according to plan 1, which one of the following must be true?

(A) Louis is assigned to project T as a result of the second reassignment.
(B) Madelyn is assigned to project Q as a result of the second reassignment.
(C) Madelyn is assigned to project T as a result of the second reassignment.
(D) Oliver is assigned to project S as a result of the second reassignment.
(E) Oliver is assigned to project T as a result of the second reassignment.

Explanation for Question 24

This item requires the test taker to identify a characteristic of the second reassignment of apprentices to projects, if the first reassignment is made according to Plan 1.

Central to the solution of this item is the fact that if Plan 1 is the plan used to make the first reassignment, then it is irrelevant whether one uses Plan 2 or Plan 3 for the second reassignment—either results in the same final assignment of apprentices to projects. Below is a table showing the initial assignments (the initial of apprentices appears below the project to which they are assigned):

Q	R	S	T
L	M	N	O

Using Plan 1 to make the first reassignment, the apprentice assigned to project Q (Louis) and the apprentice assigned to project S (Nora) are switched, while the apprentice assigned to project R (Madelyn) and the apprentice assigned to project T (Oliver) are switched. This gives us the following table:

Q	R	S	T
N	O	L	M

Using either Plan 2 or Plan 3 to make the second reassignment, the apprentice assigned to Project S (Louis) is switched with the apprentice assigned to project T (Madelyn). Since Plan 1 cannot be used again, the second reassignment must be the following:

Q	R	S	T
N	O	M	L

From this it is evident that Louis is assigned to project T as a result of the second reassignment. Thus (A) is the credited response. Simple inspection shows that none of (B) through (E) can, let alone, must, be true.

This was a "difficult" item, with 30 percent of test takers answering it correctly.

There is a strategy a test taker may use with passages such as the one upon which questions 22 and 24 are based. Sometimes the conditions given in a passage result in a limited number of possibilities. In such cases it may actually be most efficient to plot out all the possibilities and then "read-off" the answers to each question. The extra time spent plotting out all the possibilities is often made up for by the briefer time it takes to answer each question.

The test taker should note that since there is a single starting state, that is, the initial assignment of apprentices to projects is given, and since only two plans out of three are used, there can be at most six possible assignments for the entire year. Moreover, as we have seen in the explanation to question 24, two of these combinations of plans are identical, so there are only five unique possible sets of assignments for the year. These are listed below:

Possibility 1

	Q	R	S	T
Initial Assignment	L	M	N	O
Plan 1	N	O	L	M
Plan 2 (or 3)	N	O	M	L

Possibility 2

	Q	R	S	T
Initial Assignment	L	M	N	O
Plan 2	L	M	O	N
Plan 1	O	N	L	M

Possibility 3

	Q	R	S	T
Initial Assignment	L	M	N	O
Plan 2	L	M	O	N
Plan 3	M	L	O	N

Possibility 4

	Q	R	S	T
Initial Assignment	L	M	N	O
Plan 3	M	L	N	O
Plan 1	N	O	M	L

Possibility 5

	Q̲	R̲	S̲	T̲
Initial Assignment	L	M	N	O
Plan 3	M	L	N	O
Plan 2	M	L	O	N

Armed with this "solution set," answering questions is an almost trivial task. Take question 22 for example. We need only consider those possibilities that have Louis reassigned to R at some point, i.e., possibilities 3 through 5. All one has to do now is compare each response with the assignment before Louis is assigned to R, if the response option matches an assignment in any of the possibilities, then that option is the correct answer. In this case (A) matches the first reassignment of possibility 3.

If it is clear to the test taker that there are very few possibilities entailed by the conditions given in the passage, then this strategy is worth considering. If, however, one has doubts about the number of possibilities, one should avoid this strategy as it may consume far more time than is prudent.

■ Logical Reasoning Questions

Logical reasoning questions evaluate a test taker's ability to understand, analyze, criticize, and complete arguments. The arguments are contained in short passages taken from a variety of sources, including letters to the editor, speeches, advertisements, newspaper articles and editorials, informal discussions and conversations, as well as articles in the humanities, the social sciences, and the natural sciences.

Each logical reasoning question requires the examinee to read and comprehend the argument or the reasoning contained in the passage, and answer one or two questions about it. The questions test a variety of logical skills. These include:

- recognizing the point or issue of an argument or dispute;

- detecting the assumptions involved in an argument or chain of reasoning;

- drawing reasonable conclusions from given evidence or premises;

- identifying and applying principles;

- identifying the method or structure of an argument or chain of reasoning;

- detecting reasoning errors and misinterpretations;

- determining how additional evidence or argument affects an argument or conclusion; and

- identifying explanations and recognizing resolutions of conflicting facts or arguments.

The questions do not presuppose knowledge of the terminology of formal logic. For example, you will not be expected to know the meaning of specialized terms such as "ad hominem" or "syllogism." On the other hand, you will be expected to understand and critique the reasoning contained in arguments. This requires that you possess, at a minimum, a college-level understanding of widely used concepts such as argument, premise, assumption, and conclusion.

Suggested Approach

Read each question carefully. Make sure that you understand the meaning of each part of the question. Make sure that you understand the meaning of each answer choice and the ways in which it may or may not relate to the question posed.

Do not pick a response simply because it is a true statement. Although true, it may not answer the question posed.

Answer each question on the basis of the information that is given, even if you do not agree with it. Work within the context provided by the passage. LSAT questions do not involve any tricks or hidden meanings.

Ten Logical Reasoning Questions from PrepTest XI and Explanations

The questions on the following pages have been selected from the Logical Reasoning sections of PrepTest XI (Section 2, pages 42-49 and Section 4, pages 58-65). **If you wish to answer these questions before reading explanations for them, you should skip this section and return to it after you have completed your practice on Section 2 and 4 of PrepTest XI.**

Directions: The questions in this section are based on the reasoning contained in brief statements or passages. For some questions, more than one of the choices could conceivably answer the question. However, you are to choose the best answer; that is, the response that most accurately and completely answers the question. You should not make assumptions that are by commonsense standards implausible, superfluous, or incompatible with the passage. After you have chosen the best answer, blacken the corresponding space on your answer sheet.

Question 6, Section 2, page 43

6. Cigarette smoking has been shown to be a health hazard; therefore, governments should ban all advertisements that promote smoking.

    Which one of the following principles, if established, most strongly supports the argument?

    (A) Advertisements should not be allowed to show people doing things that endanger their health.
    (B) Advertisers should not make misleading claims about the healthfulness of their products.
    (C) Advertisements should disclose the health hazards associated with the products they promote.
    (D) All products should conform to strict government health and safety standards.
    (E) Advertisements should promote only healthful products.

Explanation for Question 6

This question asks the examinee to identify the principle that, if established, most strongly supports a short argument for governments banning all advertisements that promote smoking. (E) asserts that advertisements should "promote only healthful products;" that is, if an advertisement promotes a product, that product should be healthful. The only premise of the argument in the passage states that cigarette smoking has been shown to be a health hazard; thus cigarettes are not a healthful product. So if the principle in (E) were established, it would strongly support the claim that advertisements should not promote smoking, which in turn provides strong support for the argument in the passage, that "governments should ban all advertisements that promote smoking." Thus the principle in (E) provides very strong support for the argument, and (E) is the credited response.

Response (A) provides a basis for a ban of some types of cigarette advertisements, but it does not support a ban on all advertisements that promote smoking. Advertisements that promote smoking do not need to actually show people smoking or doing anything else that might endanger their health. For example, advertisements may promote smoking simply by associating smoking with a desirable lifestyle or a famous person.

Response (B) is incorrect for a similar reason. An advertisement for cigarettes may, but need not, make misleading claims about the healthfulness of that product in order to promote it. For example, showing a glamorous person holding a pack of cigarettes or even smoking a cigarette makes no claim about the healthfulness of cigarettes.

Response (C) states a principle that provides little or no support for the argument in the passage. The principle in

(C) gives no basis for banning advertisements that promote smoking; it merely makes a prescription about what those advertisements should say.

Similarly with response (D): the principle does not give a reason for banning advertisements that promote smoking. The principle in (D) supports the regulation of the product itself, not the advertisements that promote it.

Forty-two percent of examinees answered this question correctly when it appeared on the LSAT.

Question 7, Section 2, page 43

7. Every adult male woolly monkey is larger than even the largest female woolly monkey. In colonies of woolly monkeys, any adult male will dominate any female.

    If the statements above are true, which one of the following must on the basis of them be true of woolly monkeys in colonies?

    (A) Size is the primary determinant of relations of dominance among woolly monkeys.
    (B) Some large adolescent male woolly monkeys dominate some smaller females of the species.
    (C) If a male woolly monkey is larger than a female of the species, that male will dominate that female.
    (D) If a female woolly monkey dominates a male of the species, the dominated male monkey is not an adult.
    (E) An adult male woolly monkey can dominate a female of the species only if that female is also an adult.

Explanation for Question 7

This question asks the examinee to identify the response that must be true if the statements in the passage are true. A good way to approach this type of question is to attempt to determine whether it is possible for a response to be false in the same situation in which all the statements in the passage are true. If it is possible for the response to be false while the statements in the passage are true, the response is incorrect. If there is no way that the response could be false while all the statements in the passage are true, then it is the credited response.

From the second statement in the passage, it logically follows that it is false that in woolly monkey colonies, a female woolly monkey can dominate an adult male of the species. From this it follows that if a female woolly monkey dominates a male of the species, then that male is not an adult. Thus (D) must be true of woolly monkeys in colonies if the statements in the passage are true, and it is the credited response.

Response (A) need not be true even if the statements in the passage are true. The passage states that every adult male woolly monkey is larger than every female woolly monkey, and that any adult male in a woolly monkey colony will dominate any female. But given this information, it does not have to be true that size is the primary determinant of relations of dominance among woolly monkeys. For example, it may be coincidental that adult male woolly monkeys are both bigger than females and dominant over females. That is, the fact that adult males dominate females may be due to some factor other than size. Or it may be that size has nothing to do with dominance relations among woolly monkeys of the same sex as each other.

With regard to response (B), the statements in the passage give no information about the abilities of adolescent woolly monkeys to dominate others of their species. So it is entirely compatible with the information in the passage that no large adolescent male woolly monkeys dominate any smaller female woolly monkeys. Hence (B) need not be true even if the statements in the passage are true, and it is an incorrect response.

Response (C) is a statement about woolly monkeys in general, while the information in the passage is restricted to female and adult male woolly monkeys. Given that the statements in the passage are true, it is entirely possible that a female woolly monkey dominates a larger male woolly monkey who is not yet an adult. This shows that (C) does not need to be true even if the statements in the passage are true.

With regard to response (E), the passage states that adult male woolly monkeys dominate any female in their colony. This shows that it need not be true that an adult woolly monkey can dominate a female of the species only if the female is an adult; there may well be nonadult females in colonies with adult males. Hence (E) is an incorrect response.

When it appeared on the test, 54 percent of test takers answered this question correctly, making it an item of "middle difficulty."

Question 15, Section 2, page 45

15. A standard problem for computer security is that passwords that have to be typed on a computer keyboard are comparatively easy for unauthorized users to steal or guess. A new system that relies on recognizing the voices of authorized users apparently avoids this problem. In a small initial trial, the system never incorrectly accepted someone seeking access to the computer's data. Clearly, if this result can be repeated in an operational setting, then there will be a way of giving access to those people who are entitled to access and to no one else.

The reasoning above is flawed because it

(A) makes a faulty comparison, in that a security system based on voice recognition would not be expected to suffer from the same problems as one that relied on passwords entered from a keyboard

(B) bases a general conclusion on a small amount of data

(C) fails to recognize that a security system based on voice recognition could easily have applications other than computer security

(D) ignores the possibility that the system sometimes denies access to people who are entitled to access

(E) states its conclusion in a heavily qualified way

Explanation for Question 15

The task in this question is to choose the response that describes a flaw in the reasoning in the passage. The passage discusses a particular problem in computer security—that "passwords that have to be typed on a computer keyboard are comparatively easy for unauthorized users to steal or guess"—and reports on a new security system based on voice recognition that has shown favorable results in addressing this problem in an initial trial. During the initial trial of the voice-recognition security system, it "never incorrectly accepted someone seeking access to the computer's data." On the basis of this trial, it is concluded that "... if this result can be repeated in an operational setting, then there will be a way of giving access to those people who are entitled to access and to no one else." So the conclusion actually makes two claims about what will happen if the result can be repeated in an operational setting: there will be a method that both (i) gives access to those people who are entitled to access and (ii) does not give access to anyone who is not entitled to access. But the evidence presented by the argument supports only the second of these claims. In other words, even if the result of the initial trial can be repeated in an operational setting, this does not provide a reason for concluding that the system will be successful in giving access to those who are entitled to access. Response (D), the credited response, indicates this flaw: the possibility that the system sometimes denies access to people who are entitled to access is not addressed by the reasoning in the passage.

Response (A) is incorrect. To the extent that a comparison is made between the two security systems, the comparison is an appropriate one to make. After all, the matter at issue is whether the voice-recognition security system can avoid a problem found in the password security system.

Response (B) does not describe a flaw in the reasoning in the passage. The conclusion drawn in the passage is qualified by the phrase "... if this result can be repeated in an operational setting ...," so the argument itself recognizes that the amount of data is small. The flaw does not arise from the small *size* of the data relative to the generality of the conclusion. Rather, it arises from a problem with the *nature* of the data, viz., the fact that the data are not relevant to whether the new system gives access to those people who are entitled access.

Response (C) is not correct because the possibility that a voice activation security system has other applications is irrelevant to the issue at hand—the system's effectiveness with one specific application. So while the argument does ignore this possibility, its doing so is not a reasoning flaw.

Response (E) is not correct because, while it is arguably true of the passage, it does not describe a flaw in its reasoning. On the contrary, the qualified way in which the conclusion is stated is appropriate, given the small amount of data presented.

Thirty-two percent of examinees answered this question correctly, making it a "difficult" question.

Questions 20, Section 2, page 47

A recent report on an environmental improvement program was criticized for focusing solely on pragmatic solutions to the large number of significant problems that plague the program instead of seriously trying to produce a coherent vision for the future of the program. In response the report's authors granted that the critics had raised a valid point but explained that, to do anything at all, the program needed continued government funding, and that to get such funding the program first needed to regain a reputation for competence.

20. The basic position taken by the report's authors on the criticism leveled against the report is that

(A) addressing the critics' concern now would be premature
(B) the critics' motives are self-serving
(C) the notion of a coherent vision would be inappropriate to a program of the sort at issue
(D) the authors of the report are more knowledgeable than its critics
(E) giving the report a single focus is less desirable than the critics claim

Explanation for Question 20

The passage for this question outlines a criticism that has been made of a report on an environmental improvement program, and recounts the response to this criticism by the report's authors. The question asks the examinee to identify the basic position that the report's authors take on this criticism.

According to the passage, the report's authors conceded that the "critics had raised a valid point," but went on to justify their approach to the report by pointing out that the

foremost need of the program was continued government funding, and for that funding to continue, "the program first needed to regain a reputation for competence." In essence, the authors are saying that the concern for restoring the program's reputation currently takes priority over the concern raised by the critics. Response (A) expresses this position by indicating that it would be premature to deal with the critics' concern at the present time; thus (A) is the credited response.

Response (B) misses the point made by the report's authors. The authors make no suggestion at all about the critics' motives, let alone that their motives are self-serving.

Response (C) also strays quite far from the authors' position. By granting that the critics raise a valid point, the authors may very well be conceding that the notion of a coherent vision is appropriate to this program. Moreover, the authors' response to their critics does not focus on the appropriateness of the critics' approach, but rather on the rationale for their own approach.

Response (D) is incorrect. Nothing is said in the passage about the authors being or claiming to be more knowledgeable than their critics.

Response (E) is incorrect because it misrepresents the issue that the authors' reply addresses. The question at issue is not so much whether the report should have a single or multiple focus, and the critics are certainly never said to claim that a single focus is desirable, as (E) indicates. Rather, the authors' reply addresses the question of what the approach of the report should be.

When it appeared on the LSAT, 53 percent of examinees answered this question correctly, making it an item of "middle difficulty."

Question 22, Section 2, page 48

22. Oil company representative: We spent more money on cleaning the otters affected by our recent oil spill than has been spent on any previous marine mammal rescue project. This shows our concern for the environment.

Environmentalist: You have no such concern. Your real concern is evident in your admission to the press that news photographs of oil-covered otters would be particularly damaging to your public image, which plays an important role in your level of sales.

The environmentalist's conclusion would be properly drawn if it were true that the

(A) oil company cannot have more than one motive for cleaning the otters affected by the oil spill
(B) otter population in the area of the oil spill could not have survived without the cleaning project

(C)   oil company has always shown a high regard for its profits in choosing its courses of action

(D)   government would have spent the money to clean the otters if the oil company had not agreed to do it

(E)   oil company's efforts toward cleaning the affected otters have been more successful than have such efforts in previous projects to clean up oil spills

Explanation for Question 22

The task in this question is to choose one of five responses which, if it were true, would allow the conclusion of the environmentalist's argument to be properly drawn.

The environmentalist 's conclusion is that the oil company has no concern for the environment. The evidence presented is that the oil company representative has admitted that not cleaning the otters would be bad for sales. That is, by showing that the oil company is motivated by an interest in protecting its public image (and thus its sales), the environmentalist hopes to show that the oil company is not motivated by a different interest, namely, concern for the environment. If response (A) were true, the environmentalist's argument would succeed: if the oil company can have no more than one motive in this case, then demonstrating that it has a particular motive (protecting sales) is sufficient to show that it does not have any other particular motive (e.g., environmental concern). Thus (A) is the credited response.

Response (B) is incorrect because even if it is true, it leaves entirely open the possibility that the oil company is concerned for the environment, in addition to being concerned with its sales. If anything, the assertion in (B) that the survival of the otter population was dependent upon the cleanup might support the claim that the oil company has a concern for the environment in this case.

Likewise if response (C) were true, it would not make the environmentalist's conclusion be properly drawn. The oil company's acting out of a concern for the environment is entirely consistent with it being true that the "oil company has always shown a high regard for profits in choosing its courses of action." A high regard for profits is not incompatible with the oil company also holding other things in high regard, such as the environment. Even if (C) is true, it can still be true that the oil company is concerned with the environment; thus (C) is an incorrect response.

The truth of response (D) would do nothing to rule out the possibility that the oil company is acting out of concern for the environment. Even if the government would have cleaned the otters if the oil company had not, the oil company, in cleaning the otters, could still have acted out of concern for the environment. It is not unusual for two parties to be willing to do the same thing out of the same concern and the action be "overdetermined." Thus (D) is an incorrect response.

Finally, if (E) were true, the oil company certainly could still have acted out of concern for the environment when it cleaned the otters. If anything, the success of this cleanup project in relation to previous efforts might support the claim that the oil company has a concern for the environment in this case. Response (E) is thus incorrect.

Forty-three percent of examinees answered this question correctly when it appeared on the LSAT, making it a "difficult" item.

Question 23, Section 2, page 48

23.   A group of scientists studying calcium metabolism in laboratory rats discovered that removing the rats' parathyroid glands resulted in the rats' having substantially lower than normal levels of calcium in their blood. This discovery led the scientists to hypothesize that the function of the parathyroid gland is to regulate the level of calcium in the blood by raising that level when it falls below the normal range. In a further experiment, the scientists removed not only the parathyroid gland but also the adrenal gland from rats. They made the surprising discovery that the level of calcium in the rats' blood decreased much less sharply than when the parathyroid gland alone was removed.

Which one of the following, if true, explains the surprising discovery in a way most consistent with the scientists' hypothesis?

(A)   The adrenal gland acts to lower the level of calcium in the blood.

(B)   The adrenal gland and the parathyroid gland play the same role in regulating calcium blood levels.

(C)   The absence of a parathyroid gland causes the adrenal gland to increase the level of calcium in the blood.

(D)   If the adrenal gland, and no other gland, of a rat were removed, the rat's calcium level would remain stable.

(E)   The only function of the parathyroid gland is to regulate the level of calcium in the blood.

Explanation for Question 23

The passage on which this question is based describes an experimental finding: removing the parathyroid glands of rats caused the rats to have calcium levels much lower than normal; and a hypothesis scientists have based on that finding: the parathyroid gland regulates the level of calcium in the blood by raising that level whenever it falls below normal. The passage then describes another experiment whose results apparently conflict with the scientists' hypothesis. This experiment found that removing both the parathyroid gland

and the adrenal gland from rats resulted in a decrease in the level of calcium in the blood much less drastic than that for rats with only the parathyroid removed. The question asks the examinee to choose an option that, if true, explains this further finding in a way most consistent with the scientists' hypothesis.

If response (A) is true, the adrenal gland lowers the calcium level in the blood. In that case, if the adrenal gland were removed from a rat, one would expect that rat's calcium level to be higher than it would be otherwise. And this is exactly what the further experiment found—with the adrenal and parathyroid glands removed, the calcium levels are higher than with the parathyroid gland alone removed. In this way, the further experimental results are explained in a way consistent with the scientists' hypothesis: the parathyroid gland's removal and the adrenal gland's presence each individually lower the calcium levels. (A) is thus the credited response.

Response (B) does not explain the findings of the further experiment in a way consistent with the scientists' hypothesis. If (B) and the scientists' hypothesis were both true, we would expect there to be even lower levels of calcium in the blood with both glands removed than with just the parathyroid gland removed. But the findings of the experiment were just the opposite: the calcium level "decreased much less sharply," i.e., was not as low, with both glands removed as it was with just the parathyroid gland removed.

Likewise, response (C) is incorrect. If, as (C) asserts, the parathyroid gland's being absent causes the adrenal gland to increase the calcium level, we would expect a higher calcium level with the parathyroid gland removed and the adrenal gland in place than with both of the glands removed, if the scientists' hypothesis is correct. Again, the results of the further experiment were the opposite of this.

Response (D) gives no basis for explaining the finding of the further experiment. If (D) were true, removing the adrenal gland alone would have no effect on a rat's calcium level. This does not help to explain the finding that removing the adrenal gland along with the parathyroid gland caused a different calcium level than did removal of the parathyroid gland only. If anything, response (D) is at odds with the finding of the further experiment, and so (D) is an incorrect response.

Response (E) asserts only that the parathyroid gland's function is restricted to the regulation of the level of calcium in the blood. This helps not at all to explain the difference in the observed effects of removing only the parathyroid gland and removing both the parathyroid and adrenal glands. Thus, (E) is an incorrect response.

This was classified as a "difficult" question, as 32 percent of examinees answered this question correctly.

Question 11, Section 4, page 61

11. Logging industry official: Harvesting trees from old-growth forests for use in manufacture can reduce the amount of carbon dioxide in the atmosphere, since when large old trees die in the forest they decompose, releasing their stored carbon dioxide. Harvesting old-growth forests would, moreover, make room for rapidly growing young trees, which absorb more carbon dioxide from the atmosphere than do trees in old-growth forests.

Which one of the following, if true, most seriously weakens the official's argument?

(A)   Many old-growth forests are the home of thousands of animal species that would be endangered if the forests were to be destroyed.

(B)   Much of the organic matter from old-growth trees, unusable as lumber, is made into products that decompose rapidly.

(C)   A young tree contains less than half the amount of carbon dioxide that is stored in an old tree of the same species.

(D)   Much of the carbon dioxide present in forests is eventually released when wood and other organic debris found on the forest floor decompose.

(E)   It can take many years for the trees of a newly planted forest to reach the size of those found in existing old-growth forests.

Explanation for Question 11

The logging industry official in this passage argues that the amount of carbon dioxide in the atmosphere can be reduced by harvesting the trees in old-growth forests for use in manufacture. The official gives two reasons for this: when old trees die in the forest they release carbon dioxide when they decompose, and the young trees that replace old-growth trees absorb more carbon dioxide from the atmosphere than their predecessors. The task of this question is to choose the response that, if true, most seriously weakens this argument.

In order for the first reason to furnish evidence for the official's conclusion, it must at least be true that the products manufactured from the harvested old-growth timber do not release as much or more carbon dioxide into the atmosphere than the decomposition of the harvested trees in the forest would have, had they not been harvested. Response (B) calls that into question by asserting that much of the organic matter from old-growth trees, being unusable as lumber, is made into products that decompose rapidly. Since we know from the argument in the passage that decomposing trees release their stored carbon dioxide into the atmosphere, it is reasonable to believe that this decomposition of the organic matter from the trees used in manufacture will also release the stored carbon dioxide from the trees into the atmosphere. Furthermore, since the decomposition is rapid, it may result in the stored carbon dioxide being released into the atmosphere more quickly than it would be were the old trees allowed to stand in the forest. Since the trees, if not harvested, would be left standing in the forest, they may only eventually and gradually fall and decompose, releasing their stored carbon dioxide over a very extended period of time. So if (B) is true it is reasonable to think that harvesting the old-growth trees could very well result in a rapid injection of carbon dioxide into the atmosphere, over a short time, much exceeding the amount that would have been released over that time if the trees were left standing. In this way (B) weakens the argument in the passage by calling into question an assumption that must be made for one of its premises to furnish evidence for its conclusion. So (B) is the credited response.

Response (A) is incorrect because it has no bearing on the official's argument, which concludes that harvesting old-growth forests can reduce atmospheric carbon dioxide. (A) gives a reason for not destroying old-growth forests, but "old-growth forests should be destroyed" is a distinct conclusion from the one in the argument in question.

Response (C) is incorrect; what it asserts does not counteract either of the reasons that the official gives in support of the conclusion. Indeed, if anything, (C) is implied by the mechanism that the official's second reason suggests, namely, that trees absorb and store carbon dioxide from the atmosphere as they grow. So if anything, (C) would confirm the official's argument.

Response (D) is incorrect; the official's argument is actually strengthened by (D)'s being true. As trees die and decompose, they often fall to the forest floor. This is common knowledge, and it is also suggested by (D)'s specifically mentioning "wood" as part of the debris on the forest floor. So at least some of the wood and other organic debris (e.g., leaves or needles) comes from the harvestable trees, if they are not harvested. Response (D) strengthens the official's argument inasmuch as harvested trees can no longer contribute to the wood and other organic debris on the forest floor, there to decompose and release stored carbon dioxide into the atmosphere.

Response (E) is not correct because it is not relevant to the conclusion of the official's argument. Like (A), response (E) may give a reason for not harvesting old-growth trees, but it does not weaken the official's argument that harvesting old-growth forests can reduce the amount of carbon dioxide in the atmosphere.

Thirty-six percent of examinees answered this question correctly, making it a "difficult" item.

Question 15, Section 4, page 62

15. A certain experimental fungicide causes no harm to garden plants, though only if it is diluted at least to ten parts water to one part fungicide. Moreover, this fungicide is known to be so effective against powdery mildew that it has the capacity to eliminate it completely from rose plants. Thus this fungicide, as long as it is sufficiently diluted, provides a means of eliminating powdery mildew from rose plants that involves no risk of harming the plants.

Which one of the following is an assumption on which the argument depends?

(A)   There is not an alternative method, besides application of this fungicide, for eliminating powdery mildew from rose plants without harming the plants.

(B)   When the fungicide is sufficiently diluted, it does not present any risk of harm to people, animals, or beneficial insects.

(C)   Powdery mildew is the only fungal infection that affects rose plants.

(D)   If a fungicide is to be effective against powdery mildew on rose plants, it must eliminate the powdery mildew completely.

(E)   The effectiveness of the fungicide does not depend on its being more concentrated than one part in ten parts of water.

Explanation for Question 15

The argument proceeds by reporting that an experimental fungicide causes no harm to garden plants, but only when it is diluted to ten parts water (or more) to one part fungicide. Then it reports that the fungicide is capable of completely eliminating powdery mildew from rose plants. It concludes on the basis of these two statements that the fungicide, sufficiently diluted, provides a means of eliminating powdery mildew from rose plants without harming those plants. In other words, it is concluded that the use of fungicide can be both safe to the rose plants and completely effective against the mildew. However, the premises do not establish that the fungicide is safe and completely effective under the same circumstances. For example, it may be that the fungicide is completely effective only when it is so concentrated that it is not safe (i.e., more concentrated than one part fungicide to ten parts water). For the argument to succeed in proving its conclusion, this possibility must be ruled out, which is what is done in response (E). In this way, the argument depends on the assumption of (E), and (E) is the credited response.

Response (A) is incorrect since whether or not there is an alternative method for safely eliminating powdery mildew from rose plants is irrelevant to the argument. That is, if

(A) is false, this does not diminish the strength of the argument in the passage, which is just about a particular method for powdery mildew removal.

Response (B) provides an irrelevant assumption. Since the argument draws a conclusion about the safety of the fungicide to rose plants only, only the risk of harming the rose plants needs to be considered: the risk of the fungicide harming people, animals, or beneficial insects is entirely incidental to this argument.

The argument does not depend on the assumption in response (C). If (C) is false, i.e., there are other fungal infections affecting rose plants, the argument for the fungicide being safe and effective in treating powdery mildew on rose plants is no less strong. Only the fungicide's effectiveness and safety in treating powdery mildew needs to be considered.

Likewise, the argument does not depend on the assumption in response (D). To see this, imagine that (D) is not true: some fungicide is effective against powdery mildew on rose plants, but does not eliminate powdery mildew completely. But the experimental fungicide in question is not of this sort: the argument tells us that the experimental fungicide is effective against powdery mildew and can eliminate powdery mildew completely. The properties other fungicides may or may not have are not at issue.

This is considered a "difficult" question. Thirty-eight percent of test takers answered this question correctly.

Question 22, Section 4, page 65

22. Paulsville and Longtown cannot both be included in the candidate's itinerary of campaign stops. The candidate will make a stop in Paulsville unless Salisbury is made part of the itinerary. Unfortunately, a stop in Salisbury is out of the question. Clearly, then, a stop in Longtown can be ruled out.

The reasoning in the argument above most closely parallels that in which one of the following arguments?

(A) The chef never has both fresh radishes and fresh green peppers available for the chef's salad at the same time. If she uses fresh radishes, she also uses spinach. But currently there is no spinach to be had. It can be inferred, then, that she will not be using fresh green peppers.

(B) Tom will definitely support Parker if Mendoza does not apply; and Tom will not support both Parker and Chung. Since, as it turns out, Mendoza will not apply, it follows that Chung will not get Tom's support.

(C) The program committee never selects two plays by Shaw for a single season. But when they select a play by Coward, they do not select

any play by Shaw at all. For this season, the committee has just selected a play by Shaw, so they will not select any play by Coward.

(D) In agricultural pest control, either pesticides or the introduction of natural enemies of the pest, but not both, will work. Of course, neither will be needed if pest-resistant crops are planted. So if pesticides are in fact needed, it must be that there are no natural enemies of the pest.

(E) The city cannot afford to build both a new stadium and the new road that would be needed to get there. But neither of the two projects is worth doing without the other. Since the city will not undertake any but worthwhile projects, the new stadium will not be constructed at this time.

Explanation for Question 22

The argument in the passage consists of a conclusion and three reasons for that conclusion (premises). This argument can be spelled out as follows:

(1) IT IS NOT TRUE THAT BOTH <u>Paulsville is one of the candidate's campaign stops</u> AND <u>Longtown is one of the candidate's campaign stops</u>.

(2) IF <u>Salisbury is</u> NOT <u>one of the candidate's campaign stops</u> THEN <u>Paulsville is one of the candidate's campaign stops</u>. (This is another way of saying that Paulsville is one of the candidate's campaign stops UNLESS Salisbury is one of the candidate's campaign stops.)

(3) <u>Salisbury is</u> NOT <u>one of the candidate's campaign stops</u>.

Therefore,

(Conclusion) <u>Longtown is</u> NOT <u>one of the candidate's campaign stops</u>.

To see how the reasoning in this argument works, notice that from premises (2) and (3), it follows that Paulsville is one of the candidate's campaign stops. This, together with premise (1), implies that Longtown is NOT one of the candidate's campaign stops.

The argument in response (B) is the one whose reasoning is most closely parallel to that in the argument above:

(B.1) IF <u>Mendoza does</u> NOT <u>apply</u> THEN <u>Tom will definitely support Parker</u>.

(B.2) IT IS NOT TRUE THAT BOTH <u>Tom supports Parker</u> AND <u>Tom supports Chung</u>.

(B.3) <u>Mendoza will</u> NOT <u>apply</u>.

Therefore,

(B.conclusion) <u>Chung will</u> NOT <u>get Tom's support</u>.

Notice that both the logically relevant words (such as IF, THEN, NOT, BOTH, etc.) and the entities related by them—Paulsville, Longtown, and Salisbury in the passage, and Parker, Mendoza, and Chung in (B)—occur in the same pattern in the passage and in (B). The two arguments do differ with respect to the order in which the premises are listed: the premise that corresponds to premise (2) in the passage is listed first in response (B), while the premise corresponding to premise (1) in the passage is listed second. Of course this difference is not logically relevant; it does not effect the reasoning. The reasoning in no other option parallels the reasoning of the argument in the passage more closely than does the reasoning in (B), so (B) is the credited response.

(A) is an incorrect response: the reasoning in (A)'s argument is importantly different from the reasoning in the argument in the passage. (A)'s argument can be spelled out as follows:

A.1) IT IS NOT TRUE THAT BOTH <u>the chef has fresh radishes available for the chef's salad</u> AND <u>the chef has fresh green peppers available for the chef's salad</u>.
A.2) IF <u>the chef uses fresh radishes</u> THEN <u>the chef uses spinach</u>.
A.3) <u>Spinach</u> is NOT <u>available</u>.
Therefore,
(A.conclusion) <u>The chef will</u> NOT <u>use fresh green peppers</u>.

Notice that there are several differences between this argument and the one in the passage. The second premise has no "NOT" in (A), and the entities in question are arranged differently in the two arguments: in the first premise, "radishes" corresponds to "Paulsville" and "peppers" corresponds to "Longtown," but in the second premise, "radishes" corresponds to "Salisbury" and "spinach" corresponds to "Paulsville," while in the third premise, "spinach" corresponds to "Salisbury," and in the conclusion, "peppers" corresponds to "Longtown." This difference affects the argument in such a way that unlike in the arguments in the passage and option (B), the conclusion cannot be validly drawn from the premises in option (A). From the second and third premise in (A), it follows that <u>the chef does not use fresh radishes</u>. But this, together with the first premise, does not imply that <u>the chef will</u> NOT <u>use fresh green peppers</u>. While the argument in (A) is similar in some ways to that in the passage, its reasoning is not as closely parallel to the passage's reasoning as is the reasoning of (B)'s argument, so (A) is not a credited response.

Response (C) is also incorrect: its reasoning is quite different from that in the passage.

C.1) IT IS NOT TRUE THAT BOTH <u>the program committee selects one play by Shaw for a certain season</u> AND <u>the program committee selects another play by Shaw for that same season</u>.

(C.2) IF <u>the committee selects a play by Coward</u> THEN <u>the committee does</u> NOT <u>select a play by Shaw</u>.
(C.3) <u>The program committee has selected a play by Shaw for this season</u>.
Therefore,
(C.conclusion) <u>The program committee will</u> NOT <u>select a play by Coward</u>.

Notice that if (C)'s first premise is to be parallel to the first premise of the passage's argument, then "select one play by Shaw" corresponds to "Paulsville" and "select another play by Shaw" corresponds to "Longtown." But rather than occurring in the conclusion (as does "Longtown" in the passage), the term "select another play by Shaw" never occurs again in the argument in (C). In fact, and unlike in the passage and option (B), the first premise in option (C) plays no role in drawing (C)'s conclusion; (C)'s conclusion follows from the second and third premises alone.

In response (D), we need look no further than the first premise to see that the argument is quite unlike that in the passage:

(D.1) EITHER <u>pesticides will work</u> OR <u>the introduction of natural enemies of the pest will work</u> BUT IT IS NOT TRUE THAT BOTH <u>pesticides will work</u> AND <u>the introduction of natural enemies of the pest will work</u>.

Notice that this sentence is quite different in structure from the first premise of the argument in the passage. The first premise of the passage is consistent with the candidate stopping in neither Paulsville nor Longtown. But the first premise of (D)'s argument is not consistent with neither pesticides nor the introduction of natural enemies of the pest's working. Moreover, with response (D), the first premise does not connect well with the rest of the argument. That premise indicates that either of two courses of action (using pesticides or introducing natural enemies), but not both, will <u>work</u>. The remainder of the argument speaks only of the <u>needs</u> for these courses of action or a further one (planting pest-resistant crops). As a result, unlike in the arguments in the passage and option (B), the conclusion of this argument does not clearly follow from its premises.

Finally, the argument in response (E) is quite different from that in the passage. Response (E) is like the passage in that two options (building a new stadium and building the new road needed to get there) are presented as incompatible; together, they are not viable. But unlike the passage, response (E) goes on to say that either one of the options alone is also not viable. In the passage, that one of the options (Paulsville's being one of the candidates's campaign stops) is viable and will be taken follows from the second and third premises.

This is one major way in which the reasoning in the argument in (E) is not parallel to the reasoning in the argument in the passage.

Thirty-four percent of examinees answered this question correctly when it appeared on the LSAT, making it a "difficult" question.

Question 23, Section 4, page 65

23. A study of adults who suffer from migraine headaches revealed that a significant proportion of the study participants suffer from a complex syndrome characterized by a set of three symptoms. Those who suffer from the syndrome experienced excessive anxiety during early childhood. As adolescents, these people began experiencing migraine headaches. As these people approached the age of 20, they also began to experience recurring bouts of depression. Since this pattern is invariant, always with excessive anxiety at its beginning, it follows that excessive anxiety in childhood is one of the causes of migraine headaches and depression in later life.

The reasoning in the argument is vulnerable to criticism on which one of the following grounds?

(A) It does not specify the proportion of those in the general population who suffer from the syndrome.
(B) It fails to rule out the possibility that all of the characteristic symptoms of the syndrome have a common cause.
(C) It makes a generalization that is inconsistent with the evidence.
(D) It fails to demonstrate that the people who participated in the study are representative of migraine sufferers.
(E) It does not establish why the study of migraine sufferers was restricted to adult participants.

Explanation for Question 23

The passage on which this question is based describes a syndrome consisting of three symptoms occurring in succession in the lives of participants in a migraine study: anxiety during early childhood, migraines beginning in adolescence, and bouts of depression starting at approximately age twenty. It is reasoned that, because the order in which these symptoms occur does not vary, it follows that anxiety in childhood is a cause of migraine headaches and depression later on.

But the fact that one phenomenon is always followed by other phenomena does not establish that the first is the cause of the others. For example, at a railroad crossing the blinking of the red lights is followed by the lowering of the gates, which is followed by the passing of the train. But the blinking of the lights does not cause the gates to lower, much less the train to pass; rather, the train trips a sensor that causes both the flashing lights and the lowering gates. Similarly, the evidence presented in the passage is consistent with conclusions other than that drawn by the argument: for example, some other factor (a certain physiological or psychological trait perhaps) may cause both childhood anxiety and the later symptoms. If this is so, childhood anxiety is an effect of this other factor as well, not itself the cause of the later symptoms. If the reasoning in this argument were to be successful, it would need to rule out the possibility that all three of the symptoms have a common cause. Response (B) identifies this problem with the argument's reasoning, and it is the credited response.

Response (A) is incorrect because the proportion of the general population that suffers from this syndrome is irrelevant to the success or failure of the argument. The argument does not claim that all migraine sufferers have the syndrome, nor that excessive anxiety in childhood is the only cause of migraines later in life. It is stated in the argument that some people in the study suffered from the syndrome, and this information is appropriately reflected in the conclusion that the argument reaches about "… one of the causes of migraine headaches and depression.… ." Information about the proportion of persons with this syndrome in the general population is not needed.

Response (C) is incorrect because it is not an accurate criticism of the argument in question. The causal generalization made in the argument—that childhood anxiety causes the two later symptoms—is consistent with the evidence presented. Given what the passage says, childhood anxiety may cause the other symptoms; the problem with the argument is that many other generalizations are also consistent with the evidence presented.

Response (D) is incorrect because there is no need, for the purposes of the argument, to show that the persons in the study are representative of migraine sufferers. Only if the argument came to a conclusion about all causes of migraines or all migraine sufferers would it be necessary to demonstrate that those in the study are representative of migraine sufferers. But the conclusion of the argument in the passage is about only one of the causes of migraine headaches (and depression).

Response (E) is incorrect because although it is true of the passage, it gives no basis for criticizing the reasoning in its argument. Again, since the argument makes no claim to be demonstrating a general point about the causes of migraines, its evidence need not be general. That is, the fact that the study was made only of adults does not weaken the argument: its conclusion says only that the study uncovered one cause of migraines.

This was a "difficult" question. Thirty-nine percent of examinees answered this question correctly when it appeared on the LSAT.

Taking the PrepTest Under Simulated LSAT Conditions

One important way to prepare for the LSAT is to take sample tests under the same requirements and time limits you will encounter in taking an actual LSAT. This helps you to estimate the amount of time you can afford to spend on each question in a section and to determine the question types on which you may need additional practice.

Since the LSAT is a timed test, it is important to use your allotted time wisely. During the test, you may work only on the section designated by the test supervisor. You cannot devote extra time to a difficult section and make up that time on a section you find easier. In pacing yourself, and checking your answers, you should think of each section of the test as a separate minitest.

Be sure that you answer every question on the test. When you do not know the correct answer to a question, first eliminate the responses that you know are incorrect, then make your best guess among the remaining choices. Do not be afraid to guess.

When you take the sample tests that follow, abide by all the requirements specified in the directions and keep strictly within the specified time limits. Work without a rest period. When you take an actual test you will have only a short break—usually 10-15 minutes—after SECTION III. When taken under conditions as much like actual testing conditions as possible, the PrepTest provides very useful preparation for taking the LSAT.

Official directions for the four multiple-choice sections and the writing sample are included in this book so that you can approximate actual testing conditions as you practice. To take each test:

- Set a timer for 35 minutes. Answer all the questions in SECTION I. Stop working on that section when the 35 minutes have elapsed.

- Repeat, allowing yourself 35 minutes each for sections II, III, and IV.

- Set the timer for 30 minutes, then prepare your response to the writing sample at the end of this test.

- Refer to "Computing Your Score" later in this booklet for instruction on evaluating your performance. An answer key is provided for that purpose.

How these PrepTests Differ from an Actual LSAT

These sample tests are made up of the scored sections and writing samples from actual LSAT administered in June 1994, October 1994, and December 1994. However, it does not contain the extra, variable section that is used to pretest new test items of one of the three question types.

Also, you are likely to encounter the three LSAT question types in a different order when you take an actual LSAT than in these PrepTests. This is because the order of the question types is intentionally varied for each administration of the test.

The Writing Exercise

Test takers are given 30 minutes to complete a brief writing exercise, which is not scored but is used by law school admission personnel to assess writing skill. This book contains 50 writing sample prompts that are representative of the prompts that have been administered in the past and illustrative of the prompts that will be administered in the future. Some writing sample prompts, or variations of them, may be given at more than one LSAT administration.

Read the topic carefully. You will probably find it best to spend a few minutes considering the topic and organizing your thoughts before you begin writing. **Do not write on a topic other than the one specified. Writing on a topic of your own choice is not acceptable.**

There is no "right" or "wrong" position on the writing sample topic. Law schools are interested in how skillfully you support the position you take and how clearly you express that position. How well you write is much more important than how much you write. No special knowledge is required or expected. Law schools are interested in organization, vocabulary, and writing mechanics. They understand the short time available to you and the pressure under which you are writing.

Confine your writing to the lined area following the writing sample topic. You will find that you have enough space if you plan your writing carefully, write on every line, avoid wide margins, and keep your handwriting a reasonable size. Be sure that your handwriting is legible.

Scratch paper is provided for use during the writing sample portion of the test only. Scratch paper cannot be used in other sections of the LSAT.

The writing sample is photocopied and sent to law schools to which you direct your LSAT score. A pen will be provided at the test center, which must be used (for the writing sample only) to ensure a photocopy of high quality.

The Official

LSAT

PrepTest™ XI

The sample test that follows consists of
four sections corresponding to the four
scored sections of the June 1994 LSAT.

June 1994
Form 5LSS22

General Directions for the LSAT Answer Sheet

The actual testing time for this portion of the test will be 2 hours 55 minutes. There are five sections, each with a time limit of 35 minutes. The supervisor will tell you when to begin and end each section. If you finish a section before time is called, you may check your work on that section <u>only</u>; do not turn to any other section of the test book and do not work on any other section either in the test book or on the answer sheet.

There are several different types of questions on the test, and each question type has its own directions. <u>Be sure you understand the directions for each question type before attempting to answer any questions in that section.</u>

Not everyone will finish all the questions in the time allowed. Do not hurry, but work steadily and as quickly as you can without sacrificing accuracy. You are advised to use your time effectively. If a question seems too difficult, go on to the next one and return to the difficult question after completing the section. MARK THE BEST ANSWER YOU CAN FOR EVERY QUESTION. NO DEDUCTIONS WILL BE MADE FOR WRONG ANSWERS. YOUR SCORE WILL BE BASED ONLY ON THE NUMBER OF QUESTIONS YOU ANSWER CORRECTLY.

ALL YOUR ANSWERS MUST BE MARKED ON THE ANSWER SHEET. Answer spaces for each question are lettered to correspond with the letters of the potential answers to each question in the test book. After you have decided which of the answers is correct, blacken the corresponding space on the answer sheet. BE SURE THAT EACH MARK IS BLACK AND COMPLETELY FILLS THE ANSWER SPACE. Give only one answer to each question. If you change an answer, be sure that all previous marks are <u>erased completely</u>. Since the answer sheet is machine scored, incomplete erasures may be interpreted as intended answers. ANSWERS RECORDED IN THE TEST BOOK WILL NOT BE SCORED.

There may be more questions noted on this answer sheet than there are questions in a section. Do not be concerned but be certain that the section and number of the question you are answering matches the answer sheet section and question number. Additional answer spaces in any answer sheet section should be left blank. Begin your next section in the number one answer space for that section.

Score Cancellation

Complete this section only if you are absolutely certain you want to cancel your score. A CANCELLATION REQUEST CANNOT BE RESCINDED. IF YOU ARE AT ALL UNCERTAIN, YOU SHOULD NOT COMPLETE THIS SECTION; INSTEAD, YOU SHOULD USE THE TIME ALLOWED AFTER THE TEST (UP TO 5 DAYS) TO FULLY CONSIDER YOUR DECISION.

To cancel your score from this administration, you must:

A. fill in the ovals here........ ◯ ◯

B. read the following statement. Then sign your name and enter the date.

I certify that I wish to cancel my test score from this administration. I understand that my request is irreversible and that my score will not be sent to me or to the law schools to which I apply.

_____
Sign your name in full

_____
Date

HOW DID YOU PREPARE FOR THE LSAT?
(Select all that apply.)

Responses to this item are voluntary and will be used for statistical research purposes only.

◯ By studying the sample questions in the *LSAT/LSDAS Registration and Information Book.*
◯ By taking the free sample LSAT.
◯ By working through *The Official LSAT PrepTest(s), PrepBook, Workbooks,* or *PrepKit.*
◯ By using a book on how to prepare for the LSAT **not** published by Law Services.
◯ By attending a commercial test preparation or coaching course.
◯ By attending a test preparation or coaching course offered through an undergraduate institution.
◯ Self study.
◯ Other preparation.
◯ No preparation.

CERTIFYING STATEMENT
Please write (DO NOT PRINT) the following statement. Sign and date.

I certify that I am the examinee whose name appears on this answer sheet and that I am here to take the LSAT for the sole purpose of being considered for admission to law school. I further certify that I will neither assist nor receive assistance from any other candidate, and I agree not to copy or retain examination questions or to transmit them in any form to any other person.

_____
_____
_____
_____
_____
_____
_____
_____
_____

SIGNATURE: _____ TODAY'S DATE: ____ / ____ / ____
                                                              MONTH DAY YEAR

INSTRUCTIONS FOR COMPLETING THE BIOGRAPHICAL AREA ARE ON THE BACK COVER OF YOUR TEST BOOKLET.

USE ONLY A NO. 2 OR HB PENCIL TO COMPLETE THIS ANSWER SHEET. DO NOT USE INK.

1 LAST NAME | FIRST NAME | MI

(A–Z bubbles for each letter position)

2 DATE OF BIRTH

MONTH	DAY	YEAR
Jan		
Feb		
Mar	0 0	0 0
Apr	1 1	1 1
May	2 2	2 2
June	3 3	3 3
July	4	4 4
Aug	5	5 5
Sept	6	6 6
Oct	7	7 7
Nov	8	8 8
Dec	9	9 9

3 SOCIAL SECURITY NO.

(0–9 bubbles for each digit)

Right Mark:

Wrong Marks:

4 ETHNIC DESCRIPTION

- American Indian/ Alaskan Native
- Asian/Pacific Islander
- Black/African Amer.
- Canadian Aboriginal
- Caucasian/White
- Chicano/Mex. Amer.
- Hispanic
- Puerto Rican
- Other

5 GENDER

- Male
- Female

6 DOMINANT LANGUAGE

- English
- Other

7 ENGLISH FLUENCY

- Yes
- No

8 CENTER NUMBER

(0–9 bubbles for each digit)

9 TEST FORM CODE

(0–9 bubbles for each digit)

10 TEST BOOK SERIAL NO.

11 TEST FORM

12 TEST DATE

MONTH / DAY / YEAR

13 PLEASE PRINT ALL INFORMATION

LAST NAME FIRST

MAILING ADDRESS

SOCIAL SECURITY/ SOCIAL INSURANCE NO.

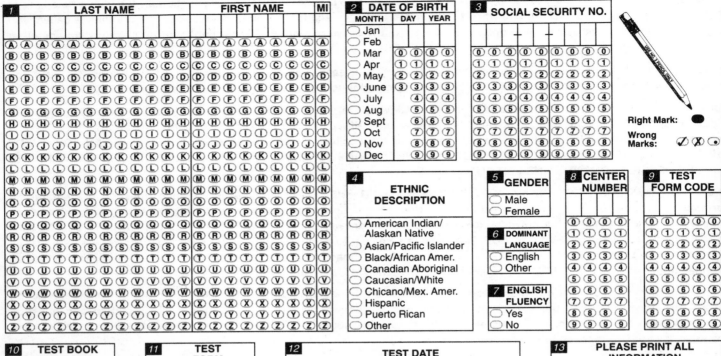

LAW SCHOOL ADMISSION TEST

MARK ONE AND ONLY ONE ANSWER TO EACH QUESTION. BE SURE TO FILL IN COMPLETELY THE SPACE FOR YOUR INTENDED ANSWER CHOICE. IF YOU ERASE, DO SO COMPLETELY. MAKE NO STRAY MARKS.

	SECTION 1	SECTION 2	SECTION 3	SECTION 4	SECTION 5
1	A B C D E	A B C D E	A B C D E	A B C D E	A B C D E
2	A B C D E	A B C D E	A B C D E	A B C D E	A B C D E
3	A B C D E	A B C D E	A B C D E	A B C D E	A B C D E
4	A B C D E	A B C D E	A B C D E	A B C D E	A B C D E
5	A B C D E	A B C D E	A B C D E	A B C D E	A B C D E
6	A B C D E	A B C D E	A B C D E	A B C D E	A B C D E
7	A B C D E	A B C D E	A B C D E	A B C D E	A B C D E
8	A B C D E	A B C D E	A B C D E	A B C D E	A B C D E
9	A B C D E	A B C D E	A B C D E	A B C D E	A B C D E
10	A B C D E	A B C D E	A B C D E	A B C D E	A B C D E
11	A B C D E	A B C D E	A B C D E	A B C D E	A B C D E
12	A B C D E	A B C D E	A B C D E	A B C D E	A B C D E
13	A B C D E	A B C D E	A B C D E	A B C D E	A B C D E
14	A B C D E	A B C D E	A B C D E	A B C D E	A B C D E
15	A B C D E	A B C D E	A B C D E	A B C D E	A B C D E
16	A B C D E	A B C D E	A B C D E	A B C D E	A B C D E
17	A B C D E	A B C D E	A B C D E	A B C D E	A B C D E
18	A B C D E	A B C D E	A B C D E	A B C D E	A B C D E
19	A B C D E	A B C D E	A B C D E	A B C D E	A B C D E
20	A B C D E	A B C D E	A B C D E	A B C D E	A B C D E
21	A B C D E	A B C D E	A B C D E	A B C D E	A B C D E
22	A B C D E	A B C D E	A B C D E	A B C D E	A B C D E
23	A B C D E	A B C D E	A B C D E	A B C D E	A B C D E
24	A B C D E	A B C D E	A B C D E	A B C D E	A B C D E
25	A B C D E	A B C D E	A B C D E	A B C D E	A B C D E
26	A B C D E	A B C D E	A B C D E	A B C D E	A B C D E
27	A B C D E	A B C D E	A B C D E	A B C D E	A B C D E
28	A B C D E	A B C D E	A B C D E	A B C D E	A B C D E
29	A B C D E	A B C D E	A B C D E	A B C D E	A B C D E
30	A B C D E	A B C D E	A B C D E	A B C D E	A B C D E

NOTE: If you have a new address, you must write Law Services at Box 2000-C, Newtown, PA 18940 or call (215) 968-1001. We cannot guarantee that all address changes will be processed before scores are mailed, so be sure to notify your post office of your forwarding address.

FOR LAW SERVICES USE ONLY
LR
LW
LCS

SECTION I
Time—35 minutes
24 Questions

Directions: Each group of questions in this section is based on a set of conditions. In answering some of the questions, it may be useful to draw a rough diagram. Choose the response that most accurately and completely answers each question and blacken the corresponding space on your answer sheet.

Questions 1–6

Eight camp counselors—Fran, George, Henry, Joan, Kathy, Lewis, Nathan, and Olga—must each be assigned to supervise exactly one of three activities—swimming, tennis, and volleyball. The assignment of counselors must conform to the following conditions:
   Each activity is supervised by at least two, but not more than three, of the eight counselors.
   Henry supervises swimming.
   Neither Kathy nor Olga supervises tennis.
   Neither Kathy nor Nathan supervises the same activity as Joan.
   If George supervises swimming, both Nathan and Olga supervise volleyball.

1. Which one of the following is an acceptable assignment of the counselors to the activities?

   (A) Swimming: Fran, George, Henry; Tennis: Joan, Lewis; Volleyball: Kathy, Nathan, Olga
   (B) Swimming: George, Henry, Olga; Tennis: Fran, Joan, Lewis; Volleyball: Kathy, Nathan
   (C) Swimming: Henry; Tennis: Fran, George, Joan, Lewis; Volleyball: Kathy, Nathan, Olga
   (D) Swimming: Henry, Joan, Kathy; Tennis: George, Nathan; Volleyball: Fran, Lewis, Olga
   (E) Swimming: Henry, Nathan; Tennis: Fran, Kathy, Lewis; Volleyball: George, Joan, Olga

2. Which one of the following is a pair of counselors who could be two of three counselors assigned to supervise swimming?

   (A) George and Nathan
   (B) George and Olga
   (C) Joan and Kathy
   (D) Joan and Nathan
   (E) Joan and Olga

3. Which one of the following is a pair of counselors who could together be assigned to supervise tennis?

   (A) Fran and Kathy
   (B) George and Nathan
   (C) Henry and Lewis
   (D) Joan and Nathan
   (E) Joan and Olga

4. If George and Kathy are two of three counselors assigned to supervise swimming, which one of the following could be true of the assignment?

   (A) Fran supervises swimming.
   (B) Henry supervises tennis.
   (C) Joan supervises volleyball.
   (D) Lewis supervises volleyball.
   (E) Nathan supervises tennis.

5. If Fran and Lewis are two of three counselors assigned to supervise swimming, which one of the following must be true of the assignment?

   (A) George supervises volleyball.
   (B) Henry supervises volleyball.
   (C) Joan supervises tennis.
   (D) Kathy supervises swimming.
   (E) Nathan supervises tennis.

6. If Joan is assigned to supervise the same activity as Olga, which one of the following CANNOT be true of the assignment?

   (A) Fran supervises swimming.
   (B) George supervises swimming.
   (C) Kathy supervises volleyball.
   (D) Lewis supervises volleyball.
   (E) Nathan supervises tennis.

GO ON TO THE NEXT PAGE.

Questions 7–11

A fire chief is determining the work schedules of five firefighters: Fuentes, Graber, Howell, Iman, and Jackson. The schedule must meet the following conditions:

Except for Saturday and Sunday, when none of them works, exactly one of the firefighters works each day.

None of the firefighters can work more than two days per week.

No firefighter works on two consecutive days.

Fuentes never works later in the week than Jackson.

If Howell works, then Graber must work on the following day.

7. Which one of the following CANNOT be a Monday-to-Friday work schedule?

(A) Fuentes, Iman, Fuentes, Jackson, Iman
(B) Fuentes, Jackson, Howell, Graber, Fuentes
(C) Graber, Fuentes, Graber, Fuentes, Jackson
(D) Graber, Howell, Graber, Fuentes, Jackson
(E) Howell, Graber, Iman, Graber, Iman

8. If each firefighter is required to have at least two consecutive days off during the Monday-to-Friday workweek, which one of the following could be a possible work schedule?

(A) Howell, Graber, Howell, Graber, Iman
(B) Howell, Howell, Graber, Fuentes, Iman
(C) Iman, Fuentes, Jackson, Iman, Iman
(D) Fuentes, Howell, Graber, Fuentes, Jackson
(E) Jackson, Howell, Graber, Iman, Fuentes

9. If both Fuentes and Jackson work during a week, which one of the following statements CANNOT be true?

(A) Fuentes works on Monday and Wednesday.
(B) Jackson works on Monday and Wednesday.
(C) Fuentes works on Tuesday and Thursday.
(D) Jackson works on Tuesday and Thursday.
(E) Jackson works on Wednesday and Friday.

10. If Fuentes works two days during the week and Jackson works on Thursday, which one of the following statements could be true?

(A) Fuentes works on Tuesday.
(B) Graber works on Tuesday.
(C) Howell works on Tuesday.
(D) Graber works on Wednesday.
(E) Howell works on Wednesday.

11. If Graber does not work during the week, which one of the following statements must be true?

(A) Fuentes works exactly one day during the week.
(B) Fuentes works exactly two days during the week.
(C) Iman works exactly one day during the week.
(D) Iman works exactly two days during the week.
(E) Jackson works exactly one day during the week.

GO ON TO THE NEXT PAGE.

Questions 12–19

A housing committee will consist of exactly five representatives, one of whom will be its chairperson. The representatives will be selected from among a group of five tenants—F, G, J, K, and M—and a group of four homeowners—P, Q, R, and S. The following conditions must be met:

The committee must include at least two representatives from each group.

The chairperson must be a representative belonging to the group from which exactly two representatives are selected.

If F is selected, Q must be selected.

If G is selected, K must be selected.

If either J or M is selected, the other must also be selected.

M and P cannot both be selected.

12. Which one of the following is an acceptable selection of representatives for the committee?

   (A)   F, G, Q, R, S
   (B)   F, J, K, P, Q
   (C)   F, P, Q, R, S
   (D)   J, K, M, Q, S
   (E)   J, M, P, Q, S

13. Which one of the following lists three representatives who could be selected together for the committee?

   (A)   F, G, J
   (B)   F, G, M
   (C)   F, J, M
   (D)   G, J, K
   (E)   G, J, M

14. If M is the chairperson of the committee, which one of the following is among the people who must also be on the committee?

   (A)   F
   (B)   G
   (C)   K
   (D)   P
   (E)   R

15. If F is the chairperson of the committee, which one of the following is among the people who must also be on the committee?

   (A)   G
   (B)   K
   (C)   P
   (D)   R
   (E)   S

16. If F is selected, any one of the following people could be the chairperson of the committee EXCEPT:

   (A)   G
   (B)   K
   (C)   P
   (D)   Q
   (E)   S

17. If neither F nor K is selected for the committee, which one of the following can be true?

   (A)   G is selected.
   (B)   P is selected.
   (C)   J is the chairperson.
   (D)   Q is the chairperson.
   (E)   S is the chairperson.

18. If the chairperson of the committee is to be a homeowner, which one of the following must be true?

   (A)   If G is selected, Q is also selected.
   (B)   If G is selected, R is also selected.
   (C)   If J is selected, F is also selected.
   (D)   If J is selected, Q is also selected.
   (E)   If J is selected, R is also selected.

19. The committee must include at least one representative from which one of the following pairs?

   (A)   F, P
   (B)   G, J
   (C)   K, Q
   (D)   M, P
   (E)   R, S

GO ON TO THE NEXT PAGE.

Questions 20–24

Four apprentices—Louis, Madelyn, Nora, and Oliver—are initially assigned to projects Q, R, S, and T, respectively. During the year in which they are apprentices, two reassignments of apprentices to projects will be made, each time according to a different one of the following plans, which can be used in any order:

Plan 1. The apprentice assigned to project Q switches projects with the apprentice assigned to project S and the apprentice assigned to project R switches projects with the apprentice assigned to project T.

Plan 2. The apprentice assigned to project S switches projects with the apprentice assigned to project T.

Plan 3. Louis and Madelyn switch projects with each other.

20. Which one of the following must be true after the second reassignment of apprentices to projects during the year if that reassignment assigns Nora to project T ?

   (A)   Louis is assigned to project S.
   (B)   Madelyn is assigned to project R.
   (C)   Madelyn is assigned to project S.
   (D)   Oliver is assigned to project R.
   (E)   Oliver is assigned to project S.

21. Which one of the following could be true after only one reassignment during the year?

   (A)   Louis is assigned to project T.
   (B)   Nora is assigned to project R.
   (C)   Oliver is assigned to project Q.
   (D)   Louis and Nora each remain assigned to the same projects as before.
   (E)   Nora and Oliver each remain assigned to the same projects as before.

22. If at some time during the year, Louis is reassigned to project R, which one of the following could have been the assignment of apprentices to the projects immediately before the reassignment?

   (A)   Q: Louis; R: Madelyn; S: Oliver; T: Nora
   (B)   Q: Louis; R: Nora; S: Oliver; T: Madelyn
   (C)   Q: Nora; R: Madelyn; S: Louis; T: Oliver
   (D)   Q: Nora; R: Oliver; S: Louis; T: Madelyn
   (E)   Q: Oliver; R: Nora; S: Louis; T: Madelyn

23. Which one of the following is an acceptable assignment of apprentices to the projects after only one reassignment during the year?

   (A)   Q: Louis; R: Madelyn; S: Nora; T: Oliver
   (B)   Q: Madelyn; R: Louis; S: Nora; T: Oliver
   (C)   Q: Madelyn; R: Oliver; S: Nora; T: Louis
   (D)   Q: Nora; R: Louis; S: Oliver; T: Madelyn
   (E)   Q: Nora; R: Madelyn; S: Oliver; T: Louis

24. If the first reassignment is made according to plan 1, which one of the following must be true?

   (A)   Louis is assigned to project T as a result of the second reassignment.
   (B)   Madelyn is assigned to project Q as a result of the second reassignment.
   (C)   Madelyn is assigned to project T as a result of the second reassignment.
   (D)   Oliver is assigned to project S as a result of the second reassignment.
   (E)   Oliver is assigned to project T as a result of the second reassignment.

S T O P

IF YOU FINISH BEFORE TIME IS CALLED, YOU MAY CHECK YOUR WORK ON THIS SECTION ONLY.
DO NOT WORK ON ANY OTHER SECTION IN THE TEST.

SECTION II

Time — 35 minutes

26 Questions

<u>Directions:</u> The questions in this section are based on the reasoning contained in brief statements or passages. For some questions, more than one of the choices could conceivably answer the question. However, you are to choose the <u>best</u> answer; that is, the response that most accurately and completely answers the question. You should not make assumptions that are by commonsense standards implausible, superfluous, or incompatible with the passage. After you have chosen the best answer, blacken the corresponding space on your answer sheet.

Questions 1–2

Sea turtles nest only at their own birthplaces. After hatching on the beach, the turtles enter the water to begin their far-ranging migration, only returning to their birthplaces to nest some 15 to 30 years later. It has been hypothesized that newborn sea turtles learn the smell of their birth environment, and it is this smell that stimulates the turtles to return to nest.

1. Which one of the following, if true, would cast the most serious doubt on the hypothesis in the passage?

    (A) Beaches on which sea turtles nest tend to be in secluded locations such as on islands.
    (B) Sea turtles exposed to a variety of environments under experimental conditions preferred the environment that contained sand from their own birthplaces.
    (C) Electronic tags attached to sea turtles did not alter their nesting patterns.
    (D) Unlike other types of turtles, sea turtles have a well-developed sense of smell.
    (E) Sea turtles that had their sense of smell destroyed by exposure to petroleum products returned to nest at their own birthplaces.

2. Which one of the following would be most important to know in evaluating the hypothesis in the passage?

    (A) how long the expected life span of sea turtles is
    (B) what the maximum migratory range of mature sea turtles is
    (C) whether many beaches on which sea turtles were hatched have since been destroyed by development
    (D) whether immediately before returning to nest, sea turtles are outside the area where the smell of their birthplace would be perceptible
    (E) whether both sexes of sea turtles are actively involved in the nesting process

3. For Juanita to get to the zoo she must take either the number 12 bus or else the subway. Everyone knows that the number 12 bus is not running this week; so although Juanita generally avoids using the subway, she must have used it today, since she was seen at the zoo this afternoon.

The method of the argument is to

    (A) assert that if something is true, it will be known to be true
    (B) demonstrate that certain possibilities are not exclusive
    (C) show that something is the case by ruling out the only alternative
    (D) explain why an apparent exception to a general rule is not a real exception
    (E) substitute a claim about what invariably occurs for a claim about what typically occurs

GO ON TO THE NEXT PAGE.

4. If the regulation of computer networks is to be modeled on past legislation, then its model must be either legislation regulating a telephone system or else legislation regulating a public broadcasting service. If the telephone model is used, computer networks will be held responsible only for ensuring that messages get transmitted. If the public broadcast model is used, computer networks will additionally be responsible for the content of those messages. Yet a computer network serves both these sorts of functions: it can serve as a private message service or as a publicly accessible information service. Thus neither of these models can be appropriate for computer networks.

The passage is structured to lead to which one of the following conclusions?

(A)   Regulation of computer networks is required in order to ensure the privacy of the messages transmitted through such networks.
(B)   The regulation of computer networks should not be modeled on any single piece of past legislation.
(C)   Computer networks were developed by being modeled on both telephone systems and television networks.
(D)   Legislators who do not have extensive experience with computers should not attempt to write legislation regulating computer networks.
(E)   A computer network merely duplicates the functions of a telephone system and a television network.

5. The government has proposed a plan requiring young people to perform services to correct various current social ills, especially those in education and housing. Government service, however, should be compelled only in response to a direct threat to the nation's existence. For that reason, the proposed program should not be implemented.

Which one of the following is an assumption on which the argument depends?

(A)   Government-required service by young people cannot correct all social ills.
(B)   The nation's existence is directly threatened only in times of foreign attack.
(C)   Crises in education and housing constitute a threat to the nation's existence.
(D)   The nation's young people believe that current social ills pose no direct threat to the nation's existence.
(E)   Some of the social ills that currently afflict the nation do not pose a direct threat to the nation's existence.

6. Cigarette smoking has been shown to be a health hazard; therefore, governments should ban all advertisements that promote smoking.

Which one of the following principles, if established, most strongly supports the argument?

(A)   Advertisements should not be allowed to show people doing things that endanger their health.
(B)   Advertisers should not make misleading claims about the healthfulness of their products.
(C)   Advertisements should disclose the health hazards associated with the products they promote.
(D)   All products should conform to strict government health and safety standards.
(E)   Advertisements should promote only healthful products.

7. Every adult male woolly monkey is larger than even the largest female woolly monkey. In colonies of woolly monkeys, any adult male will dominate any female.

If the statements above are true, which one of the following must on the basis of them be true of woolly monkeys in colonies?

(A)   Size is the primary determinant of relations of dominance among woolly monkeys.
(B)   Some large adolescent male woolly monkeys dominate some smaller females of the species.
(C)   If a male woolly monkey is larger than a female of the species, that male will dominate that female.
(D)   If a female woolly monkey dominates a male of the species, the dominated male monkey is not an adult.
(E)   An adult male woolly monkey can dominate a female of the species only if that female is also an adult.

GO ON TO THE NEXT PAGE.

8. S: Our nation is becoming too averse to risk.
       We boycott any food reported to contain
       a toxic chemical, even though the risk, as
       a mathematical ratio, might be minimal.
       With this mentality, Columbus would never
       have sailed west.

    T: A risk-taker in one context can be risk-averse in
       another: the same person can drive recklessly,
       but refuse to eat food not grown organically.

    T responds to S by showing that

    (A) a distinction should be made between
        avoidable and unavoidable risks
    (B) aversion to risk cannot be reliably assessed
        without reference to context
    (C) there is confusion about risk in the minds of
        many members of the public
    (D) mathematical odds concerning risk give an
        unwarranted impression of precision
    (E) risk cannot be defined in relation to perceived
        probable benefit

9. Any announcement authorized by the head of the
    department is important. However, announcements
    are sometimes issued, without authorization, by
    people other than the head of the department, so
    some announcements will inevitably turn out not to
    be important.

    The reasoning is flawed because the argument

    (A) does not specify exactly which communications
        are to be classified as announcements
    (B) overlooks the possibility that people other than
        the head of the department have the authority
        to authorize announcements
    (C) leaves open the possibility that the head of the
        department never, in fact, authorizes any
        announcements
    (D) assumes without warrant that just because
        satisfying a given condition is enough to
        ensure an announcement's importance,
        satisfying that condition is necessary for its
        importance
    (E) fails to distinguish between the importance of
        the position someone holds and the importance
        of what that person may actually be announcing
        on a particular occasion

Questions 10–11

The labeling of otherwise high-calorie foods as
"sugar-free," based on the replacement of all sugar by
artificial sweeteners, should be prohibited by law. Such a
prohibition is indicated because many consumers who
need to lose weight will interpret the label "sugar-free" as
synonymous with "low in calories" and harm themselves
by building weight-loss diets around foods labeled
"sugar-free." Manufacturers of sugar-free foods are well
aware of this tendency on the part of consumers.

10. Which one of the following principles, if established,
    most helps to justify the conclusion in the passage?

    (A) Product labels that are literally incorrect
        should be prohibited by law, even if reliance
        on those labels is not likely to cause harm to
        consumers.
    (B) Product labels that are literally incorrect, but
        in such an obvious manner that no rational
        consumer would rely on them, should
        nevertheless be prohibited by law.
    (C) Product labels that are literally correct but
        cannot be interpreted by the average buyer
        of the product without expert help should be
        prohibited by law.
    (D) Product labels that are literally correct but will
        predictably be misinterpreted by some buyers
        of the product to their own harm should be
        prohibited by law.
    (E) Product labels that are literally correct, but
        only on one of two equally accurate
        interpretations, should be prohibited by law
        if buyers tend to interpret the label in the way
        that does not match the product's actual
        properties.

11. Which one of the following, if true, provides the
    strongest basis for challenging the conclusion in the
    passage?

    (A) Food manufacturers would respond to a ban
        on the label "sugar-free" by reducing the
        calories in sugar-free products by enough to
        be able to promote those products as diet
        foods.
    (B) Individuals who are diabetic need to be able to
        identify products that contain no sugar by
        reference to product labels that expressly state
        that the product contains no sugar.
    (C) Consumers are sometimes slow to notice changes
        in product labels unless those changes are
        themselves well advertised.
    (D) Consumers who have chosen a particular
        weight-loss diet tend to persist with this diet if
        they have been warned not to expect very
        quick results.
    (E) Exactly what appears on a product label is less
        important to consumer behavior than is the
        relative visual prominence of the different
        pieces of information that the label contains.

GO ON TO THE NEXT PAGE.

12. In the Centerville Botanical Gardens, all tulip trees are older than any maples. A majority, but not all, of the garden's sycamores are older than any of its maples. All the garden's maples are older than any of its dogwoods.

If the statements above are true, which one of the following must also be true of trees in the Centerville Botanical Gardens?

(A) Some dogwoods are as old as the youngest tulip trees.
(B) Some dogwoods are as old as the youngest sycamores.
(C) Some sycamores are not as old as the oldest dogwoods.
(D) Some tulip trees are not as old as the oldest sycamores.
(E) Some sycamores are not as old as the youngest tulip trees.

13. Emissions from automobiles that burn gasoline and automobiles that burn diesel fuel are threatening the quality of life on our planet, contaminating both urban air and global atmosphere. Therefore, the only effective way to reduce such emissions is to replace the conventional diesel fuel and gasoline used in automobiles with cleaner-burning fuels, such as methanol, that create fewer emissions.

Which one of the following is an assumption on which the argument depends?

(A) Reducing the use of automobiles would not be a more effective means to reduce automobile emissions than the use of methanol.
(B) There is no fuel other than methanol that is cleaner-burning than both diesel fuel and gasoline.
(C) If given a choice of automobile fuels, automobile owners would not select gasoline over methanol.
(D) Automobile emissions constitute the most serious threat to the global environment.
(E) At any given time there is a direct correlation between the level of urban air pollution and the level of contamination present in the global atmosphere.

14. Dr. Libokov: Certain islands near New Zealand are home to the tuatara, reptiles that are the sole surviving members of the sphenodontidans. Sphenodontidans were plentiful throughout the world during the age of the dinosaurs. But the survival of sphenodontidans near New Zealand, and their total disappearance elsewhere, is no mystery. New Zealand and nearby islands have no native land mammals. Land mammals, plentiful elsewhere, undoubtedly became major predators of sphenodontidans and their eggs, leading to their extinction.

Dr. Santos: In fact, the tuatara thrive only on a few islands near New Zealand. On all those where land mammals, such as rats, dogs, or cats, have been introduced in recent years, the tuatara are now extinct or nearly so.

Which one of the following most accurately characterizes Dr. Santos' response to the hypothesis advanced by Dr. Libokov?

(A) It identifies a flaw in Dr. Libokov's reasoning.
(B) It restates Dr. Libokov's major hypothesis and thus adds nothing to it.
(C) It contradicts one of Dr. Libokov's assertions.
(D) It offers a hypothesis that is incompatible with Dr. Libokov's position.
(E) It provides additional evidence in support of Dr. Libokov's hypothesis.

15. A standard problem for computer security is that passwords that have to be typed on a computer keyboard are comparatively easy for unauthorized users to steal or guess. A new system that relies on recognizing the voices of authorized users apparently avoids this problem. In a small initial trial, the system never incorrectly accepted someone seeking access to the computer's data. Clearly, if this result can be repeated in an operational setting, then there will be a way of giving access to those people who are entitled to access and to no one else.

The reasoning above is flawed because it

(A) makes a faulty comparison, in that a security system based on voice recognition would not be expected to suffer from the same problems as one that relied on passwords entered from a keyboard
(B) bases a general conclusion on a small amount of data
(C) fails to recognize that a security system based on voice recognition could easily have applications other than computer security
(D) ignores the possibility that the system sometimes denies access to people who are entitled to access
(E) states its conclusion in a heavily qualified way

GO ON TO THE NEXT PAGE.

16. Body temperature varies over a 24-hour period, with a low point roughly between 4 a.m. and 5 a.m. Speed of reaction varies in line with body temperature, such that whenever body temperature is low, speed of reaction is low. If low body temperature caused slow reaction, the speed of reaction should increase if we artificially raised body temperature during the period 4 a.m. to 5 a.m. But the speed of reaction does not increase.

Which one of the following conclusions can properly be drawn from the above statements?

(A) Low speeds of reaction cause low body temperature.
(B) Low speeds of reaction do not cause low body temperature.
(C) Low body temperatures do not cause low speeds of reaction.
(D) Low body temperatures cause low speeds of reaction.
(E) Artificially raising body temperature causes increased speed of reaction.

17. Of the two proposals for solving the traffic problems on Main Street, Chen's plan is better for the city as a whole, as is clear from the fact that the principal supporter of Ripley's plan is Smith Stores. Smith Stores, with its highly paid consultants, knows where its own interest lies and, moreover, has supported its own interests in the past, even to the detriment of the city as a whole.

The faulty reasoning in which one of the following is most parallel to that in the argument above?

(A) Surely Centreville should oppose adoption of the regional planning commission's new plan since it is not in Centreville's interest, even though it might be in the interest of some towns in the region.
(B) The school board should support the plan for the new high school since this plan was recommended by the well-qualified consultants whom the school board hired at great expense.
(C) Of the two budget proposals, the mayor's is clearly preferable to the city council's, since the mayor's budget addresses the needs of the city as a whole, whereas the city council is protecting special interests.
(D) Nomura is clearly a better candidate for college president than Miller, since Nomura has the support of the three deans who best understand the president's job and with whom the president will have to work most closely.
(E) The planned light-rail system will clearly serve suburban areas well, since its main opponent is the city government, which has always ignored the needs of the suburbs and sought only to protect the interests of the city.

GO ON TO THE NEXT PAGE.

Questions 18–19

The format of network television news programs generally allows advocates of a point of view only 30 seconds to convey their message. Consequently, regular watchers become accustomed to thinking of issues in terms only of slogans and catch phrases, and so the expectation of careful discussion of public issues gradually disappears from their awareness. The format of newspaper stories, on the other hand, leads readers to pursue details of stories headed by the most important facts and so has the opposite effect on regular readers—that of maintaining the expectation of careful discussion of public issues. Therefore, in contrast to regular newspaper reading, regular watching of network television news programs increases the tendency to think of public issues in oversimplified terms.

18.   The argument assumes which one of the following?

(A)   Viewers of network television news programs would be interested in seeing advocates of opposing views present their positions at length.

(B)   Since it is not possible to present striking images that would symbolize events for viewers, and since images hold sway over words in television, television must oversimplify.

(C)   It is not possible for television to present public issues in a way that allows for the nuanced presentation of diverse views and a good-faith interchange between advocates of opposing views.

(D)   In network television news reports, it is not usual for a reporter to offer additional factual evidence and background information to develop a story in which opposing views are presented briefly by their advocates.

(E)   Television news reporters introduce more of their own biases into news stories than do newspaper reporters.

19.   Which one of the following, if true, most seriously weakens the argument?

(A)   Regular watchers of network television news programs are much more likely than other people to be habitual readers of newspapers.

(B)   Including any 30-second quotations from proponents of diverse views, the total amount of time devoted to a single topic on regular network television news programs averages less than one and a half minutes.

(C)   The format of network television news programs does not include roundtable discussion of issues among informed proponents of diverse views.

(D)   Television news reports tend to devote equal time to discussion of opposing views.

(E)   People who watch the most television, measured in average number of hours of watching per week, tend not to be regular readers of newspapers.

Questions 20–21

A recent report on an environmental improvement program was criticized for focusing solely on pragmatic solutions to the large number of significant problems that plague the program instead of seriously trying to produce a coherent vision for the future of the program. In response the report's authors granted that the critics had raised a valid point but explained that, to do anything at all, the program needed continued government funding, and that to get such funding the program first needed to regain a reputation for competence.

20.   The basic position taken by the report's authors on the criticism leveled against the report is that

(A)   addressing the critics' concern now would be premature

(B)   the critics' motives are self-serving

(C)   the notion of a coherent vision would be inappropriate to a program of the sort at issue

(D)   the authors of the report are more knowledgeable than its critics

(E)   giving the report a single focus is less desirable than the critics claim

21.   Which one of the following, if true, would best serve the critics of the report in their attempt to undermine the position taken by the report's authors?

(A)   The government does not actually provide a full 100 percent of the program's funding.

(B)   The program will continue to have numerous serious problems precisely because it lacks a coherent vision for its future.

(C)   The program had a coherent vision at its inception, but that vision has proved impossible to sustain.

(D)   The government has threatened to cut off funding for the program but has not acted yet on this threat.

(E)   The program has acquired a worse reputation for incompetence than it deserves.

GO ON TO THE NEXT PAGE.

22. Oil company representative: We spent more money on cleaning the otters affected by our recent oil spill than has been spent on any previous marine mammal rescue project. This shows our concern for the environment.

Environmentalist: You have no such concern. Your real concern is evident in your admission to the press that news photographs of oil-covered otters would be particularly damaging to your public image, which plays an important role in your level of sales.

The environmentalist's conclusion would be properly drawn if it were true that the

(A) oil company cannot have more than one motive for cleaning the otters affected by the oil spill

(B) otter population in the area of the oil spill could not have survived without the cleaning project

(C) oil company has always shown a high regard for its profits in choosing its courses of action

(D) government would have spent the money to clean the otters if the oil company had not agreed to do it

(E) oil company's efforts toward cleaning the affected otters have been more successful than have such efforts in previous projects to clean up oil spills

23. A group of scientists studying calcium metabolism in laboratory rats discovered that removing the rats' parathyroid glands resulted in the rats' having substantially lower than normal levels of calcium in their blood. This discovery led the scientists to hypothesize that the function of the parathyroid gland is to regulate the level of calcium in the blood by raising that level when it falls below the normal range. In a further experiment, the scientists removed not only the parathyroid gland but also the adrenal gland from rats. They made the surprising discovery that the level of calcium in the rats' blood decreased much less sharply than when the parathyroid gland alone was removed.

Which one of the following, if true, explains the surprising discovery in a way most consistent with the scientists' hypothesis?

(A) The adrenal gland acts to lower the level of calcium in the blood.

(B) The adrenal gland and the parathyroid gland play the same role in regulating calcium blood levels.

(C) The absence of a parathyroid gland causes the adrenal gland to increase the level of calcium in the blood.

(D) If the adrenal gland, and no other gland, of a rat were removed, the rat's calcium level would remain stable.

(E) The only function of the parathyroid gland is to regulate the level of calcium in the blood.

24. Since Mayor Drabble always repays her political debts as soon as possible, she will almost certainly appoint Lee to be the new head of the arts commission. Lee has wanted that job for a long time, and Drabble owes Lee a lot for his support in the last election.

Which one of the following is an assumption on which the argument depends?

(A) Mayor Drabble has no political debt that is both of longer standing than the one she owes to Lee and could as suitably be repaid by an appointment to be the new head of the arts commission.

(B) There is no one to whom Mayor Drabble owes a greater political debt for support in the last election than the political debt she owes to Lee.

(C) Lee is the only person to whom Mayor Drabble owes a political debt who would be willing to accept an appointment from her as the new head of the arts commission.

(D) Whether Lee is qualified to head the arts commission is irrelevant to Mayor Drabble's decision.

(E) The only way that Mayor Drabble can adequately repay her political debt to Lee is by appointing him to head the arts commission.

GO ON TO THE NEXT PAGE.

25. The fact that tobacco smoke inhaled by smokers harms the smokers does not prove that the much smaller amount of tobacco smoke inhaled by nonsmokers who share living space with smokers harms the nonsmokers to some degree. Many substances, such as vitamin A, are toxic in large quantities but beneficial in small quantities.

In which one of the following is the pattern of reasoning most similar to that in the argument above?

(A) The fact that a large concentration of bleach will make fabric very white does not prove that a small concentration of bleach will make fabric somewhat white. The effect of a small concentration of bleach may be too slight to change the color of the fabric.

(B) Although a healthful diet should include a certain amount of fiber, it does not follow that a diet that includes large amounts of fiber is more healthful than one that includes smaller amounts of fiber. Too much fiber can interfere with proper digestion.

(C) The fact that large amounts of chemical fertilizers can kill plants does not prove that chemical fertilizers are generally harmful to plants. It proves only that the quantity of chemical fertilizer used should be adjusted according to the needs of the plants and the nutrients already in the soil.

(D) From the fact that five professional taste testers found a new cereal product tasty, it does not follow that everyone will like it. Many people find broccoli a tasty food, but other people have a strong dislike for the taste of broccoli.

(E) Although watching television for half of every day would be a waste of time, watching television briefly every day is not necessarily even a small waste of time. After all, it would be a waste to sleep half of every day, but some sleep every day is necessary.

26. Why should the government, rather than industry or universities, provide the money to put a network of supercomputers in place? Because there is a range of problems that can be attacked only with the massive data-managing capacity of a supercomputer network. No business or university has the resources to purchase by itself enough machines for a whole network, and no business or university wants to invest in a part of a network if no mechanism exists for coordinating establishment of the network as a whole.

Which one of the following indicates a weakness in the argument?

(A) It does not furnish a way in which the dilemma concerning the establishment of the network can be resolved.

(B) It does not establish the impossibility of creating a supercomputer network as an international network.

(C) It fails to address the question of who would maintain the network if the government, rather than industry or universities, provides the money for establishing it.

(D) It takes for granted and without justification that it would enhance national preeminence in science for the government to provide the network.

(E) It overlooks the possibility that businesses or universities, or both, could cooperate to build the network.

S T O P

IF YOU FINISH BEFORE TIME IS CALLED, YOU MAY CHECK YOUR WORK ON THIS SECTION ONLY.
DO NOT WORK ON ANY OTHER SECTION IN THE TEST.

SECTION III

Time — 35 minutes

27 Questions

<u>Directions:</u> Each passage in this section is followed by a group of questions to be answered on the basis of what is <u>stated</u> or <u>implied</u> in the passage. For some of the questions, more than one of the choices could conceivably answer the question. However, you are to choose the <u>best</u> answer; that is, the response that most accurately and completely answers the question, and blacken the corresponding space on your answer sheet.

Nearly every writer on the philosophy of civil rights activist Martin Luther King, Jr., makes a connection between King and Henry David Thoreau, usually via Thoreau's famous essay,
(5) "Civil Disobedience" (1849). In his book *Stride Toward Freedom* (1958), King himself stated that Thoreau's essay was his first intellectual contact with the theory of passive resistance to governmental laws that are perceived as morally unjust. However,
(10) this emphasis on Thoreau's influence on King is unfortunate: first, King would not have agreed with many other aspects of Thoreau's philosophy, including Thoreau's ultimate acceptance of violence as a form of protest; second, an overemphasis on
(15) the influence of one essay has kept historians from noting other correspondences between King's philosophy and transcendentalism. "Civil Disobedience" was the only example of transcendentalist writing with which King was
(20) familiar, and in many other transcendentalist writings, including works by Ralph Waldo Emerson and Margaret Fuller, King would have found ideas more nearly akin to his own.

The kind of civil disobedience King had in
(25) mind was, in fact, quite different from Thoreau's view of civil disobedience. Thoreau, like most other transcendentalists, was primarily interested in reform of the individual, whereas King was primarily interested in reform of society. As a protest against
(30) the Mexican War, Thoreau refused to pay taxes, but he did not hope by his action to force a change in national policy. While he encouraged others to adopt similar protests, he did not attempt to mount any mass protest action against unjust laws. In
(35) contrast to Thoreau, King began to advocate the use of mass civil disobedience to effect revolutionary changes within the social system.

However, King's writings suggest that, without realizing it, he was an incipient transcendentalist.
(40) Most transcendentalists subscribed to the concept of "higher law" and included civil disobedience to unjust laws as part of their strategy. They often invoked the concept of higher law to justify their opposition to slavery and to advocate disobedience
(45) to the strengthened Fugitive Slave Law of 1850. In his second major book, King's discussion of just and unjust laws and the responsibility of the individual is very similar to the transcendentalists' discussion of higher law. In reference to how one
(50) can advocate breaking some laws and obeying

others, King notes that there are two types of laws, just and unjust; he describes a just law as a "code that squares with the moral law" and an unjust law as a "code that is out of harmony with the moral
(55) law." Thus, King's opposition to the injustice of legalized segregation in the twentieth century is philosophically akin to the transcendentalists' opposition to the Fugitive Slave Law in the nineteenth century.

1. Which one of the following best states the main idea of the passage?

   (A) King's philosophy was more influenced by Thoreau's essay on civil disobedience than by any other writing of the transcendentalists.
   (B) While historians may have overestimated Thoreau's influence on King, King was greatly influenced by a number of the transcendentalist philosophers.
   (C) Thoreau's and King's views on civil disobedience differed in that King was more concerned with the social reform than with the economic reform of society.
   (D) Although historians have overemphasized Thoreau's influence on King, there are parallels between King's philosophy and transcendentalism that have not been fully appreciated.
   (E) King's ideas about law and civil disobedience were influenced by transcendentalism in general and Thoreau's essays in particular.

2. Which one of the following statements about "Civil Disobedience" would the author consider most accurate?

   (A) It was not King's first contact with the concept of passive resistance to unjust laws.
   (B) It was one of many examples of transcendentalist writing with which King was familiar.
   (C) It provided King with a model for using passive resistance to effect social change.
   (D) It contains a number of ideas with which other transcendentalists strongly disagreed.
   (E) It influenced King's philosophy on passive resistance to unjust laws.

GO ON TO THE NEXT PAGE.

3. In the first paragraph, the author is primarily concerned with

(A) chronicling the development of King's philosophy on passive resistance to unjust law
(B) suggesting that a common emphasis on one influence on King's philosophy has been misleading
(C) providing new information about the influence of twentieth-century philosophers on King's work
(D) summarizing the work of historians on the most important influences on King's philosophy
(E) providing background information about nineteenth-century transcendentalist philosophers

4. According to the passage, which one of the following is true of Emerson and Fuller?

(A) Some of their ideas were less typical of transcendentalism than were some of Thoreau's ideas.
(B) They were more concerned with the reform of society than with the reform of the individual.
(C) They would have been more likely than Thoreau to agree with King on the necessity of mass protest in civil disobedience.
(D) Their ideas about civil disobedience and unjust laws are as well known as Thoreau's are.
(E) Some of their ideas were more similar to King's than were some of Thoreau's.

5. According to the passage, King differed from most transcendentalists in that he

(A) opposed violence as a form of civil protest
(B) opposed war as an instrument of foreign policy under any circumstances
(C) believed that just laws had an inherent moral value
(D) was more interested in reforming society than in reforming the individual
(E) protested social and legal injustice in United States society rather than United States foreign policy

6. The passage suggests which one of the following about Thoreau?

(A) He was the first to develop fully the theory of civil disobedience.
(B) His work has had a greater influence on contemporary thinkers than has the work of Emerson and Fuller.
(C) His philosophy does not contain all of the same elements as the philosophies of the other transcendentalists.
(D) He advocated using civil disobedience to force the federal government to change its policies on war.
(E) He is better known for his ideas on social and legal reform than for his ideas on individual reform.

7. The passage provides support for which one of the following statements about the quotations in lines 52-55 ?

(A) They are an example of a way in which King's ideas differed from Thoreau's but were similar to the ideas of other transcendentalists.
(B) They provide evidence that proves that King's philosophy was affected by transcendentalist thought.
(C) They suggest that King, like the transcendentalists, judged human laws by ethical standards.
(D) They suggest a theoretical basis for King's philosophy of government.
(E) They provide a paraphrase of Thoreau's position on just and unjust laws.

GO ON TO THE NEXT PAGE.

In *Democracy and its Critics*, Robert Dahl defends both democratic values and pluralist democracies, or polyarchies (a rough shorthand term for Western political systems). Dahl argues
(5) convincingly that the idea of democracy rests on political equality—the equal capacity of all citizens to determine or influence collective decisions. Of course, as Dahl recognizes, if hierarchical ordering is inevitable in any structure of government, and if
(10) no society can guarantee perfect equality in the resources that may give rise to political influence, the democratic principle of political equality is incapable of full realization. So actual systems can be deemed democratic only as approximations to
(15) the ideal. It is on these grounds that Dahl defends polyarchy.

As a representative system in which elected officials both determine government policy and are accountable to a broad-based electorate, polyarchy
(20) reinforces a diffusion of power away from any single center and toward a variety of individuals, groups, and organizations. It is this centrifugal characteristic, Dahl argues, that makes polyarchy the nearest possible approximation to the democratic
(25) ideal. Polyarchy achieves this diffusion of power through party competition and the operation of pressure groups. Competing for votes, parties seek to offer different sections of the electorate what they most want; they do not ask what the majority
(30) thinks of an issue, but what policy commitments will sway the electoral decisions of particular groups. Equally, groups that have strong feelings about an issue can organize in pressure groups to influence public policy.

(35) During the 1960s and 1970s, criticism of the theory of pluralist democracy was vigorous. Many critics pointed to a gap between the model and the reality of Western political systems. They argued that the distribution of power resources other than
(40) the vote was so uneven that the political order systematically gave added weight to those who were already richer or organizationally more powerful. So the power of some groups to exclude issues altogether from the political agenda effectively
(45) countered any diffusion of influence on decision-making.

Although such criticism became subdued during the 1980s, Dahl himself seems to support some of the earlier criticism. Although he regrets that some
(50) Western intellectuals demand more democracy from polyarchies than is possible, and is cautious about the possibility of further democratization, he nevertheless ends his book by asking what changes in structures and consciousness might make political
(55) life more democratic in present polyarchies. One answer, he suggests, is to look at the economic order of polyarchies from the point of view of the citizen as well as from that of producers and consumers. This would require a critical examination
(60) of both the distribution of those economic resources

that are at the same time political resources, and the relationship between political structures and economic enterprises.

8. The characterization of polyarchies as "centrifugal" (line 22) emphasizes the

(A) way in which political power is decentralized in a polyarchy
(B) central role of power resources in a polyarchy
(C) kind of concentrated power that political parties generate in a polyarchy
(D) dynamic balance that exists between economic enterprises and elected officials in a polyarchy
(E) dynamic balance that exists between voters and elected officials in a polyarchy

9. In the third paragraph, the author of the passage refers to criticism of the theory of pluralist democracy primarily in order to

(A) refute Dahl's statement that Western intellectuals expect more democracy from polyarchies than is possible
(B) advocate the need for rethinking the basic principles on which the theory of democracy rests
(C) suggest that the structure of government within pluralist democracies should be changed
(D) point out a flaw in Dahl's argument that the principle of political equality cannot be fully realized
(E) point out an objection to Dahl's defense of polyarchy

10. According to the passage, the aim of a political party in a polyarchy is to do which one of the following?

(A) determine what the position of the majority of voters is on a particular issue
(B) determine what position on an issue will earn the support of particular groups of voters
(C) organize voters into pressure groups in order to influence public policy on a particular issue
(D) ensure that elected officials accurately represent the position of the party on specific issues
(E) ensure that elected officials accurately represent the position of the electorate on specific issues

GO ON TO THE NEXT PAGE.

11. It can be inferred from the passage that Dahl assumes which one of the following in his defense of polyarchies?

   (A) Polyarchies are limited in the extent to which they can embody the idea of democracy.

   (B) The structure of polyarchical governments is free of hierarchical ordering.

   (C) The citizens of a polyarchy have equal access to the resources that provide political influence.

   (D) Polyarchy is the best political system to foster the growth of political parties.

   (E) Polyarchy is a form of government that is not influenced by the interests of economic enterprises.

12. Which one of the following is most closely analogous to pluralist democracies as they are described in relation to the democratic principle of political equality?

   (A) an exact copy of an ancient artifact that is on display in a museum

   (B) a performance of a musical score whose range of tonality cannot be completely captured by any actual instruments

   (C) a lecture by a former astronaut to a class of young students who would like to be astronauts

   (D) the commemoration of a historical event each year by a historian presenting a lecture on a topic related to the event

   (E) the mold from which a number of identical castings of a sculpture are made

13. Which one of the following, if true, would most strengthen Dahl's defense of polyarchy?

   (A) The political agenda in a polyarchy is strongly influenced by how power resources other than the vote are distributed.

   (B) The outcome of elections is more often determined by the financial resources candidates are able to spend during campaigns than by their stands on political issues.

   (C) Public policy in a polyarchy is primarily determined by decision-makers who are not accountable to elected officials.

   (D) Political parties in a polyarchy help concentrate political power in the central government.

   (E) Small and diverse pressure groups are able to exert as much influence on public policy in a polyarchy as are large and powerful groups.

14. The passage can best be described as

   (A) an inquiry into how present-day polyarchies can be made more democratic

   (B) a commentary on the means pressure groups employ to exert influence within polyarchies

   (C) a description of the relationship between polyarchies and economic enterprises

   (D) a discussion of the strengths and weaknesses of polyarchy as a form of democracy

   (E) an overview of the similarities between political parties and pressure groups in a polyarchy

GO ON TO THE NEXT PAGE.

The old belief that climatic stability accounts for the high level of species diversity in the Amazon River basin of South America emerged, strangely enough, from observations of the deep sea. Sanders
(5) discovered high diversity among the mud-dwelling animals of the deep ocean. He argued that such diversity could be attributed to the absence of significant fluctuations in climate and physical conditions, without which the extinction of species
(10) should be rare. In the course of time new species would continue to evolve, and so the rate of speciation would be greater than the rate of extinction, resulting in the accumulation of great diversity. Sanders argued that the Amazon tropical
(15) rain forest is analogous to the deep sea: because the rain forest has a stable climate, extinction should be rare. Evidence that some species of rain-forest trees have persisted for some 30 million years in the Amazon basin, added to the absence of
(20) winter and glaciation, supports this view.

Recently, however, several observations have cast doubt on the validity of the stability hypothesis and suggest that the climate of the Amazon basin has fluctuated significantly in the past. Haffer
(25) noted that different species of birds inhabit different corners of the basin in spite of the fact that essentially unbroken green forest spreads from the western edge to the eastern edge of the region. This pattern presented a puzzle to biologists
(30) studying the distributions of plants and animals: why would different species inhabit different parts of the forest if the habitat in which they lived had a stable climate?

Haffer proposed a compelling explanation for
(35) the distribution of species. Observing that species found on high ground are different from those on low ground, and knowing that in the Amazon lowlands are drier than uplands, he proposed that during the ice ages the Amazon lowlands became a
(40) near-desert arid plain; meanwhile, the more elevated regions became islands of moisture and hence served as refuges for the fauna and flora of the rain forest. Populations that were once continuous diverged and became permanently
(45) separated. Haffer's hypothesis appears to explain the distribution of species as well as the unusual species diversity. The ice-age refuges would have protected existing species from extinction. But the periodic geographic isolation of related populations
(50) (there have been an estimated 13 ice ages to date) would have facilitated the development of new species as existing species on the lowlands adapted to changing climates.

Although no conclusive proof has yet been
(55) found to support Haffer's hypothesis, it has led other researchers to gauge the effects of climatic changes, such as storms and flooding, on species diversity in the Amazon basin. Their research suggests that climatic disturbances help account for
(60) the splendid diversity of the Amazon rain forest today.

15. As discussed in the first paragraph of the passage, Sanders' analogy between the deep sea and the Amazon basin involves which one of the following assumptions?

(A) Both the Amazon basin and the deep sea support an unusually high rate of speciation.
(B) Both the rain-forest trees in the Amazon basin and the mud-dwelling animals in the deep sea have survived for 30 million years.
(C) Both the deep sea and the Amazon basin have not experienced dramatic changes in climate or physical conditions.
(D) A dependable supply of water to the Amazon basin and the deep sea has moderated the rate of extinction in both habitats.
(E) The rate of speciation in the Amazon basin is equivalent to the rate of speciation in the deep sea.

16. The author of the passage would most likely agree with which one of the following statements about Haffer's hypothesis?

(A) It provides an intriguing and complete explanation for the high rate of species diversity in the Amazon basin.
(B) It is partially correct in that a number of climatic disturbances account for species diversity in the Amazon basin.
(C) It has not yet been verified, but it has had an influential effect on current research on species diversity in the Amazon basin.
(D) It is better than Sanders' theory in accounting for the low rate of species extinction in the Amazon basin.
(E) It provides a compelling explanation for the distribution of species in the Amazon basin but does not account for the high species diversity.

17. According to the passage, lowlands in the Amazon basin currently differ from uplands in which one of the following respects?

(A) Lowlands are desertlike, whereas uplands are lush.
(B) Lowlands are less vulnerable to glaciation during the ice ages than are uplands.
(C) Uplands support a greater diversity of species than do lowlands.
(D) Uplands are wetter than are lowlands.
(E) Uplands are more densely populated than are lowlands.

GO ON TO THE NEXT PAGE.

18. Which one of the following best describes the organization of the passage?

(A) A hypothesis is discussed, evidence that undercuts that hypothesis is presented, and a new hypothesis that may account for the evidence is described.

(B) A recently observed phenomenon is described, an explanation for that phenomenon is discussed, and the explanation is evaluated in light of previous research findings.

(C) Several hypotheses that may account for a puzzling phenomenon are described and discounted, and a more promising hypothesis is presented.

(D) A hypothesis and the assumptions on which it is based are described, and evidence is provided to suggest that the hypothesis is only partially correct.

(E) Two alternative explanations for a phenomenon are presented and compared, and experiments designed to test each theory are described.

19. The author of the passage mentions the number of ice ages in the third paragraph most probably in order to

(A) provide proof that cooler and drier temperatures are primarily responsible for the distribution of species in the Amazon

(B) explain how populations of species were protected from extinction in the Amazon basin

(C) explain how most existing species were able to survive periodic climatic disturbances in the Amazon basin

(D) suggest that certain kinds of climatic disturbances cause more species diversity than do other kinds of climatic disturbances

(E) suggest that geographic isolation may have occurred often enough to cause high species diversity in the Amazon basin

20. The passage suggests that which one of the following is true of Sanders' hypothesis?

(A) He underestimated the effects of winter and glaciation in the Amazon basin on the tropical rain forest.

(B) He failed to recognize the similarity in physical conditions of the Amazon lowlands and the Amazon uplands.

(C) He failed to take into account the relatively high rate of extinction during the ice ages in the Amazon basin.

(D) He overestimated the length of time that species have survived in the Amazon basin.

(E) He failed to account for the distribution of species in the Amazon basin.

21. Which one of the following is evidence that would contribute to the "proof" mentioned in line 54 ?

(A) Accurately dated sediment cores from a freshwater lake in the Amazon indicate that the lake's water level rose significantly during the last ice age.

(B) Data based on radiocarbon dating of fossils suggest that the Amazon uplands were too cold to support rain forests during the last ice age.

(C) Computer models of climate during global ice ages predict only insignificant reductions of monsoon rains in tropical areas such as the Amazon.

(D) Fossils preserved in the Amazon uplands during the last ice age are found together with minerals that are the products of an arid landscape.

(E) Fossilized pollen from the Amazon lowlands indicates that during the last ice age the Amazon lowlands supported vegetation that needs little water rather than the rain forests they support today.

GO ON TO THE NEXT PAGE.

Although surveys of medieval legislation, guild organization, and terminology used to designate different medical practitioners have demonstrated that numerous medical specialities were recognized
(5) in Europe during the Middle Ages, most historians continue to equate the term "woman medical practitioner," wherever they encounter it in medieval records, with "midwife." This common practice obscures the fact that, although women
(10) were not represented on all levels of medicine equally, they were represented in a variety of specialties throughout the broad medical community. A reliable study by Wickersheimer and Jacquart documents that, of 7,647 medical practitioners in
(15) France during the twelfth through fifteenth centuries, 121 were women; of these, only 44 were identified as midwives, while the rest practiced as physicians, surgeons, apothecaries, barbers, and other healers.

While preserving terminological distinctions
(20) somewhat increases the quality of the information extracted from medieval documents concerning women medical practitioners, scholars must also reopen the whole question of why documentary evidence for women medical practitioners
(25) comprises such a tiny fraction of the evidence historians of medieval medicine usually present. Is this due to the limitations of the historical record, as has been claimed, or does it also result from the methods historians use? Granted, apart from
(30) medical licenses, the principal sources of information regarding medical practitioners available to researchers are wills, property transfers, court records, and similar documents, all of which typically underrepresent women because of
(35) restrictive medieval legal traditions. Nonetheless, the parameters researchers choose when they define their investigations may contribute to the problem. Studies focusing on the upper echelons of "learned" medicine, for example, tend to exclude healers on
(40) the legal and social fringes of medical practice, where most women would have been found.

The advantages of broadening the scope of such studies is immediately apparent in Pelling and Webster's study of sixteenth-century London.
(45) Instead of focusing solely on officially recognized and licensed practitioners, the researchers defined a medical practitioner as "any individual whose occupation is basically concerned with the care of the sick." Using this definition, they found primary
(50) source information suggesting that there were 60 women medical practitioners in the city of London in 1560. Although this figure may be slightly exaggerated, the evidence contrasts strikingly with that of Gottfried, whose earlier survey identified
(55) only 28 women medical practitioners in all of England between 1330 and 1530.

Finally, such studies provide only statistical information about the variety and prevalence of women's medical practice in medieval Europe.
(60) Future studies might also make profitable use of analyses developed in other areas of women's history as a basis for exploring the social context of women's medical practice. Information about economic rivalry in medicine, women's literacy, and
(65) the control of medical knowledge could add much to our growing understanding of women medical practitioners' role in medieval society.

22. Which one of the following best expresses the main point of the passage?

(A) Recent studies demonstrate that women medical practitioners were more common in England than in the rest of Western Europe during the Middle Ages.

(B) The quantity and quality of the information historians uncover concerning women's medical practice in medieval Europe would be improved if they changed their methods of study.

(C) The sparse evidence for women medical practitioners in studies dealing with the Middle Ages is due primarily to the limitations of the historical record.

(D) Knowledge about the social issues that influenced the role women medical practitioners played in medieval society has been enhanced by several recent studies.

(E) Analyses developed in other areas of women's history could probably be used to provide more information about the social context of women's medical practice during the Middle Ages.

23. Which one of the following is most closely analogous to the error the author believes historians make when they equate the term "woman medical practitioner" with "midwife"?

(A) equating pear with apple
(B) equating science with biology
(C) equating supervisor with subordinate
(D) equating member with nonmember
(E) equating instructor with trainee

GO ON TO THE NEXT PAGE.

24. It can be inferred from the passage that the author would be most likely to agree with which one of the following assertions regarding Gottfried's study?

    (A) Gottfried's study would have recorded a much larger number of women medical practitioners if the time frame covered by the study had included the late sixteenth century.
    (B) The small number of women medical practitioners identified in Gottfried's study is due primarily to problems caused by inaccurate sources.
    (C) The small number of women medical practitioners identified in Gottfried's study is due primarily to the loss of many medieval documents.
    (D) The results of Gottfried's study need to be considered in light of the social changes occurring in Western Europe during the fourteenth and fifteenth centuries.
    (E) In setting the parameters for his study, Gottfried appears to have defined the term "medical practitioner" very narrowly.

25. The passage suggests that a future study that would be more informative about medieval women medical practitioners might focus on which one of the following?

    (A) the effect of social change on the political and economic structure of medieval society
    (B) the effect of social constraints on medieval women's access to a medical education
    (C) the types of medical specialties that developed during the Middle Ages
    (D) the reasons why medieval historians tend to equate the term "woman medical practitioner" with midwife
    (E) the historical developments responsible for the medieval legal tradition's restrictions on women

26. The author refers to the study by Wickersheimer and Jacquart in order to

    (A) demonstrate that numerous medical specialties were recognized in Western Europe during the Middle Ages
    (B) demonstrate that women are often underrepresented in studies of medieval medical practitioners
    (C) prove that midwives were officially recognized as members of the medical community during the Middle Ages
    (D) prove that midwives were only a part of a larger community of women medical practitioners during the Middle Ages
    (E) prove that the existence of midwives can be documented in Western Europe as early as the twelfth century

27. In the passage, the author is primarily concerned with doing which one of the following?

    (A) describing new methodological approaches
    (B) revising the definitions of certain concepts
    (C) comparing two different analyses
    (D) arguing in favor of changes in method
    (E) chronicling certain historical developments

S T O P

IF YOU FINISH BEFORE TIME IS CALLED, YOU MAY CHECK YOUR WORK ON THIS SECTION ONLY.
DO NOT WORK ON ANY OTHER SECTION IN THE TEST.

SECTION IV

Time—35 minutes

24 Questions

<u>Directions:</u> The questions in this section are based on the reasoning contained in brief statements or passages. For some questions, more than one of the choices could conceivably answer the question. However, you are to choose the <u>best</u> answer; that is, the response that most accurately and completely answers the question. You should not make assumptions that are by commonsense standards implausible, superfluous, or incompatible with the passage. After you have chosen the best answer, blacken the corresponding space on your answer sheet.

1. Megatrash Co., the country's largest waste-disposal company, has been sued by environmental groups who have accused the firm of negligent handling of hazardous waste. The fines and legal fees that have resulted from the legal attacks against Megatrash have cost the company substantial amounts of money. Surprisingly, as successful lawsuits against the company have increased in number, the company has grown stronger and more profitable.

Which one of the following, if true, does the most to resolve the apparent paradox?

(A) Although waste-disposal firms merely handle but do not generate toxic waste, these firms have been held legally responsible for environmental damage caused by this waste.

(B) Megatrash has made substantial contributions to environmental causes, as have other large waste-disposal companies.

(C) Some of the judgments against Megatrash have legally barred it from entering the more profitable areas of the waste-management business.

(D) The example of Megatrash's legal entanglements has driven most of the company's competitors from the field and deterred potential rivals from entering it.

(E) In cases in which Megatrash has been acquitted of charges of negligence, the company has paid more in legal fees than it would have been likely to pay in fines.

2. Lewis: Those who do not learn from past mistakes —their own and those of others—are condemned to repeat them. In order to benefit from the lessons of history, however, we first have to know history. That is why the acquisition of broad historical knowledge is so important.

Morris: The trouble is that the past is infinitely various. From its inexhaustible storehouse of events it is possible to prove anything or its contrary.

The issue that Morris raises in objecting to Lewis' view is whether

(A) there are any uncontested historical facts

(B) historical knowledge can be too narrow to be useful

(C) history teaches any unequivocal lessons

(D) there are conventional criteria for calling a past action a mistake

(E) events in the present are influenced by past events

3. A group of scientists who have done research on the health effects of food irradiation has discovered no evidence challenging its safety. Supporters of food irradiation have cited this research as certain proof that food irradiation is a safe practice.

A flaw in the reasoning of the supporters of food irradiation is that they

(A) assume that the scientists doing the research set out to prove that food irradiation is an unsafe practice

(B) are motivated by a biased interest in proving the practice to be safe

(C) overlook the possibility that objections about safety are not the only possible objections to the practice

(D) neglect to provide detailed information about the evidence used to support the conclusion

(E) use the lack of evidence contradicting a claim as conclusive evidence for that claim

4. Cooking teacher: Lima beans generally need about an hour of boiling to reach the proper degree of doneness. The precise amount of time it takes depends on size: larger beans require a longer cooking time than smaller beans do. It is important that lima beans not be overcooked since overcooking robs beans of many of their nutrients. Undercooking should also be avoided, since undercooked beans cannot be completely digested.

If the statements above are true, they most strongly support which one of the following?

(A) Lima beans that are completely digestible have lost many of their nutrients in cooking.

(B) The nutrients that are lost when lima beans are overcooked are the same as those that the body fails to assimilate when lima beans are not completely digested.

(C) Large lima beans, even when fully cooked, are more difficult to digest than small lima beans.

(D) Lima beans that are added to the pot together should be as close to the same size as possible if they are to yield their full nutritional value.

(E) From the standpoint of good nutrition, it is better to overcook than to undercook lima beans.

GO ON TO THE NEXT PAGE.

Questions 5–6

Large quantities of lead dust can be released during renovations in houses with walls painted with lead-based paint. Because the dust puts occupants at high risk of lead poisoning, such renovations should be done only in unoccupied houses by contractors who are experienced in removing all traces of lead from houses and who have the equipment to protect themselves from lead dust. Even when warned, however, many people will not pay to have someone else do renovations they believe they could do less expensively themselves. Therefore, *Homeowners' Journal* should run an article giving information to homeowners on how to reduce the risk of lead poisoning associated with do-it-yourself renovation.

5. Which one of the following, if true, argues most strongly against the passage's recommendation about an article?

(A) Most homeowners know whether or not the walls of their houses are painted with lead-based paint, even if the walls were painted by previous owners.

(B) Most people who undertake do-it-yourself renovation projects do so for the satisfaction of doing the work themselves and so are unlikely to hire a professional to do that sort of work.

(C) Whenever information on do-it-yourself home renovation is published, many people who would otherwise hire professionals decide to perform the renovations themselves, even when there are risks involved.

(D) In many areas, it is difficult to find professional renovators who have the equipment and qualifications to perform safely renovations involving lead dust.

(E) When professionally done home renovations are no more expensive than do-it-yourself renovations, most people choose to have their homes renovated by professionals.

6. Which one of the following principles most helps to justify the passage's recommendation about an article?

(A) Potentially dangerous jobs should always be left to those who have the training and experience to perform them safely, even if additional expense results.

(B) If people refuse to change their behavior even when warned that they are jeopardizing their health, information that enables them to minimize the risks of that behavior should be made available to them.

(C) A journal for homeowners should provide its readers with information on do-it-yourself projects only if such projects do not entail substantial risks.

(D) No one should be encouraged to perform a potentially dangerous procedure if doing so could place any other people at risk.

(E) People who are willing to do work themselves and who are competent to do so should not be discouraged from doing that work.

GO ON TO THE NEXT PAGE.

7. The scientific theory of evolution has challenged the view of human origin as divine creation and sees us as simply descended from the same ancestors as the apes. While science and technology have provided brilliant insights into our world and eased our everyday life, they have simultaneously deprived us of a view in which our importance is assured. Thus, while science has given us many things, it has taken away much that is also greatly valued.

Which one of the following is assumed in the passage?

(A) Science and technology are of less value than religion.
(B) People have resisted the advances of science and technology.
(C) The assurance that people are important is highly valued.
(D) The world was a better place before the advent of science and technology.
(E) The need of people to feel important is now met by science and technology.

Questions 8–9

That long-term cigarette smoking can lead to health problems including cancer and lung disease is a scientifically well-established fact. Contrary to what many people seem to believe, however, it is not necessary to deny this fact in order to reject the view that tobacco companies should be held either morally or legally responsible for the poor health of smokers. After all, excessive consumption of candy undeniably leads to such health problems as tooth decay, but no one seriously believes that candy eaters who get cavities should be able to sue candy manufacturers.

8. The main point of the argument is that

(A) no one should feel it necessary to deny the scientifically well-established fact that long-term cigarette smoking can lead to health problems
(B) people who get cavities should not be able to sue candy manufacturers
(C) the fact that smokers' health problems can be caused by their smoking is not enough to justify holding tobacco companies either legally or morally responsible for those problems
(D) excessive consumption of candy will lead to health problems just as surely as long-term cigarette smoking will
(E) if candy manufacturers were held responsible for tooth decay among candy eaters then tobacco companies should also be held responsible for health problems suffered by smokers

9. The reasoning in the argument is most vulnerable to criticism on the grounds that it

(A) fails to establish that the connection between tooth decay and candy eating is as scientifically well documented as that between smoking and the health problems suffered by smokers
(B) depends on the obviously false assumption that everyone who gets cavities does so only as a result of eating too much candy
(C) leaves undefined such critical qualifying terms as "excessive" and "long-term"
(D) attributes certain beliefs to "many people" without identifying the people who allegedly hold those beliefs
(E) fails to address the striking differences in the nature of the threat to health posed by tooth decay on the one hand and cancer and lung disease on the other

GO ON TO THE NEXT PAGE.

10. Lydia: Each year, thousands of seabirds are injured when they become entangled in equipment owned by fishing companies. Therefore, the fishing companies should assume responsibility for funding veterinary treatment for the injured birds.

Jonathan: Your feelings for the birds are admirable. Your proposal, however, should not be adopted because treatment of the most seriously injured birds would inhumanely prolong the lives of animals no longer able to live in the wild, as all wildlife should.

Jonathan uses which one of the following techniques in his response to Lydia?

(A) He directs a personal attack against her rather than addressing the argument she advances.

(B) He suggests that her proposal is based on self-interest rather than on real sympathy for the injured birds.

(C) He questions the appropriateness of interfering with wildlife in any way, even if the goal of the interference is to help.

(D) He attempts to discredit her proposal by discussing its implications for only those birds that it serves least well.

(E) He evades discussion of her proposal by raising the issue of whether her feelings about the birds are justified.

11. Logging industry official: Harvesting trees from old-growth forests for use in manufacture can reduce the amount of carbon dioxide in the atmosphere, since when large old trees die in the forest they decompose, releasing their stored carbon dioxide. Harvesting old-growth forests would, moreover, make room for rapidly growing young trees, which absorb more carbon dioxide from the atmosphere than do trees in old-growth forests.

Which one of the following, if true, most seriously weakens the official's argument?

(A) Many old-growth forests are the home of thousands of animal species that would be endangered if the forests were to be destroyed.

(B) Much of the organic matter from old-growth trees, unusable as lumber, is made into products that decompose rapidly.

(C) A young tree contains less than half the amount of carbon dioxide that is stored in an old tree of the same species.

(D) Much of the carbon dioxide present in forests is eventually released when wood and other organic debris found on the forest floor decompose.

(E) It can take many years for the trees of a newly planted forest to reach the size of those found in existing old-growth forests.

12. A survey of a group of people between the ages of 75 and 80 found that those who regularly played the card game bridge tended to have better short-term memory than those who did not play bridge. It was originally concluded from this that playing bridge can help older people to retain and develop their memory. However, it may well be that bridge is simply a more enjoyable game for people who already have good short-term memory and who are thus more inclined to play.

In countering the original conclusion the reasoning above uses which one of the following techniques?

(A) challenging the representativeness of the sample surveyed

(B) conceding the suggested relationship between playing bridge and short-term memory, but questioning whether any conclusion about appropriate therapy can be drawn

(C) arguing that the original conclusion relied on an inaccurate understanding of the motives that the people surveyed have for playing bridge

(D) providing an alternative hypothesis to explain the data on which the original conclusion was based

(E) describing a flaw in the reasoning on which the original conclusion was based

13. There are tests to detect some of the rare genetic flaws that increase the likelihood of certain diseases. If these tests are performed, then a person with a rare genetic flaw that is detected can receive the appropriate preventive treatment. Since it costs the health-care system less to prevent a disease than to treat it after it has occurred, widespread genetic screening will reduce the overall cost of health care.

The argument assumes which one of the following?

(A) The cost of treating patients who would, in the absence of screening, develop diseases that are linked to rare genetic flaws would be more than the combined costs of widespread screening and preventive treatment.

(B) Most diseases linked to rare genetic flaws are preventable.

(C) The resources allocated by hospitals to the treatment of persons with diseases linked to genetic flaws will increase once screening is widely available.

(D) Even if the genetic tests are performed, many people whose rare genetic flaws are detected will develop diseases linked to the flaws as a consequence of not receiving the appropriate preventive treatment.

(E) If preventive treatment is given to patients with rare genetic flaws, additional funds will be available for treating the more common diseases.

14. In the 1960s paranoia was viewed by social scientists as ungrounded fear of powerlessness, and the theme of paranoia as it relates to feelings of powerlessness was dominant in films of that period. In the 1970s paranoia instead was viewed by social scientists as a response to real threats from society. Films of this period portray paranoia as a legitimate response to a world gone mad.

Which one of the following is a conclusion that the statements above, if true, most strongly support?

(A) Images of paranoia presented in films made in a period reflect trends in social science of that period.
(B) Responses to real threats can, and often do, degenerate into groundless fears.
(C) The world is becoming more and more threatening.
(D) Paranoia is a condition that keeps changing along with changes in society.
(E) The shift in perception by social scientists from the 1960s to the 1970s resulted from an inability to find a successful cure for paranoia.

15. A certain experimental fungicide causes no harm to garden plants, though only if it is diluted at least to ten parts water to one part fungicide. Moreover, this fungicide is known to be so effective against powdery mildew that it has the capacity to eliminate it completely from rose plants. Thus this fungicide, as long as it is sufficiently diluted, provides a means of eliminating powdery mildew from rose plants that involves no risk of harming the plants.

Which one of the following is an assumption on which the argument depends?

(A) There is not an alternative method, besides application of this fungicide, for eliminating powdery mildew from rose plants without harming the plants.
(B) When the fungicide is sufficiently diluted, it does not present any risk of harm to people, animals, or beneficial insects.
(C) Powdery mildew is the only fungal infection that affects rose plants.
(D) If a fungicide is to be effective against powdery mildew on rose plants, it must eliminate the powdery mildew completely.
(E) The effectiveness of the fungicide does not depend on its being more concentrated than one part in ten parts of water.

16. When glass products are made from recycled glass, the resulting products can be equal in quality to glass products made from quartz sand, the usual raw material. When plastics are recycled, however, the result is inevitably a plastic of a lower grade than the plastic from which it is derived. Moreover, no applications have been found for grades of plastic that are lower than the currently lowest commercial grade.

Which one of the following is a conclusion that can be properly drawn from the statements above?

(A) Products cannot presently be made out of plastic recycled entirely from the currently lowest commercial grade.
(B) It is impossible to make glass products from recycled glass that are equal in quality to the best glass products made from the usual raw material.
(C) Glass products made from recycled glass are less expensive than comparable products made from quartz sand.
(D) Unless recycled plastic bears some symbol revealing its origin, not even materials scientists can distinguish it from virgin plastic.
(E) The difference in quality between different grades of glass is not as great as that between different grades of plastic.

GO ON TO THE NEXT PAGE.

Questions 17–18

Teacher: Journalists who conceal the identity of the sources they quote stake their professional reputations on what may be called the logic of anecdotes. This is so because the statements reported by such journalists are dissociated from the precise circumstances in which they were made and thus will be accepted for publication only if the statements are high in plausibility or originality or interest to a given audience—precisely the properties of a good anecdote.

Student: But what you are saying, then, is that the journalist need not bother with sources in the first place. Surely, any reasonably resourceful journalist can invent plausible, original, or interesting stories faster than they can be obtained from unidentified sources.

17. The student's response contains which one of the following reasoning flaws?

(A) confusing a marginal journalistic practice with the primary work done by journalists
(B) ignoring the possibility that the teacher regards as a prerequisite for the publication of an unattributed statement that the statement have actually been made
(C) confusing the characteristics of reported statements with the characteristics of the situations in which the statements were made
(D) judging the merits of the teacher's position solely by the most extreme case to which the position applies
(E) falsely concluding that if three criteria, met jointly, assure an outcome, then each criterion, met individually, also assures that outcome

18. Which one of the following, if true, most strengthens the teacher's argument?

(A) A journalist undermines his or her own professional standing by submitting for publication statements that, not being attributed to a named source, are rejected for being implausible, unoriginal, or dull.
(B) Statements that are attributed to a fully identified source make up the majority of reported statements included by journalists in stories submitted for publication.
(C) Reported statements that are highly original will often seem implausible unless submitted by a journalist who is known for solid, reliable work.
(D) Reputable journalists sometimes do not conceal the identity of their sources from their publishers but insist that the identity of those sources be concealed from the public.
(E) Journalists who have special access to sources whose identity they must conceal are greatly valued by their publishers.

19. The proposal to extend clinical trials, which are routinely used as systematic tests of pharmaceutical innovations, to new surgical procedures should not be implemented. The point is that surgical procedures differ in one important respect from medicinal drugs: a correctly prescribed drug depends for its effectiveness only on the drug's composition, whereas the effectiveness of even the most appropriate surgical procedure is transparently related to the skills of the surgeon who uses it.

The reasoning in the argument is flawed because the argument

(A) does not consider that new surgical procedures might be found to be intrinsically more harmful than the best treatment previously available
(B) ignores the possibility that the challenged proposal is deliberately crude in a way designed to elicit criticism to be used in refining the proposal
(C) assumes that a surgeon's skills remain unchanged throughout the surgeon's professional life
(D) describes a dissimilarity without citing any scientific evidence for the existence of that dissimilarity
(E) rejects a proposal presumably advanced in good faith without acknowledging any such good faith

GO ON TO THE NEXT PAGE.

20. If the majority of the residents of the apartment complex complain that their apartments are infested with ants, then the management of the complex will have to engage the services of an exterminator. But the majority of the residents of the complex indicate that their apartments are virtually free of ants. Therefore, the management of the complex will not have to engage the services of an exterminator.

Which one of the following arguments contains a flawed pattern of reasoning parallel to that contained in the argument above?

(A) A theater will be constructed in the fall if funds collected are at least sufficient to cover its cost. To date, the funds collected exceed the theater's cost, so the theater will be constructed in the fall.

(B) The number of flights operated by the airlines cannot be reduced unless the airlines can collect higher airfares. But people will not pay higher airfares, so it is not the case that the number of flights will be reduced.

(C) In order for the company to start the proposed building project, both the town council and the mayor must approve. Since the mayor has already approved, the building project will be started soon.

(D) Most employees will attend the company picnic if the entertainment committee is successful in getting a certain band to play at the picnic. But that band will be out of the country on the day of the picnic, so it is not true that most employees will attend.

(E) Either the school's principal or two-thirds of the parent council must approve a change in the school dress code in order for the code to be changed. Since the principal will not approve a change in the dress code, the code will not be changed.

21. When the supply of a given resource dwindles, alternative technologies allowing the use of different resources develop, and demand for the resource that was in short supply naturally declines. Then the existing supplies of that resource satisfy whatever demand remains. Among the once-dwindling resources that are now in more than adequate supply are flint for arrowheads, trees usable for schooner masts, and good mules. Because new technologies constantly replace old ones, we can never run out of important natural resources.

Which one of the following, if true, most seriously undermines the conclusion?

(A) The masts and hulls of some sailing ships built today are still made of wood.

(B) There are considerably fewer mules today than there were 100 years ago.

(C) The cost of some new technologies is often so high that the companies developing them might actually lose money at first.

(D) Dwindling supplies of a natural resource often result in that resource's costing more to use.

(E) The biological requirements for substances like clean air and clean water are unaffected by technological change.

GO ON TO THE NEXT PAGE.

22. Paulsville and Longtown cannot both be included in the candidate's itinerary of campaign stops. The candidate will make a stop in Paulsville unless Salisbury is made part of the itinerary. Unfortunately, a stop in Salisbury is out of the question. Clearly, then, a stop in Longtown can be ruled out.

The reasoning in the argument above most closely parallels that in which one of the following arguments?

(A) The chef never has both fresh radishes and fresh green peppers available for the chef's salad at the same time. If she uses fresh radishes, she also uses spinach. But currently there is no spinach to be had. It can be inferred, then, that she will not be using fresh green peppers.

(B) Tom will definitely support Parker if Mendoza does not apply; and Tom will not support both Parker and Chung. Since, as it turns out, Mendoza will not apply, it follows that Chung will not get Tom's support.

(C) The program committee never selects two plays by Shaw for a single season. But when they select a play by Coward, they do not select any play by Shaw at all. For this season, the committee has just selected a play by Shaw, so they will not select any play by Coward.

(D) In agricultural pest control, either pesticides or the introduction of natural enemies of the pest, but not both, will work. Of course, neither will be needed if pest-resistant crops are planted. So if pesticides are in fact needed, it must be that there are no natural enemies of the pest.

(E) The city cannot afford to build both a new stadium and the new road that would be needed to get there. But neither of the two projects is worth doing without the other. Since the city will not undertake any but worthwhile projects, the new stadium will not be constructed at this time.

23. A study of adults who suffer from migraine headaches revealed that a significant proportion of the study participants suffer from a complex syndrome characterized by a set of three symptoms. Those who suffer from the syndrome experienced excessive anxiety during early childhood. As adolescents, these people began experiencing migraine headaches. As these people approached the age of 20, they also began to experience recurring bouts of depression. Since this pattern is invariant, always with excessive anxiety at its beginning, it follows that excessive anxiety in childhood is one of the causes of migraine headaches and depression in later life.

The reasoning in the argument is vulnerable to criticism on which one of the following grounds?

(A) It does not specify the proportion of those in the general population who suffer from the syndrome.

(B) It fails to rule out the possibility that all of the characteristic symptoms of the syndrome have a common cause.

(C) It makes a generalization that is inconsistent with the evidence.

(D) It fails to demonstrate that the people who participated in the study are representative of migraine sufferers.

(E) It does not establish why the study of migraine sufferers was restricted to adult participants.

24. Mainstream economic theory holds that manufacturers, in deciding what kinds of products to manufacture and what form those products should have, simply respond to the needs and desires of consumers. However, most major manufacturers manipulate and even create consumer demand, as anyone who watches television knows. Since even mainstream economic theorists watch television, their motive in advancing this theory must be something other than disinterested concern for scientific truth.

The claim that manufacturers manipulate and create consumer demand plays which one of the following roles in the argument?

(A) It is one of the claims on which the conclusion is based.

(B) It is the conclusion of the argument.

(C) It states the position argued against.

(D) It states a possible objection to the argument's conclusion.

(E) It provides supplementary background information.

S T O P

IF YOU FINISH BEFORE TIME IS CALLED, YOU MAY CHECK YOUR WORK ON THIS SECTION ONLY.
DO NOT WORK ON ANY OTHER SECTION IN THE TEST.

SIGNATURE_____ / /

LSAT WRITING SAMPLE TOPIC

The publisher of *Willow Creek Dispatch*, the morning newspaper in the small town of Willow Creek, is hiring a new editor in chief. Write an argument favoring one candidate over the other based on the following considerations:

- The *Dispatch* wants to gain a reputation as a leader among small town newspapers.
- The *Dispatch* needs an editor in chief who understands the issues that are important to the residents of Willow Creek.

Amanda Fitzgerald is currently the editor of the local news section of a major city newspaper, where she worked as a reporter for over a decade before becoming an editor eight years ago. While a reporter, she won five national journalism awards for articles on public housing, community control of schools, and the demise of neighborhood businesses. Her colleagues describe her as "an advocate for excellence" as an editor. She grew up in Forest Knolls, a small town near Willow Creek; though she has not lived there for 23 years, she returns occasionally to visit her brother and his family.

Molly Chu was born and raised in a large city. She is the editor in chief of the *Lumberton Gazette*, the morning paper in Lumberton, a nearby town of comparable size to Willow Creek. She has worked at the *Gazette* for the past eleven years, becoming the editor in chief two years ago after a highly praised stint as the newspaper's only staff reporter. The Association of Small Town Newspapers awarded her third place in last year's editorial competition. In addition, parts of her article about health care in small towns were quoted in a story about health care that was the lead article in a national magazine.

Directions:

1. Use the Answer Key on the next page to check your answers.

2. Use the Scoring Worksheet below to compute your raw score.

3. Use the Score Conversion Chart to convert your raw score into the 120-180 scale.

Scoring Worksheet

1. Enter the number of questions you answered correctly in each section.

	Number Correct
SECTION I	_____
SECTION II	_____
SECTION III	_____
SECTION IV	_____

2. Enter the sum here: _____
   This is your Raw Score.

Conversion Chart

For Converting Raw Score to the 120-180 LSAT Scaled Score
LSAT Form 5LSS22

Reported Score	Raw Score Lowest	Raw Score Highest
180	99	101
179	—*	—*
178	98	98
177	97	97
176	96	96
175	95	95
174	94	94
173	93	93
172	92	92
171	91	91
170	90	90
169	89	89
168	88	88
167	86	87
166	85	85
165	84	84
164	82	83
163	81	81
162	79	80
161	77	78
160	76	76
159	74	75
158	72	73
157	71	71
156	69	70
155	67	68
154	65	66
153	63	64
152	61	62
151	59	60
150	58	58
149	56	57
148	54	55
147	52	53
146	50	51
145	48	49
144	46	47
143	44	45
142	43	43
141	41	42
140	39	40
139	37	38
138	36	36
137	34	35
136	32	33
135	30	31
134	29	29
133	27	28
132	26	26
131	24	25
130	23	23
129	22	22
128	20	21
127	19	19
126	18	18
125	17	17
124	16	16
123	15	15
122	14	14
121	13	13
120	0	12

*There is no raw score that will produce this scaled score for this form.

SECTION I

1.	A	8.	D	15.	B	22.	A
2.	E	9.	B	16.	A	23.	B
3.	B	10.	B	17.	C	24.	A
4.	D	11.	D	18.	A		
5.	C	12.	D	19.	C		
6.	B	13.	C	20.	E		
7.	B	14.	E	21.	E		

SECTION II

1.	E	8.	B	15.	D	22.	A
2.	D	9.	D	16.	C	23.	A
3.	C	10.	D	17.	E	24.	A
4.	B	11.	B	18.	D	25.	E
5.	E	12.	E	19.	A	26.	E
6.	E	13.	A	20.	A		
7.	D	14.	E	21.	B		

SECTION III

1.	D	8.	A	15.	C	22.	B
2.	E	9.	E	16.	C	23.	B
3.	B	10.	B	17.	D	24.	E
4.	E	11.	A	18.	A	25.	B
5.	D	12.	B	19.	E	26.	D
6.	C	13.	E	20.	E	27.	D
7.	C	14.	D	21.	E		

SECTION IV

1.	D	8.	C	15.	E	22.	B
2.	C	9.	E	16.	A	23.	B
3.	E	10.	D	17.	B	24.	A
4.	D	11.	B	18.	A		
5.	C	12.	D	19.	A		
6.	B	13.	A	20.	D		
7.	C	14.	A	21.	E		

The Official
LSAT
PrepTest™ XII

The sample test that follows consists of
four sections corresponding to the four
scored sections of the October 1994 LSAT.

October 1994
Form 4LSS26

General Directions for the LSAT Answer Sheet

The actual testing time for this portion of the test will be 2 hours 55 minutes. There are five sections, each with a time limit of 35 minutes. The supervisor will tell you when to begin and end each section. If you finish a section before time is called, you may check your work on that section only; do not turn to any other section of the test book and do not work on any other section either in the test book or on the answer sheet.

There are several different types of questions on the test, and each question type has its own directions. Be sure you understand the directions for each question type before attempting to answer any questions in that section.

Not everyone will finish all the questions in the time allowed. Do not hurry, but work steadily and as quickly as you can without sacrificing accuracy. You are advised to use your time effectively. If a question seems too difficult, go on to the next one and return to the difficult question after completing the section. MARK THE BEST ANSWER YOU CAN FOR EVERY QUESTION. NO DEDUCTIONS WILL BE MADE FOR WRONG ANSWERS. YOUR SCORE WILL BE BASED ONLY ON THE NUMBER OF QUESTIONS YOU ANSWER CORRECTLY.

ALL YOUR ANSWERS MUST BE MARKED ON THE ANSWER SHEET. Answer spaces for each question are lettered to correspond with the letters of the potential answers to each question in the test book. After you have decided which of the answers is correct, blacken the corresponding space on the answer sheet. BE SURE THAT EACH MARK IS BLACK AND COMPLETELY FILLS THE ANSWER SPACE. Give only one answer to each question. If you change an answer, be sure that all previous marks are erased completely. Since the answer sheet is machine scored, incomplete erasures may be interpreted as intended answers. ANSWERS RECORDED IN THE TEST BOOK WILL NOT BE SCORED.

There may be more questions noted on this answer sheet than there are questions in a section. Do not be concerned but be certain that the section and number of the question you are answering matches the answer sheet section and question number. Additional answer spaces in any answer sheet section should be left blank. Begin your next section in the number one answer space for that section.

Score Cancellation

Complete this section only if you are absolutely certain you want to cancel your score. A CANCELLATION REQUEST CANNOT BE RESCINDED. IF YOU ARE AT ALL UNCERTAIN, YOU SHOULD NOT COMPLETE THIS SECTION; INSTEAD, YOU SHOULD USE THE TIME ALLOWED AFTER THE TEST (UP TO 5 DAYS) TO FULLY CONSIDER YOUR DECISION.

To cancel your score from this administration, you must:

A. fill in the ovals here........ ◯ ◯

B. read the following statement. Then sign your name and enter the date.

I certify that I wish to cancel my test score from this administration. I understand that my request is irreversible and that my score will not be sent to me or to the law schools to which I apply.

_____
Sign your name in full

_____
Date

HOW DID YOU PREPARE FOR THE LSAT?
(Select all that apply.)

Responses to this item are voluntary and will be used for statistical research purposes only.

- ◯ By studying the sample questions in the *LSAT/LSDAS Registration and Information Book*.
- ◯ By taking the free sample LSAT.
- ◯ By working through *The Official LSAT PrepTest(s), PrepBook, Workbooks, or PrepKit*.
- ◯ By using a book on how to prepare for the LSAT **not** published by Law Services.
- ◯ By attending a commercial test preparation or coaching course.
- ◯ By attending a test preparation or coaching course offered through an undergraduate institution.
- ◯ Self study.
- ◯ Other preparation.
- ◯ No preparation.

CERTIFYING STATEMENT

Please write (DO NOT PRINT) the following statement. Sign and date.

I certify that I am the examinee whose name appears on this answer sheet and that I am here to take the LSAT for the sole purpose of being considered for admission to law school. I further certify that I will neither assist nor receive assistance from any other candidate, and I agree not to copy or retain examination questions or to transmit them in any form to any other person.

_____
_____
_____
_____
_____
_____
_____
_____

SIGNATURE: _____ TODAY'S DATE: ___/___/___
                                                    MONTH DAY YEAR

INSTRUCTIONS FOR COMPLETING THE BIOGRAPHICAL AREA ARE ON THE BACK COVER OF YOUR TEST BOOKLET.
USE ONLY A NO. 2 OR HB PENCIL TO COMPLETE THIS ANSWER SHEET. DO NOT USE INK.

1 LAST NAME / FIRST NAME / MI

(Grid of bubbles A–Z for each letter position)

2 DATE OF BIRTH

MONTH	DAY	YEAR
○ Jan		
○ Feb		
○ Mar		
○ Apr		
○ May		
○ June		
○ July		
○ Aug		
○ Sept		
○ Oct		
○ Nov		
○ Dec		

(Number bubbles 0–9)

3 SOCIAL SECURITY NO.

(Number bubbles 0–9)

Right Mark: ●
Wrong Marks: ⊘ ⊗ ⊙

4 ETHNIC DESCRIPTION

- ○ American Indian/ Alaskan Native
- ○ Asian/Pacific Islander
- ○ Black/African Amer.
- ○ Canadian Aboriginal
- ○ Caucasian/White
- ○ Chicano/Mex. Amer.
- ○ Hispanic
- ○ Puerto Rican
- ○ Other

5 GENDER
- ○ Male
- ○ Female

6 DOMINANT LANGUAGE
- ○ English
- ○ Other

7 ENGLISH FLUENCY
- ○ Yes
- ○ No

8 CENTER NUMBER

(Number bubbles 0–9)

9 TEST FORM CODE

(Number bubbles 0–9)

10 TEST BOOK SERIAL NO.

11 TEST FORM

12 TEST DATE

_____ / _____ / _____
MONTH   DAY   YEAR

13 PLEASE PRINT ALL INFORMATION

LAST NAME   FIRST

MAILING ADDRESS

SOCIAL SECURITY/ SOCIAL INSURANCE NO.

NOTE: If you have a new address, you must write Law Services at Box 2000-C, Newtown, PA 18940 or call (215) 968-1001. We cannot guarantee that all address changes will be processed before scores are mailed, so be sure to notify your post office of your forwarding address.

═══ LAW SCHOOL ADMISSION TEST ═══

MARK ONE AND ONLY ONE ANSWER TO EACH QUESTION. BE SURE TO FILL IN COMPLETELY THE SPACE FOR YOUR INTENDED ANSWER CHOICE. IF YOU ERASE, DO SO COMPLETELY. MAKE NO STRAY MARKS.

SECTION 1 / SECTION 2 / SECTION 3 / SECTION 4 / SECTION 5

Questions 1–30 in each section with answer bubbles (A) (B) (C) (D) (E)

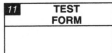

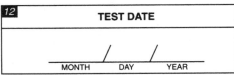

FOR LAW SERVICES USE ONLY

LR	
LW	
LCS	

Copyright © 1994 BY LAW SCHOOL ADMISSION SERVICES, INC. ALL RIGHTS RESERVED. PRINTED IN U.S.A.

SECTION I

Time—35 minutes

26 Questions

Directions: The questions in this section are based on the reasoning contained in brief statements or passages. For some questions, more than one of the choices could conceivably answer the question. However, you are to choose the best answer; that is, the response that most accurately and completely answers the question. You should not make assumptions that are by commonsense standards implausible, superfluous, or incompatible with the passage. After you have chosen the best answer, blacken the corresponding space on your answer sheet.

1. It is probably within the reach of human technology to make the climate of Mars inhabitable. It might be several centuries before people could live there, even with breathing apparatuses, but some of the world's great temples and cathedrals took centuries to build. Research efforts now are justified if there is even a chance of making another planet inhabitable. Besides, the intellectual exercise of understanding how the Martian atmosphere might be changed could help in understanding atmospheric changes inadvertently triggered by human activity on Earth.

The main point of the argument is that

(A) it is probably technologically possible for humankind to alter the climate of Mars
(B) it would take several centuries to make Mars even marginally inhabitable
(C) making Mars inhabitable is an effort comparable to building a great temple or cathedral
(D) research efforts aimed at discovering how to change the climate of Mars are justified
(E) efforts to change the climate of Mars could facilitate understanding of the Earth's climate

Questions 2–3

Adults have the right to vote; so should adolescents. Admittedly, adolescents and adults are not the same. But to the extent that adolescents and adults are different, adults cannot be expected to represent the interests of adolescents. If adults cannot represent the interests of adolescents, then only by giving adolescents the vote will these interests be represented.

2. The argument relies on which one of the following assumptions?

(A) The right to vote is a right that all human beings should have.
(B) Adolescents and adults differ in most respects that are important.
(C) Adolescents should have their interests represented.
(D) Anyone who has the right to vote has all the rights an adult has.
(E) Adolescents have never enjoyed the right to vote.

3. The statement that adolescents and adults are not the same plays which one of the following roles in the argument?

(A) It presents the conclusion of the argument.
(B) It makes a key word in the argument more precise.
(C) It illustrates a consequence of one of the claims that are used to support the conclusion.
(D) It distracts attention from the point at issue.
(E) It concedes a point that is then used to support the conclusion.

GO ON TO THE NEXT PAGE.

4. When deciding where to locate or relocate, businesses look for an educated work force, a high level of services, a low business-tax rate, and close proximity to markets and raw materials. However, although each of these considerations has approximately equal importance, the lack of proximity either to markets or to raw materials often causes municipalities to lose prospective businesses, whereas having a higher-than-average business-tax rate rarely has this effect.

Which one of the following, if true, most helps to resolve the apparent discrepancy in the statements above?

(A) Taxes paid by businesses constitute only a part of the tax revenue collected by most municipalities.

(B) In general, the higher the rate at which municipalities tax businesses, the more those municipalities spend on education and on providing services to businesses.

(C) Businesses sometimes leave a municipality after that municipality has raised its taxes on businesses.

(D) Members of the work force who are highly educated are more likely to be willing to relocate to secure work than are less highly educated workers.

(E) Businesses have sometimes tried to obtain tax reductions from municipalities by suggesting that without such a reduction the business might be forced to relocate elsewhere.

Questions 5–6

Oscar: I have been accused of plagiarizing the work of Ethel Myers in my recent article. But that accusation is unwarranted. Although I admit I used passages from Myers' book without attribution, Myers gave me permission in private correspondence to do so.

Millie: Myers cannot give you permission to plagiarize. Plagiarism is wrong, not only because it violates authors' rights to their own words, but also because it misleads readers: it is fundamentally a type of lie. A lie is no less a lie if another person agrees to the deception.

5. Which one of the following principles, if established, would justify Oscar's judgment?

(A) A writer has no right to quote passages from another published source if the author of that other source has not granted the writer permission to do so.

(B) The writer of an article must cite the source of all passages that were not written by that writer if those passages are more than a few sentences long.

(C) Plagiarism is never justified, but writers are justified in occasionally quoting without attribution the work of other writers if the work quoted has not been published.

(D) An author is entitled to quote freely without attribution the work of a writer if that writer relinquishes his or her exclusive right to the material.

(E) Authors are entitled to quote without attribution passages that they themselves have written and published in other books or articles.

6. Millie uses which one of the following argumentative strategies in contesting Oscar's position?

(A) analyzing plagiarism in a way that undermines Oscar's position

(B) invoking evidence to show that Oscar did quote Myers' work without attribution

(C) challenging Oscar's ability to prove that he had received Myers' permission to quote Myers' work without attribution

(D) citing a theory of rights that prohibits plagiarism and suggesting that Oscar is committed to that theory

(E) showing that Oscar's admission demonstrates his lack of credibility

GO ON TO THE NEXT PAGE.

7. Soil scientists studying the role of compost in horticulture have found that, while compost is useful for building soil structure, it does not supply large enough quantities of the nutrients essential for plant growth to make it a replacement for fertilizer. Many home gardeners, however, have found they can grow healthy and highly productive plants in soil that lacked essential nutrients by enriching the soil with nothing but compost.

Which one of the following, if true, most helps to explain the discrepant findings of the soil scientists and the home gardeners?

(A) The findings of soil scientists who are employed by fertilizer manufacturers do not differ widely from those of scientists employed by the government or by universities.

(B) Compost used in research projects is usually made from leaves and grass clippings only, whereas compost used in home gardens is generally made from a wide variety of ingredients.

(C) Most plants grown in home gardens and in scientists' test plots need a favorable soil structure, as well as essential nutrients, in order to thrive.

(D) The soil in test plots, before it is adjusted in the course of experiments, tends to contain about the same quantities of plant nutrients as does soil in home gardens to which no compost or fertilizer has been added.

(E) Some of the varieties of plants grown by home gardeners require greater quantities of nutrients in order to be healthy than do the varieties of plants generally grown by the soil scientists in test plots.

8. At Happywell, Inc., last year the average annual salary for dieticians was $50,000, while the average annual salary for physical therapists was $42,000. The average annual salary for all Happywell employees last year was $40,000.

If the information above is correct, which one of the following conclusions can properly be drawn on the basis of it?

(A) There were more physical therapists than dieticians at Happywell last year.

(B) There was no dietician at Happywell last year who earned less than the average for a physical therapist.

(C) At least one Happywell employee earned less than the average for a physical therapist last year.

(D) At least one physical therapist earned less than the lowest-paid Happywell dietician last year.

(E) At least one dietician earned more than the highest-paid Happywell physical therapist last year.

9. Since multinational grain companies operate so as to maximize profits, they cannot be relied on to initiate economic changes that would reform the world's food-distribution system. Although it is true that the actions of multinational companies sometimes do result in such economic change, this result is incidental, arising not from the desire for reform but from the desire to maximize profits. The maximization of profits normally depends on a stable economic environment, one that discourages change.

The main point of the argument is that

(A) the maximization of profits depends on a stable economic environment

(B) when economic change accompanies business activity, that change is initiated by concern for the profit motive

(C) multinational grain companies operate so as to maximize profits

(D) the world's current food-distribution system is not in need of reform

(E) multinational grain companies cannot be relied on to initiate reform of the world's food-distribution system

10. Stage performances are judged to be realistic to the degree that actors reproduce on stage the behaviors generally associated by audiences with the emotional states of the characters portrayed. Traditional actors imitate those behaviors, whereas Method actors, through recollection of personal experience, actually experience the same emotions that their characters are meant to be experiencing. Audiences will therefore judge the performances of Method actors to be more realistic than the performances of traditional actors.

Which one of the following is an assumption on which the argument depends?

(A) Performances based on an actor's own experience of emotional states are more likely to affect an audience's emotions than are performances based on imitations of the behaviors generally associated with those emotional states.

(B) The behavior that results when a Method actor feels a certain emotion will conform to the behavior that is generally associated by audiences with that emotion.

(C) Realism is an essential criterion for evaluating the performances of both traditional actors and Method actors.

(D) Traditional actors do not aim to produce performances that are realistic representations of a character's emotional states.

(E) In order to portray a character, a Method actor need not have had experiences identical to those of the character portrayed.

GO ON TO THE NEXT PAGE.

11. The demand for used cars has risen dramatically in Germany in recent years. Most of this demand is generated by former East Germans who cannot yet afford new cars and for whom cars were generally unavailable prior to unification. This demand has outstripped supply and thus has exerted an upward pressure on the prices of used cars. Consequently, an increasing number of former West Germans, in order to take advantage of the improved market, will be selling the cars they have owned for several years. Hence, the German new-car market will most likely improve soon as well.

Which one of the following, if true, would most help to support the conclusion about the German new-car market?

(A) The demand for old cars in former West Germany is greater than the demand for new cars in former East Germany.
(B) In most European countries, the sale of a used car is subject to less tax than is the sale of a new car.
(C) Most Germans own very few cars in the course of their lives.
(D) Most former West Germans purchase new cars once they sell their used cars.
(E) Many former East Germans prefer to buy cars imported from North America because they are generally larger than European cars.

12. In 1980 health officials began to publicize the adverse effects of prolonged exposure to the sun, and since then the number of people who sunbathe for extended periods of time has decreased considerably each year. Nevertheless, in 1982 there was a dramatic rise in newly reported cases of melanoma, a form of skin cancer found mostly in people who have had prolonged exposure to the sun.

Which one of the following, if true, helps to resolve the apparent discrepancy in the information above?

(A) Before 1980 a considerable number of the people who developed melanoma as a result of prolonged exposure to the sun were over forty years of age.
(B) Before 1980, when most people had not yet begun to avoid prolonged exposure to the sun, sunbathing was widely thought to be healthful.
(C) In 1982 scientists reported that the body's need for exposure to sunlight in order to produce vitamin D, which helps prevent the growth of skin cancers, is less than was previously thought.
(D) In 1982 medical researchers perfected a diagnostic technique that allowed them to detect the presence of melanoma much earlier than had previously been possible.
(E) Since 1980, those people who have continued to sunbathe for extended periods of time have used sunblocks that effectively screen out the ultraviolet rays that help cause melanoma.

13. The tiny country of Minlandia does not produce its own television programming. Instead, the citizens of Minlandia, who generally are fluent not only in their native Minlandian, but also in Boltese, watch Boltese-language television programs from neighboring Bolta. Surveys show that the Minlandians spend on average more hours per week reading for pleasure and fewer hours per week watching television than people anywhere else in the world. A prominent psychologist accounts for the survey results by explaining that people generally prefer to be entertained in their native language, even if they are perfectly fluent in other languages.

The explanation offered by the psychologist accounts for the Minlandians' behavior only if which one of the following is assumed?

(A) Some Minlandians derive no pleasure from watching television in a language other than their native Minlandian.
(B) The study of Boltese is required of Minlandian children as part of their schooling.
(C) The proportion of bilingual residents to total population is greater in Minlandia than anywhere else in the world.
(D) At least some of what the Minlandians read for pleasure is in the Minlandian language.
(E) When Minlandians watch Boltese television programs, they tend to ignore the fact that they are hearing a foreign language spoken.

14. Morris High School has introduced a policy designed to improve the working conditions of its new teachers. As a result of this policy, only one-quarter of all part-time teachers now quit during their first year. However, a third of all full-time teachers now quit during their first year. Thus, more full-time than part-time teachers at Morris now quit during their first year.

The argument's reasoning is questionable because the argument fails to rule out the possibility that

(A) before the new policy was instituted, more part-time than full-time teachers at Morris High School used to quit during their first year
(B) before the new policy was instituted, the same number of full-time teachers as part-time teachers at Morris High School used to quit during their first year
(C) Morris High School employs more new full-time teachers than new part-time teachers
(D) Morris High School employs more new part-time teachers than new full-time teachers
(E) Morris High School employs the same number of new part-time as new full-time teachers

GO ON TO THE NEXT PAGE.

Questions 15–16

Salmonella is a food-borne microorganism that can cause intestinal illness. The illness is sometimes fatal, especially if not identified quickly and treated. Conventional *Salmonella* tests on food samples are slow and can miss unusual strains of the microorganism. A new test identifies the presence or absence of *Salmonella* by the one piece of genetic material common to all strains. Clearly, public health officials would be well advised to replace the previous *Salmonella* tests with the new test.

15. Which one of the following, if true, most strengthens the argument?

(A) The level of skill required for laboratory technicians to perform the new test is higher than that required to perform previous tests for *Salmonella*.

(B) The new test returns results very soon after food samples are submitted for testing.

(C) A proposed new treatment for *Salmonella* poisoning would take effect faster than the old treatment.

(D) *Salmonella* poisoning is becoming less frequent in the general population.

(E) Some remedies for *Salmonella* poisoning also cure intestinal disorders caused by other microorganisms.

16. Which one of the following, if true, most substantially weakens the argument?

(A) The new test identifies genetic material from *Salmonella* organisms only and not from similar bacteria.

(B) The new test detects the presence of *Salmonella* at levels that are too low to pose a health risk to people.

(C) *Salmonella* is only one of a variety of food-borne microorganisms that can cause intestinal illness.

(D) The new test has been made possible only recently by dramatic advances in biological science.

(E) Symptoms of *Salmonella* poisoning are often mistaken for those of other common intestinal illnesses.

17. On average, city bus drivers who are using the new computerized fare-collection system have a much better on-time record than do drivers using the old fare-collection system. Millicent Smith has the best on-time record of any bus driver in the city. Therefore, she must be using the computerized fare-collection system.

Which one of the following contains flawed reasoning most similar to that contained in the argument above?

(A) All the city's solid-waste collection vehicles acquired after 1988 have a larger capacity than any of those acquired before 1988. This vehicle has the largest capacity of any the city owns, so it must have been acquired after 1988.

(B) The soccer players on the blue team are generally taller than the players on the gold team. Since Henri is a member of the blue team, he is undoubtedly taller than most of the members of the gold team.

(C) This tomato is the largest of this year's crop. Since the tomatoes in the experimental plot are on average larger than those grown in the regular plots, this tomato must have been grown in the experimental plot.

(D) Last week's snowstorm in Toronto was probably an average storm for the area. It was certainly heavier than any snowstorm known to have occurred in Miami, but any average snowstorm in Toronto leaves more snow than ever falls in Miami.

(E) Lawn mowers powered by electricity generally require less maintenance than do lawn mowers powered by gasoline. This lawn mower is powered by gasoline, so it will probably require a lot of maintenance.

GO ON TO THE NEXT PAGE.

18. Frieda: Lightning causes fires and damages electronic equipment. Since lightning rods can prevent any major damage, every building should have one.

    Erik: Your recommendation is pointless. It is true that lightning occasionally causes fires, but faulty wiring and overloaded circuits cause far more fires and damage to equipment than lightning does.

Erik's response fails to establish that Frieda's recommendation should not be acted on because his response

(A)   does not show that the benefits that would follow from Frieda's recommendation would be offset by any disadvantages
(B)   does not offer any additional way of lessening the risk associated with lightning
(C)   appeals to Frieda's emotions rather than to her reason
(D)   introduces an irrelevant comparison between overloaded circuits and faulty wiring
(E)   confuses the notion of preventing damage with that of causing inconvenience

19. The use of automobile safety seats by children aged 4 and under has nearly doubled in the past 8 years. It is clear that this increase has prevented child fatalities that otherwise would have occurred, because although the number of children aged 4 and under who were killed while riding in cars involved in accidents rose 10 percent over the past 8 years, the total number of serious automobile accidents rose by 20 percent during that period.

Which one of the following, if true, most strengthens the argument?

(A)   Some of the automobile safety seats purchased for children under 4 continue to be used after the child reaches the age of 5.
(B)   The proportion of serious automobile accidents involving child passengers has remained constant over the past 8 years.
(C)   Children are taking more trips in cars today than they were 8 years ago, but the average total time they spend in cars has remained constant.
(D)   The sharpest increase in the use of automobile safety seats over the past 8 years has been for children over the age of 2.
(E)   The number of fatalities among adults involved in automobile accidents rose by 10 percent over the past 8 years.

Questions 20–21

The new perfume Aurora smells worse to Joan than any comparably priced perfume, and none of her friends likes the smell of Aurora as much as the smell of other perfumes. However, she and her friends must have a defect in their sense of smell, since Professor Jameson prefers the smell of Aurora to that of any other perfume and she is one of the world's foremost experts on the physiology of smell.

20. The reasoning is flawed because it

(A)   calls into question the truthfulness of the opponent rather than addressing the point at issue
(B)   ignores the well-known fact that someone can prefer one thing to another without liking either very much
(C)   fails to establish that there is widespread agreement among the experts in the field
(D)   makes an illegitimate appeal to the authority of an expert
(E)   misrepresents the position against which it is directed

21. From the information presented in support of the conclusion, it can be properly inferred that

(A)   none of Joan's friends is an expert on the physiology of smell
(B)   Joan prefers all other perfumes to Aurora
(C)   Professor Jameson is not one of Joan's friends
(D)   none of Joan's friends likes Aurora perfume
(E)   Joan and her friends all like the same kinds of perfumes

GO ON TO THE NEXT PAGE.

22. At the end of the year, Wilson's Department Store awards free merchandise to its top salespeople. When presented with the fact that the number of salespeople receiving these awards has declined markedly over the past fifteen years, the newly appointed president of the company responded, "In that case, since our award criterion at present is membership in the top third of our sales force, we can also say that the number of salespeople passed over for these awards has similarly declined."

Which one of the following is an assumption that would allow the company president's conclusion to be properly drawn?

(A) Policies at Wilson's with regard to hiring salespeople have not become more lax over the past fifteen years.

(B) The number of salespeople at Wilson's has increased over the past fifteen years.

(C) The criterion used by Wilson's for selecting its award recipients has remained the same for the past fifteen years.

(D) The average total sales figures for Wilson's salespeople have been declining for fifteen years.

(E) Wilson's calculates its salespeople's sales figures in the same way as it did fifteen years ago.

23. The capture of a wild animal is justified only as a last resort to save that animal's life. But many wild animals are captured not because their lives are in any danger but so that they can be bred in captivity. Hence, many animals that have been captured should not have been captured.

Which one of the following arguments is most similar in its pattern of reasoning to the argument above?

(A) Punishing a child is justified if it is the only way to reform poor behavior. But punishment is never the only way to reform poor behavior. Hence, punishing a child is never justified.

(B) Parents who never punish a child are not justified in complaining if the child regularly behaves in ways that disturb them. But many parents who prefer not to punish their children complain regularly about their children's behavior. Hence, many parents who complain about their children have no right to complain.

(C) Punishing a young child is justified only if it is done out of concern for the child's future welfare. But many young children are punished not in order to promote their welfare but to minimize sibling rivalry. Hence, many children who are punished should not have been punished.

(D) A teacher is entitled to punish a child only if the child's parents have explicitly given the teacher the permission to do so. But many parents never give their child's teacher the right to punish their child. Hence, many teachers should not punish their pupils.

(E) Society has no right to punish children for deeds that would be crimes if the children were adults. But society does have the right to protect itself from children who are known threats. Hence, confinement of such children does not constitute punishment.

GO ON TO THE NEXT PAGE.

24. Until recently it was thought that ink used before the sixteenth century did not contain titanium. However, a new type of analysis detected titanium in the ink of the famous Bible printed by Johannes Gutenberg and in that of another fifteenth-century Bible known as B-36, though not in the ink of any of numerous other fifteenth-century books analyzed. This finding is of great significance, since it not only strongly supports the hypothesis that B-36 was printed by Gutenberg but also shows that the presence of titanium in the ink of the purportedly fifteenth-century Vinland Map can no longer be regarded as a reason for doubting the map's authenticity.

The reasoning in the passage is vulnerable to criticism on the ground that

(A) the results of the analysis are interpreted as indicating that the use of titanium as an ingredient in fifteenth-century ink both was, and was not, extremely restricted

(B) if the technology that makes it possible to detect titanium in printing ink has only recently become available, it is unlikely that printers or artists in the fifteenth century would know whether their ink contained titanium or not

(C) it is unreasonable to suppose that determination of the date and location of a document's printing or drawing can be made solely on the basis of the presence or absence of a single element in the ink used in the document

(D) both the B-36 Bible and the Vinland Map are objects that can be appreciated on their own merits whether or not the precise date of their creation or the identity of the person who made them is known

(E) the discovery of titanium in the ink of the Vinland Map must have occurred before titanium was discovered in the ink of the Gutenberg Bible and the B-36 Bible

25. All actors are exuberant people and all exuberant people are extroverts, but nevertheless it is true that some shy people are actors.

If the statements above are true, each of the following must also be true EXCEPT:

(A) Some shy people are extroverts.
(B) Some shy extroverts are not actors.
(C) Some exuberant people who are actors are shy.
(D) All people who are not extroverts are not actors.
(E) Some extroverts are shy.

26. Science Academy study: It has been demonstrated that with natural methods, some well-managed farms are able to reduce the amounts of synthetic fertilizer and pesticide and also of antibiotics they use without necessarily decreasing yields; in some cases yields can be increased.

Critics: Not so. The farms the academy selected to study were the ones that seemed most likely to be successful in using natural methods. What about the farmers who have tried such methods and failed?

Which one of the following is the most adequate evaluation of the logical force of the critics' response?

(A) Success and failure in farming are rarely due only to luck, because farming is the management of chance occurrences.

(B) The critics show that the result of the study would have been different if twice as many farms had been studied.

(C) The critics assume without justification that the failures were not due to soil quality.

(D) The critics demonstrate that natural methods are not suitable for the majority of farmers.

(E) The issue is only to show that something is possible, so it is not relevant whether the instances studied were representative.

S T O P

IF YOU FINISH BEFORE TIME IS CALLED, YOU MAY CHECK YOUR WORK ON THIS SECTION ONLY.
DO NOT WORK ON ANY OTHER SECTION IN THE TEST.

SECTION II

Time—35 minutes

24 Questions

Directions: Each group of questions in this section is based on a set of conditions. In answering some of the questions, it may be useful to draw a rough diagram. Choose the response that most accurately and completely answers each question and blacken the corresponding space on your answer sheet.

Questions 1–6

A piano instructor will schedule exactly one lesson for each of six students—Grace, Henry, Janet, Steve, Tom, and Una—one lesson per day for six consecutive days. The schedule must conform to the following conditions:

Henry's lesson is later in the schedule than Janet's lesson.

Una's lesson is later in the schedule than Steve's lesson.

Steve's lesson is exactly three days after Grace's lesson.

Janet's lesson is on the first day or else the third day.

1. If Janet's lesson is scheduled for the first day, then the lesson for which one of the following students must be scheduled for the sixth day?

   (A) Grace
   (B) Henry
   (C) Steve
   (D) Tom
   (E) Una

2. For which one of the following students is there an acceptable schedule in which the student's lesson is on the third day and another acceptable schedule in which the student's lesson is on the fifth day?

   (A) Grace
   (B) Henry
   (C) Steve
   (D) Tom
   (E) Una

3. Which one of the following is a complete and accurate list of the students any one of whom could be the student whose lesson is scheduled for the second day?

   (A) Grace
   (B) Tom
   (C) Grace, Tom
   (D) Henry, Tom
   (E) Grace, Henry, Tom

4. If Henry's lesson is scheduled for a day either immediately before or immediately after Tom's lesson, then Grace's lesson must be scheduled for the

   (A) first day
   (B) second day
   (C) third day
   (D) fourth day
   (E) fifth day

5. If Janet's lesson is scheduled for the third day, which one of the following could be true?

   (A) Grace's lesson is scheduled for a later day than Henry's lesson.
   (B) Grace's lesson is scheduled for a later day than Una's lesson.
   (C) Henry's lesson is scheduled for a later day than Una's lesson.
   (D) Tom's lesson is scheduled for a later day than Henry's lesson.
   (E) Tom's lesson is scheduled for a later day than Una's lesson.

6. Which one of the following is a complete and accurate list of days any one of which could be the day for which Tom's lesson is scheduled?

   (A) first, second, third
   (B) second, third, fourth
   (C) second, fifth, sixth
   (D) first, second, third, fourth
   (E) second, third, fourth, sixth

GO ON TO THE NEXT PAGE.

Questions 7–11

Five children—F, G, H, J, and K—and four adults—Q, R, S, and T—are planning a canoeing trip. The canoeists will be divided into three groups—groups 1, 2, and 3—of three canoeists each, according to the following conditions:

There must be at least one adult in each group.
F must be in the same group as J.
G cannot be in the same group as T.
H cannot be in the same group as R.
Neither H nor T can be in group 2.

7. If F is in group 1, which one of the following could be true?

   (A) G and K are in group 3.
   (B) G and R are in group 3.
   (C) J and S are in group 2.
   (D) K and R are in group 1.
   (E) Q and S are in group 2.

8. If F and S are in group 3, which one of the following must be true?

   (A) G is in group 2.
   (B) H is in group 3.
   (C) K is in group 1.
   (D) Q is in group 2.
   (E) R is in group 1.

9. If G and K are in group 3, which one of the following must be true?

   (A) H is in group 3.
   (B) J is in group 1.
   (C) R is in group 2.
   (D) S is in group 3.
   (E) T is in group 1.

10. If Q is in group 1 and S is in group 3, which one of the following CANNOT be true?

   (A) G is in group 2.
   (B) T is in group 1.
   (C) There is exactly one child in group 1.
   (D) There is exactly one child in group 2.
   (E) There is exactly one child in group 3.

11. If G is the only child in group 1, which one of the following must be true?

   (A) F is in group 3.
   (B) K is in group 3.
   (C) Q is in group 2.
   (D) R is in group 1.
   (E) S is in group 2.

GO ON TO THE NEXT PAGE.

Questions 12–17

Lara, Mendel, and Nastassia each buy at least one kind of food from a street vendor who sells only fruit cups, hot dogs, pretzels, and shish kebabs. They make their selections in accordance with the following restrictions:
 None of the three buys more than one portion of each kind of food.
 If any of the three buys a hot dog, that person does not also buy a shish kebab.
 At least one of the three buys a hot dog, and at least one buys a pretzel.
 Mendel buys a shish kebab.
 Nastassia buys a fruit cup.
 Neither Lara nor Nastassia buys a pretzel.
 Mendel does not buy any kind of food that Nastassia buys.

12. Which one of the following statements must be true?

 (A) Lara buys a hot dog.
 (B) Lara buys a shish kebab.
 (C) Mendel buys a hot dog.
 (D) Mendel buys a pretzel.
 (E) Nastassia buys a hot dog.

13. If the vendor charges $1 for each portion of food, what is the minimum amount the three people could spend?

 (A) $3
 (B) $4
 (C) $5
 (D) $6
 (E) $7

14. If the vendor charges $1 for each portion of food, what is the greatest amount the three people could spend?

 (A) $5
 (B) $6
 (C) $7
 (D) $8
 (E) $9

15. If Lara and Mendel buy exactly two kinds of food each, which one of the following statements must be true?

 (A) Lara buys a fruit cup.
 (B) Lara buys a hot dog.
 (C) Mendel buys a fruit cup.
 (D) There is exactly one kind of food that Lara and Mendel both buy.
 (E) There is exactly one kind of food that Lara and Nastassia both buy.

16. If Lara buys a shish kebab, which one of the following statements must be true?

 (A) Lara buys a fruit cup.
 (B) Mendel buys a fruit cup.
 (C) Nastassia buys a hot dog.
 (D) Nastassia buys exactly one kind of food.
 (E) Exactly one person buys a fruit cup.

17. Assume that the condition is removed that prevents a customer who buys a hot dog from buying a shish kebab but all other conditions remain the same. If the vendor charges $1 for each portion of food, what is the maximum amount the three people could spend?

 (A) $5
 (B) $6
 (C) $7
 (D) $8
 (E) $9

GO ON TO THE NEXT PAGE.

Questions 18–24

A science student has exactly four flasks—1, 2, 3, and 4—originally containing a red, a blue, a green, and an orange chemical, respectively. An experiment consists of mixing exactly two of these chemicals together by completely emptying the contents of one of the flasks into another of the flasks. The following conditions apply:

The product of an experiment cannot be used in further experiments.

Mixing the contents of 1 and 2 produces a red chemical.

Mixing the contents of 2 and 3 produces an orange chemical.

Mixing the contents of 3 with the contents of either 1 or 4 produces a blue chemical.

Mixing the contents of 4 with the contents of either 1 or 2 produces a green chemical.

18. If the student performs exactly one experiment, which one of the following could be the colors of the chemicals in the resulting three nonempty flasks?

(A) blue, blue, green
(B) blue, orange, orange
(C) blue, orange, red
(D) green, green, red
(E) green, orange, orange

19. If the student performs exactly two experiments, which one of the following could be the colors of the chemicals in the resulting two nonempty flasks?

(A) blue, blue
(B) blue, orange
(C) blue, red
(D) green, red
(E) orange, orange

20. If the student performs exactly one experiment and none of the resulting three nonempty flasks contains a red chemical, which one of the following could be the colors of the chemicals in the three flasks?

(A) blue, blue, green
(B) blue, green, green
(C) blue, green, orange
(D) blue, orange, orange
(E) green, green, orange

21. If the student performs exactly one experiment and exactly one of the resulting three nonempty flasks contains a blue chemical, which one of the following must be the colors of the chemicals in the other two flasks?

(A) both green
(B) both orange
(C) both red
(D) one green and one red
(E) one orange and one red

22. If the student will perform exactly two experiments and after the first experiment exactly one of the resulting three nonempty flasks contains an orange chemical, then in the second experiment the student could mix together the contents of flasks

(A) 1 and 2
(B) 1 and 3
(C) 1 and 4
(D) 2 and 3
(E) 3 and 4

23. If the student performs exactly one experiment and none of the resulting three nonempty flasks contains an orange chemical, then the student must have mixed the contents of

(A) flask 1 with flask 2
(B) flask 1 with flask 4
(C) flask 2 with flask 4
(D) flask 2 with one of the other flasks
(E) flask 4 with one of the other flasks

24. If the student performs exactly two experiments and exactly one of the resulting two nonempty flasks contains an orange chemical, then it must be true that the contents of the other nonempty flask is

(A) obtained by mixing flasks 1 and 2
(B) obtained by mixing flasks 2 and 4
(C) blue
(D) green
(E) red

S T O P

IF YOU FINISH BEFORE TIME IS CALLED, YOU MAY CHECK YOUR WORK ON THIS SECTION ONLY.
DO NOT WORK ON ANY OTHER SECTION IN THE TEST.

SECTION III

Time—35 minutes

27 Questions

Directions: Each passage in this section is followed by a group of questions to be answered on the basis of what is <u>stated</u> or <u>implied</u> in the passage. For some of the questions, more than one of the choices could conceivably answer the question. However, you are to choose the <u>best</u> answer; that is, the response that most accurately and completely answers the question, and blacken the corresponding space on your answer sheet.

Modern architecture has been criticized for emphasizing practical and technical issues at the expense of aesthetic concerns. The high-rise buildings constructed throughout the industrialized
(5) world in the 1960s and 1970s provide ample evidence that cost-efficiency and utility have become the overriding concerns of the modern architect. However, Otto Wagner's seminal text on modern architecture, first published in Germany in
(10) 1896, indicates that the failures of modern architecture cannot be blamed on the ideals of its founders.

Wagner's *Modern Architecture* called for a new style based on modern technologies and modes of
(15) construction. He insisted that there could be no return to traditional, preindustrial models; only by accepting wholeheartedly the political and technological revolutions of the nineteenth century could the architect establish the forms appropriate
(20) to a modern, urban society. "All modern creations," Wagner wrote, "must correspond to the new materials and demands of the present. . .must illustrate our own better, democratic, self-confident, ideal nature," and must incorporate the new
(25) "colossal technical and scientific achievements" of the age. This would indeed seem to be the basis of a purely materialist definition of architecture, a prototype for the simplistic form-follows-function dogma that opponents have identified as the
(30) intellectual basis of modern architecture.

But the picture was more complex, for Wagner was always careful to distinguish between art and engineering. Ultimately, he envisaged the architect developing the skills of the engineer without losing
(35) the powers of aesthetic judgment that Wagner felt were unique to the artist. "Since the engineer is seldom a born artist and the architect must learn as a rule to be an engineer, architects will in time succeed in extending their influence into the realm
(40) occupied by the engineers, so that legitimate aesthetic demands can be met in a satisfactory way." In this symbiotic relationship essential to Modernism, art was to exercise the controlling influence.

(45) No other prospect was imaginable for Wagner, who was firmly rooted as a designer and, indeed, as a teacher in the Classical tradition. The apparent inconsistency of a confessed Classicist advising against the mechanical imitation of historical
(50) models and arguing for new forms appropriate to

the modern age created exactly the tension that made Wagner's writings and buildings so interesting. While he justified, for example, the choice of a circular ground plan for churches in
(55) terms of optimal sight-lines and the technology of the gasometer, the true inspiration was derived from the centralized churches of the Italian Renaissance. He acknowledged as a rationalist that there was no way back to the social and
(60) technological conditions that had produced the work of Michelangelo or Fischer von Erlach, but he recognized his emotional attachment to the great works of the Italian Renaissance and Austrian Baroque.

1. Which one of the following best expresses the main idea of the passage?

(A) Modern architecture has been criticized for emphasizing practical and technical issues and for failing to focus on aesthetic concerns.

(B) Critics have failed to take into account the technological innovations and aesthetic features that architects have incorporated into modern buildings.

(C) Wagner's *Modern Architecture* provides architects with a chronicle of the origins of modern architecture.

(D) Wagner's *Modern Architecture* indicates that the founders of modern architecture did not believe that practical issues should supersede the aesthetic concerns of the past.

(E) Wagner's seminal text, *Modern Architecture*, provides the intellectual basis for the purely materialistic definition of modern architecture.

GO ON TO THE NEXT PAGE.

2. According to the passage, Wagner asserts which one of the following about the roles of architect and engineer?

    (A) The architect should make decisions about aesthetic issues and leave decisions about technical matters to the engineer.
    (B) The engineer has often developed the powers of aesthetic judgment previously thought to be unique to the architect.
    (C) The judgment of the engineer should be as important as the judgment of the architect when decisions are made about aesthetic issues.
    (D) The technical judgment of the engineer should prevail over the aesthetic judgment of the architect in the design of modern buildings.
    (E) The architect should acquire the knowledge of technical matters typically held by the engineer.

3. The passage suggests that Wagner would be LEAST likely to agree with which one of the following statements about classical architecture and the modern architect?

    (A) The modern architect should avoid the mechanical imitation of the models of the Italian Renaissance and Austrian Baroque.
    (B) The modern architect cannot design buildings appropriate to a modern, urban society and still retain emotional attachments to the forms of the Italian Renaissance and Austrian Baroque.
    (C) The modern architect should possess knowledge of engineering as well as of the architecture of the past.
    (D) The modern architect should not base designs on the technological conditions that underlay the designs of the models of the Italian Renaissance and Austrian Baroque.
    (E) The designs of modern architects should reflect political ideals different from those reflected in the designs of classical architecture.

4. The passage suggests which one of the following about the quotations from *Modern Architecture* cited in the second paragraph?

    (A) They represent the part of Wagner's work that has had the least influence on the architects who designed the high-rise buildings of the 1960s and 1970s.
    (B) They describe the part of Wagner's work that is most often evoked by proponents of Wagner's ideas on art and technology.
    (C) They do not adequately reflect the complexity of Wagner's ideas on the use of modern technology in architecture.
    (D) They reflect Wagner's active participation in the political revolutions of the nineteenth century.
    (E) They provide an overview of Wagner's ideas on the relationship between art and technology.

5. The author of the passage states which one of the following about the concerns of modern architecture?

    (A) Cost-efficiency, utility, and aesthetic demands are the primary concerns of the modern architect.
    (B) Practical issues supersede aesthetic concerns in the design of many modern buildings.
    (C) Cost-efficiency is more important to the modern architect than are other practical concerns.
    (D) The design of many new buildings suggests that modern architects are still inspired by architectural forms of the past.
    (E) Many modern architects use current technology to design modern buildings that are aesthetically pleasing.

6. The author mentions Wagner's choice of a "circular ground plan for churches" (line 54) most likely in order to

    (A) provide an example of the kinds of technological innovations Wagner introduced into modern architecture
    (B) provide an example of Wagner's dismissal of historical forms from the Italian Renaissance
    (C) provide an example of a modern building where technological issues were much less significant than aesthetic demands
    (D) provide evidence of Wagner's tendency to imitate Italian Renaissance and Austrian Baroque models
    (E) provide evidence of the tension between Wagner's commitment to modern technology and to the Classical tradition

7. The passage is primarily concerned with

    (A) summarizing the history of a debate
    (B) explaining a traditional argument
    (C) describing and evaluating a recent approach
    (D) justifying a recent criticism by presenting new evidence
    (E) supporting an assertion by discussing an important work

GO ON TO THE NEXT PAGE.

In order to explain the socioeconomic achievement, in the face of disadvantages due to racial discrimination, of Chinese and Japanese immigrants to the United States and their

(5) descendants, sociologists have typically applied either culturally based or structurally based theories—but never both together. To use an economic metaphor, culturally based explanations assert the importance of the supply side of the labor

(10) market, emphasizing the qualities immigrant groups bring with them for competition in the United States labor market. Such explanations reflect a human-capital perspective in which status attainment is seen as a result of individuals' ability

(15) to generate resources. Structurally based explanations, on the other hand, examine the market condition of the immigrants' host society, particularly its discriminatory practices and their impact on the status attainment process of

(20) immigrant groups. In the economic metaphor, structural explanations assert the importance of the demand side of the labor market.

In order to understand the socioeconomic mobility of Chinese and Japanese immigrants and

(25) their descendants, only an analysis of supply-side and demand-side factors together, in the context of historical events, will suffice. On the cultural or supply side, differences in immigration pattern and family formation resulted in different rates of

(30) socioeconomic achievement for Chinese and Japanese immigrants. For various reasons, Chinese immigrants remained sojourners and did not (except for urban merchants) establish families. They were also hampered by ethnic conflict in the

(35) labor market. Japanese immigrants, on the other hand, were less constrained, made the transition from sojourner to settler within the first two decades of immigration, and left low-wage labor to establish small businesses based on a household

(40) mode of production. Chinese sojourners without families were more vulnerable to demoralization, whereas Japanese immigrants faced societal hostility with the emotional resources provided by a stable family life. Once Chinese immigrants began

(45) to establish nuclear families and produce a second generation, instituting household production similar to that established by Japanese immigrants, their socioeconomic attainment soon paralleled that of Japanese immigrants and their descendants.

(50) On the structural or demand side, changes in institutional constraints, immigration laws, labor markets, and societal hostility were rooted in the dynamics of capitalist economic development. Early capitalist development generated a demand for

(55) low-wage labor that could not be fulfilled. Early Chinese and Japanese immigration was a response to this demand. In an advanced capitalist economy, the demand for immigrant labor is more differentiated: skilled professional and technical

(60) labor fills empty positions in the primary labor

market and, with the traditional unskilled low-wage labor, creates two immigrant streams. The high levels of education attained by the descendants of Chinese and Japanese immigrants and their

(65) concentration in strategic states such as California paved the way for the movement of the second generation into the expanding primary labor market in the advanced capitalist economy that existed after the Second World War.

8. Which one of the following best expresses the main idea of the passage?

(A) The socioeconomic achievement of Chinese and Japanese immigrants and their descendants is best explained by a historical examination of the economic structures prevalent in the United States when such immigrant groups arrived.

(B) The socioeconomic achievement of Chinese and Japanese immigrants and their descendants is best explained by an examination of their cultural backgrounds, in particular their level of educational attainment.

(C) The socioeconomic achievement of Chinese and Japanese immigrants and their descendants has taken place in the context of a culturally based emphasis on the economic welfare of the nuclear family.

(D) Only the market structure of the capitalist economy of the United States in which supply has historically been regulated by demand can account for the socioeconomic achievement of Chinese and Japanese immigrants and their descendants.

(E) Only an analysis that combines an examination of the culture of Chinese and Japanese immigrant groups and the socioeconomic structure of the host country can adequately explain the socioeconomic achievement of Chinese and Japanese immigrants and their descendants.

9. Which one of the following can best be described as a supply-side element in the labor market, as such elements are explained in the passage?

(A) concentration of small businesses in a given geographical area
(B) need for workers with varying degrees of skill
(C) high value placed by immigrants on work
(D) expansion of the primary labor market
(E) development of an advanced capitalist economy

GO ON TO THE NEXT PAGE.

10. Which one of the following best states the function of the author's mention of "two immigrant streams" (line 62)?

    (A) It demonstrates the effects of changes in human capital.
    (B) It illustrates the operation of the primary labor market.
    (C) It explains the nature of early Chinese and Japanese immigration.
    (D) It characterizes the result of changing demand-side factors.
    (E) It underscores an influence on the labor market.

11. It can be inferred that the author's analysis of the socioeconomic achievement of Chinese and Japanese immigrants and their descendants differs from that of most sociologists primarily in that most sociologists

    (A) address the effects of the interaction of causal factors
    (B) exclude the factor of a developing capitalist economy
    (C) do not apply an economic metaphor
    (D) emphasize the disadvantageous effects of racial discrimination
    (E) focus on a single type of theoretical explanation

12. It can be inferred that which one of the following was an element of the experience of both Chinese and Japanese immigrants in the United States?

    (A) initial status as sojourners
    (B) slow accumulation of capital
    (C) quick transition from laborer to manager
    (D) rapid establishment of nuclear families
    (E) rapid acquisition of technical skills

13. The author is primarily concerned with

    (A) advancing a synthesis of approaches to an issue
    (B) challenging a tentative answer to a question
    (C) evaluating the soundness of theories
    (D) resolving the differences between schools of thought
    (E) outlining the achievements of a group

GO ON TO THE NEXT PAGE.

Although the legal systems of England and the United States are superficially similar, they differ profoundly in their approaches to and uses of legal reasons: substantive reasons are more common (5) than formal reasons in the United States, whereas in England the reverse is true. This distinction reflects a difference in the visions of law that prevail in the two countries. In England the law has traditionally been viewed as a system of rules; the (10) United States favors a vision of law as an outward expression of the community's sense of right and justice.

Substantive reasons, as applied to law, are based on moral, economic, political, and other (15) considerations. These reasons are found both "in the law" and "outside the law," so to speak. Substantive reasons inform the content of a large part of the law: constitutions, statutes, contracts, verdicts, and the like. Consider, for example, a (20) statute providing that "no vehicles shall be taken into public parks." Suppose that no specific rationales or purposes were explicitly written into this statute, but that it was clear (from its legislative history) that the substantive purpose of the statute (25) was to ensure quiet and safety in the park. Now suppose that a veterans' group mounts a World War II jeep (in running order but without a battery) as a war memorial on a concrete slab in the park, and charges are brought against its members. Most (30) judges in the United States would find the defendants not guilty because what they did had no adverse effect on park quiet and safety.

Formal reasons are different in that they frequently prevent substantive reasons from coming (35) into play, even when substantive reasons are explicitly incorporated into the law at hand. For example, when a document fails to comply with stipulated requirements, the court may render the document legally ineffective. A will requiring (40) written witness may be declared null and void and, therefore, unenforceable for the formal reason that the requirement was not observed. Once the legal rule—that a will is invalid for lack of proper witnessing—has been clearly established, and the (45) legality of the rule is not in question, application of that rule precludes from consideration substantive arguments in favor of the will's validity or enforcement.

Legal scholars in England and the United States (50) have long bemused themselves with extreme examples of formal and substantive reasoning. On the one hand, formal reasoning in England has led to wooden interpretations of statutes and an unwillingness to develop the common law through (55) judicial activism. On the other hand, freewheeling substantive reasoning in the United States has resulted in statutory interpretations so liberal that the texts of some statutes have been ignored altogether.

14. Which one of the following best describes the content of the passage as a whole?

(A) an analysis of similarities and differences between the legal systems of England and the United States
(B) a reevaluation of two legal systems with the use of examples
(C) a contrast between the types of reasons embodied in the United States and English legal systems
(D) an explanation of how two distinct visions of the law shaped the development of legal reasoning
(E) a presentation of two types of legal reasons that shows the characteristics they have in common

15. It can be inferred from the passage that English judges would be likely to find the veterans' group discussed in the second paragraph guilty of violating the statute because

(A) not to do so would encourage others to act as the group did
(B) not to do so would be to violate the substantive reasons underlying the law
(C) the veterans failed to comply with the substantive purpose of the statute
(D) the veterans failed to demonstrate that their activities had no adverse effect on the public
(E) the veterans failed to comply with the stipulated requirements of the statute

16. From the discussion of wills in the third paragraph it can be inferred that substantive arguments as to the validity of a will might be considered under which one of the following circumstances?

(A) The legal rule requiring that a will be witnessed in writing does not stipulate the format of the will.
(B) The legal rule requiring that a will be witnessed stipulates that the will must be witnessed in writing by two people.
(C) The legal ruling requiring that a will be witnessed in writing stipulates that the witnessing must be done in the presence of a judge.
(D) A judge rules that the law requires a will to be witnessed in writing regardless of extenuating circumstances.
(E) A judge rules that the law can be interpreted to allow for a verbal witness to a will in a case involving a medical emergency.

GO ON TO THE NEXT PAGE.

17. The author of the passage makes use of all of the following in presenting the discussion of the English and the United States legal systems EXCEPT

   (A) comparison and contrast
   (B) generalization
   (C) explication of terms
   (D) a chronology of historical developments
   (E) a hypothetical case

18. Which one of the following best describes the function of the last paragraph of the passage?

   (A) It presents the consequences of extreme interpretations of the two types of legal reasons discussed by the author.
   (B) It shows how legal scholars can incorrectly use extreme examples to support their views.
   (C) It corrects inaccuracies in legal scholars' views of the nature of the two types of legal systems.
   (D) It suggests how characterizations of the two types of legal reasons can become convoluted and inaccurate.
   (E) It presents scholars' characterizations of both legal systems that are only partially correct.

19. The author of the passage suggests that in English law a substantive interpretation of a legal rule might be warranted under which one of the following circumstances?

   (A) Social conditions have changed to the extent that to continue to enforce the rule would be to decide contrary to present-day social norms.
   (B) The composition of the legislature has changed to the extent that to enforce the rule would be contrary to the views of the majority in the present legislative assembly.
   (C) The legality of the rule is in question and its enforcement is open to judicial interpretation.
   (D) Individuals who have violated the legal rule argue that application of the rule would lead to unfair judicial interpretations.
   (E) Superior court judges have consistently ruled in decisions regarding the interpretation of the legal rule.

20. According to the passage, which one of the following statements about substantive reasons is true?

   (A) They may be written into laws, but they may also exert an external influence on the law.
   (B) They must be explicitly written into the law in order to be relevant to the application of the law.
   (C) They are legal in nature and determine particular applications of most laws.
   (D) They often provide judges with specific rationales for disregarding the laws of the land.
   (E) They are peripheral to the law, whereas formal reasons are central to the law.

GO ON TO THE NEXT PAGE.

How does the brain know when carbohydrates
have been or should be consumed? The answer to
this question is not known, but one element in the
explanation seems to be the neurotransmitter
(5) serotonin, one of a class of chemical mediators that
may be released from a presynaptic neuron and that
cause the transmission of a nerve impulse across a
synapse to an adjacent postsynaptic neuron. In
general, it has been found that drugs that selectively
(10) facilitate serotonin-mediated neurotransmission
tend to cause weight loss, whereas drugs that block
serotonin-mediated transmission often have the
opposite effect: they often induce carbohydrate
craving and consequent weight gain.
(15)　　Serotonin is a derivative of tryptophan, an amino
acid that is normally present at low levels in the
bloodstream. The rate of conversion is affected by
the proportion of carbohydrates in an individual's
diet: carbohydrates stimulate the secretion of
(20) insulin, which facilitates the uptake of most amino
acids into peripheral tissues, such as muscles. Blood
tryptophan levels, however, are unaffected by
insulin, so the proportion of tryptophan in the
blood relative to the other amino acids increases
(25) when carbohydrates are consumed. Since
tryptophan competes with other amino acids for
transport across the blood–brain barrier into the
brain, insulin secretion indirectly speeds
tryptophan's entry into the central nervous system
(30) where, in a special cluster of neurons, it is
converted into serotonin.
　　The level of serotonin in the brain in turn affects
the amount of carbohydrate an individual chooses
to eat. Rats that are allowed to choose among
(35) synthetic foods containing different proportions of
carbohydrate and protein will normally alternate
between foods containing mostly protein and those
containing mostly carbohydrate. However, if rats
are given drugs that enhance the effect of serotonin,
(40) the rats' carbohydrate intake is reduced. On the
other hand, when rats are given drugs that interrupt
serotonin-mediated neurotransmission, their brains
fail to respond when carbohydrates are eaten, so
the desire for them persists.
(45)　　In human beings a serotoninlike drug,
d-fenfluramine (which releases serotonin into brain
synapses and then prolongs its action by blocking its
reabsorption into the presynaptic neuron),
selectively suppresses carbohydrate snacking (and
(50) its associated weight gain) in people who crave
carbohydrates. In contrast, drugs that block
serotonin-mediated transmission or that interact
with neurotransmitters other than serotonin have
the opposite effect: they often induce carbohydrate
(55) craving and subsequent weight gain. People who
crave carbohydrates report feeling refreshed and
invigorated after eating a carbohydrate-rich meal
(which would be expected to increase brain
serotonin levels). In contrast, those who do not
(60) crave carbohydrates become sleepy following a

high-carbohydrate meal. These findings suggest that
serotonin has other effects that may be useful
indicators of serotonin levels in human beings.

21. Which one of the following best states the main idea
of the passage?

(A) The body's need for carbohydrates varies with
the level of serotonin in the blood.
(B) The body's use of carbohydrates can be
regulated by the administration of
serotoninlike drugs.
(C) The role of serotonin in regulating the
consumption of carbohydrates is similar in
rats and in humans.
(D) The body's desire for carbohydrates can be
influenced by serotonin or serotoninlike
drugs.
(E) Tryptophan initiates a chain of events that
regulates the body's use of carbohydrates.

22. The term "rate" (line 17) refers to the rate at which

(A) serotonin is produced from tryptophan
(B) carbohydrates are taken into the body
(C) carbohydrates stimulate the secretion of
insulin
(D) insulin facilitates the uptake of amino acids
into peripheral tissues
(E) tryptophan enters the bloodstream

23. It can be inferred that a person is likely to crave
carbohydrates when

(A) the amount of insulin produced is too high
(B) the amount of serotonin in the brain is too low
(C) more tryptophan than usual crosses the
blood–brain barrier
(D) neurotransmission by neurotransmitters other
than serotonin is interrupted
(E) amino acids other than tryptophan are taken
up by peripheral tissues

GO ON TO THE NEXT PAGE.

24. The information in the passage indicates that if human beings were given a drug that inhibits the action of serotonin, which one of the following might be expected to occur?

    (A) Subjects would probably show a preference for carbohydrate-rich snacks rather than protein-rich snacks.
    (B) Subjects would probably become sleepy after eating a carbohydrate-rich meal.
    (C) Subjects would be more likely to lose weight than before they took the drug.
    (D) Subjects' blood tryptophan levels would probably increase.
    (E) Subjects' desire for both carbohydrates and proteins would increase.

25. The primary purpose of the second paragraph in the passage is to

    (A) provide an overview of current research concerning the effect of serotonin on carbohydrate consumption
    (B) contrast the role of tryptophan in the body with that of serotonin
    (C) discuss the role of serotonin in the transmission of neural impulses
    (D) explain how the brain knows that carbohydrates should be consumed
    (E) establish a connection between carbohydrate intake and the production of serotonin

26. It can be inferred that after a person has taken *d*-fenfluramine, he or she will probably be

    (A) inclined to gain weight
    (B) sleepy much of the time
    (C) unlikely to crave carbohydrates
    (D) unable to sleep as much as usual
    (E) likely to secrete more insulin than usual

27. The author's primary purpose is to

    (A) defend a point of view
    (B) correct a misconception
    (C) assess conflicting evidence
    (D) suggest new directions for investigation
    (E) provide information that helps explain a phenomenon

S T O P

**IF YOU FINISH BEFORE TIME IS CALLED, YOU MAY CHECK YOUR WORK ON THIS SECTION ONLY.
DO NOT WORK ON ANY OTHER SECTION IN THE TEST.**

SECTION IV
Time—35 minutes
24 Questions

Directions: The questions in this section are based on the reasoning contained in brief statements or passages. For some questions, more than one of the choices could conceivably answer the question. However, you are to choose the best answer; that is, the response that most accurately and completely answers the question. You should not make assumptions that are by commonsense standards implausible, superfluous, or incompatible with the passage. After you have chosen the best answer, blacken the corresponding space on your answer sheet.

1. Most regular coffee is made from arabica coffee beans because the great majority of consumers prefer its generally richer flavor to that of coffee made from robusta beans. Coffee drinkers who switch to decaffeinated coffee, however, overwhelmingly prefer coffee made from robusta beans, which are unlike arabica beans in that their flavor is not as greatly affected by decaffeination. Depending on the type of bean involved, decaffeination reduces or removes various substances, most of which are flavor-neutral but one of which contributes to the richness of the coffee's flavor.

The statements above provide the most support for which one of the following conclusions?

(A) The annual world crop of arabica beans is not large enough to satisfy completely the world demand for regular coffee.

(B) Arabica beans contain more caffeine per unit of weight than do robusta beans.

(C) Coffee drinkers who drink decaffeinated coffee almost exclusively are the ones who prefer regular coffee made from robusta beans to regular coffee made from arabica beans.

(D) Decaffeination of arabica beans extracts more of the substance that enhances a coffee's flavor than does decaffeination of robusta beans.

(E) There are coffee drinkers who switch from drinking regular coffee made from arabica beans to drinking decaffeinated coffee made from arabica beans because coffee made from arabica beans is less costly.

2. For the past 13 years, high school guidance counselors nationwide have implemented an aggressive program to convince high school students to select careers requiring college degrees. The government reported that the percentage of last year's high school graduates who went on to college was 15 percent greater than the percentage of those who graduated 10 years ago and did so. The counselors concluded from this report that the program had been successful.

The guidance counselors' reasoning depends on which one of the following assumptions about high school graduates?

(A) The number of graduates who went on to college remained constant each year during the 10-year period.

(B) Any college courses that the graduates take will improve their career prospects.

(C) Some of the graduates who went on to college never received guidance from a high school counselor.

(D) There has been a decrease in the number of graduates who go on to college without career plans.

(E) Many of last year's graduates who went on to college did so in order to prepare for careers requiring college degrees.

GO ON TO THE NEXT PAGE.

3. Insectivorous plants, which unlike other plants have the ability to trap and digest insects, can thrive in soils that are too poor in minerals to support noninsectivorous plants. Yet the mineral requirements of insectivorous plants are not noticeably different from the mineral requirements of noninsectivorous plants.

The statements above, if true, most strongly support which one of the following hypotheses?

(A) The insects that insectivorous plants trap and digest are especially abundant where the soil is poor in minerals.

(B) Insectivorous plants thrive only in soils that are too poor in minerals to support noninsectivorous plants.

(C) The types of minerals required by noninsectivorous plants are more likely than are the types of minerals required by insectivorous plants to be found in soils poor in minerals.

(D) The number of different environments in which insectivorous plants thrive is greater than the number of different environments in which noninsectivorous plants thrive.

(E) Insectivorous plants can get some of the minerals they require from the insects they trap and digest.

4. The region's water authority is responding to the current drought by restricting residential water use. Yet reservoir levels are now at the same height they were during the drought ten years ago when no restrictions were put into effect and none proved necessary. Therefore, imposing restrictions now is clearly premature.

Which one of the following, if true, most seriously calls the conclusion above into question?

(A) There are now more water storage reservoirs in the region than there were ten years ago.

(B) The population of the region is approximately three times greater than it was ten years ago.

(C) The region currently has more sources outside the drought-stricken area from which to draw water than it did ten years ago.

(D) The water-consuming home appliances and fixtures sold today are designed to use water more efficiently than those sold ten years ago.

(E) The price of water for residential use is significantly higher in the region than it is in regions that are not drought-stricken.

5. Montgomery, a biologist who is also well read in archaeology, has recently written a book on the origin and purpose of ancient monumental architecture. This book has received much positive attention in the popular press but has been severely criticized by many professional archaeologists for being too extreme. Montgomery's views do not deserve a negative appraisal, however, since those views are no more extreme than the views of some professional archaeologists.

The argument is most vulnerable to which one of the following criticisms?

(A) It fails to establish that professional archaeologists' views that are at least as extreme as Montgomery's views do not deserve negative appraisal for that reason.

(B) It assumes without warrant that many professional archaeologists consider biologists unqualified to discuss ancient architecture.

(C) It overlooks the possibility that many professional archaeologists are unfamiliar with Montgomery's views.

(D) It provides no independent evidence to show that the majority of professional archaeologists do not support Montgomery's views.

(E) It attempts to support its position by calling into question the motives of anyone who supports an opposing position.

6. Chronic fatigue syndrome is characterized by prolonged fatigue, muscular pain, and neurological problems. It is not known whether these symptoms are all caused by a single virus or whether each symptom is the result of a separate viral infection. A newly synthesized drug has been tested on those who suffer from chronic fatigue syndrome. Although the specific antiviral effects of this drug are unknown, it has lessened the severity of all of the symptoms of chronic fatigue syndrome. Thus there is evidence that chronic fatigue syndrome is, in fact, caused by one virus.

The argument assumes which one of the following?

(A) All those who suffer from prolonged fatigue also suffer from neurological problems.

(B) It is more likely that the new drug counteracts one virus than that it counteracts several viruses.

(C) The symptoms of chronic fatigue syndrome are dissimilar to those of any other syndrome.

(D) Most syndromes that are characterized by related symptoms are each caused by a single viral infection.

(E) An antiviral medication that eliminates the most severe symptoms of chronic fatigue syndrome thereby cures chronic fatigue syndrome.

GO ON TO THE NEXT PAGE.

7. DataCom, a company that filed many patents last year, was financially more successful last year than were its competitors, none of which filed many patents. It is therefore likely that DataCom owed its greater financial success to the fact that it filed many patents last year.

The argument is most vulnerable to criticism on the grounds that it

(A) presupposes what it sets out to demonstrate about the relationship between the financial success of DataCom's competitors and the number of patents they filed

(B) confuses a company's financial success with its technological innovativeness

(C) fails to establish whether any one of DataCom's competitors was financially more successful last year than was any other

(D) gives no reason to exclude the possibility that other differences between DataCom and its competitors accounted for its comparative financial success

(E) applies a generalization to an exceptional case

8. A history book written hundreds of years ago contains several inconsistencies. Some scholars argue that because the book contains inconsistencies, the author must have been getting information from more than one source.

The conclusion cited does not follow unless

(A) authors generally try to reconcile discrepancies between sources

(B) the inconsistencies would be apparent to the average reader of the history book at the present time

(C) the history book's author used no source that contained inconsistencies repeated in the history book

(D) the author of the history book was aware of the kinds of inconsistencies that can arise when multiple sources are consulted

(E) the author of the history book was familiar with all of the available source material that was relevant to the history book

9. Some games, such as chess and soccer, are competitive and played according to rules, but others, such as children's games of make believe, are neither. Therefore, being competitive and involving rules are not essential to being a game.

Which one of the following is most similar in its logical features to the argument above?

(A) Both the gourmet and the glutton enjoy eating. However, one can be a glutton, but not a gourmet, without having an educated palate. Therefore, having an educated palate is essential to being a gourmet, but enjoying food is not.

(B) All North American bears eat meat. Some taxonomists, however, have theorized that the giant panda, which eats only bamboo shoots, is a kind of bear. Either these taxonomists are wrong or eating meat is not essential to being a bear.

(C) It is true that dogs occasionally eat vegetation, but if dogs were not carnivorous they would be shaped quite differently from the way they are. Therefore, being carnivorous is essential to being a dog.

(D) Most automobiles, and nearly all of those produced today, are gasoline-fueled and four-wheeled, but others, such as some experimental electric cars, are neither. Therefore, being gasoline-fueled and having four wheels are not essential to being an automobile.

(E) Montréal's most vaunted characteristics, such as its cosmopolitanism and its vitality, are all to be found in many other cities. Therefore, cosmopolitanism and vitality are not essential properties of Montréal.

GO ON TO THE NEXT PAGE.

Questions 10–11

Household indebtedness, which some theorists regard as causing recession, was high preceding the recent recession, but so was the value of assets owned by households. Admittedly, if most of the assets were owned by quite affluent households, and most of the debt was owed by low-income households, high household debt levels could have been the cause of the recession despite high asset values: low-income households might have decreased spending in order to pay off debts while the quite affluent ones might simply have failed to increase spending. But, in fact, quite affluent people must have owed most of the household debt, since money is not lent to those without assets. Therefore, the real cause must lie elsewhere.

10. The argument is structured to lead to which one of the following conclusions?

(A) High levels of household debt did not cause the recent recession.
(B) Low-income households succeeded in paying off their debts despite the recent recession.
(C) Affluent people probably increased their spending levels during the recent recession.
(D) High levels of household debt have little impact on the economy.
(E) When people borrowed money prior to the recent recession, they did not use it to purchase assets.

11. Which one of the following, if true, casts the most doubt on the argument?

(A) Prior to the recent recession, middle-income households owed enough debt that they had begun to decrease spending.
(B) The total value of the economy's household debt is exceeded by the total value of assets held by households.
(C) Low-income households somewhat decreased their spending during the recent recession.
(D) During a recession the affluent usually borrow money only in order to purchase assets.
(E) Household debt is the category of debt least likely to affect the economy.

12. Fossil-fuel emissions, considered a key factor in the phenomenon known as global warming, contain two gases, carbon dioxide and sulfur dioxide, that have opposite effects on atmospheric temperatures. Carbon dioxide traps heat, tending to warm the atmosphere, whereas sulfur dioxide turns into sulfate aerosols that reflect sunlight back toward space, thereby tending to cool the atmosphere. Given that the heat-trapping effect is stronger than the cooling effect, cutting fossil-fuel emissions might be expected to slow the rise in global temperatures. Yet, surprisingly, if fossil-fuel emissions were cut today, global warming would actually be enhanced for more than three decades before the temperature rise began to slow.

Which one of the following, if true, most helps to explain the claim made in the last sentence above?

(A) Carbon dioxide stays in the atmosphere for many decades, while the sulfate aerosols fall out within days.
(B) Sulfur pollution is not spread evenly around the globe but is concentrated in the Northern Hemisphere, where there is a relatively high concentration of industry.
(C) While it has long been understood that sulfur dioxide is a harmful pollutant, it has been understood only recently that carbon dioxide might also be a harmful pollutant.
(D) Carbon dioxide is produced not only by automobiles but also by power plants that burn fossil fuels.
(E) Because fossil-fuel emissions contain sulfur dioxide, they contribute not only to global warming but also to acid rain.

GO ON TO THE NEXT PAGE.

13. Police published a "wanted" poster for a criminal fugitive in a medical journal, because the fugitive was known to have a certain acute noninfectious skin problem that would eventually require a visit to a doctor. The poster asked for information about the whereabouts of the fugitive. A physician's responding to the poster's request for information would not violate medical ethics, since physicians are already subject to requirements to report gunshot wounds to police and certain infectious diseases to health authorities. These exceptions to confidentiality are clearly ethical.

Which one of the following principles, while remaining compatible with the requirements cited above, supports the view that a physician's responding to the request would violate medical ethics?

(A) Since a physician acts both as a professional person and as a citizen, it is not ethical for a physician to conceal information about patients from duly constituted law enforcement agencies that have proper jurisdiction.

(B) Since a patient comes to a physician with the expectation that the patient's visit and medical condition will remain confidential, it is not ethical for a physician to share this information with anyone except personnel within the physician's office.

(C) Since the primary concern of medicine is individual and public health, it is not ethical for a physician, except in the case of gunshot wounds, to reduce patients' willingness to come for treatment by a policy of disclosing their identities to law-enforcement agencies.

(D) Except as required by the medical treatment of the patient, physicians cannot ethically disclose to others information about a patient's identity or medical condition without the patient's consent.

(E) Except to other medical personnel working to preserve or restore the health of a patient or of other persons, physicians cannot ethically disclose information about the identity of patients or their medical condition.

14. Ingrid: Rock music has produced no songs as durable as the songs of the 1940s, which continue to be recorded by numerous performers.

Jerome: True, rock songs are usually recorded only once. If the original recording continues to be popular, however, that fact can indicate durability, and the best rock songs will prove to be durable.

Jerome responds to Ingrid's claim by

(A) intentionally misinterpreting the claim

(B) showing that the claim necessarily leads to a contradiction

(C) undermining the truth of the evidence that Ingrid presents

(D) suggesting an alternative standard for judging the point at issue

(E) claiming that Ingrid's knowledge of the period under discussion is incomplete

15. Health insurance insulates patients from the expense of medical care, giving doctors almost complete discretion in deciding the course of most medical treatments. Moreover, with doctors being paid for each procedure performed, they have an incentive to overtreat patients. It is thus clear that medical procedures administered by doctors are frequently prescribed only because these procedures lead to financial rewards.

The argument uses which one of the following questionable techniques?

(A) assigning responsibility for a certain result to someone whose involvement in the events leading to that result was purely coincidental

(B) inferring the performance of certain actions on no basis other than the existence of both incentive and opportunity for performing those actions

(C) presenting as capricious and idiosyncratic decisions that are based on the rigorous application of well-defined principles

(D) depicting choices as having been made arbitrarily by dismissing without argument reasons that have been given for these choices

(E) assuming that the irrelevance of a consideration for one participant in a decision makes that consideration irrelevant for each participant in the decision

GO ON TO THE NEXT PAGE.

16. Chlorofluorocarbons are the best possible solvents to have in car engines for cleaning the electronic sensors in modern automobile ignition systems. These solvents have contributed significantly to automakers' ability to meet legally mandated emission standards. Now automakers will have to phase out the use of chlorofluorocarbons at the same time that emission standards are becoming more stringent.

If under the circumstances described above cars continue to meet emission standards, which one of the following is the most strongly supported inference?

(A) As emission standards become more stringent, automakers will increasingly cooperate with each other in the area of emission control.
(B) Car engines will be radically redesigned so as to do away with the need for cleaning the electronic ignition sensors.
(C) There will be a marked shift toward smaller, lighter cars that will have less powerful engines but will use their fuel more efficiently.
(D) The solvents developed to replace chlorofluorocarbons in car engines will be only marginally less effective than the chlorofluorocarbons themselves.
(E) Something other than the cleansers for electronic ignition sensors will make a relatively greater contribution to meeting emission standards than at present.

Questions 17–18

Two alternative drugs are available to prevent blood clots from developing after a heart attack. According to two major studies, drug Y does this no more effectively than the more expensive drug Z, but drug Z is either no more or only slightly more effective than drug Y. Drug Z's manufacturer, which has engaged in questionable marketing practices such as offering stock options to doctors who participate in clinical trials of drug Z, does not contest the results of the studies but claims that they do not reveal drug Z's advantages. However, since drug Z does not clearly treat the problem more effectively than drug Y, there is no established medical reason for doctors to use drug Z rather than drug Y on their heart-attack victims.

17. A major flaw in the argument is that the argument

(A) does not consider drugs or treatments other than drug Y and drug Z that may be used to prevent blood clotting in heart-attack patients
(B) neglects to compare the marketing practices of drug Y's manufacturer with those of drug Z's manufacturer
(C) fails to recognize that there may be medical criteria relevant to the choice between the two drugs other than their effectiveness as a treatment
(D) assumes without proof that the two drugs are similar in their effectiveness as treatments because they are similar in their chemical composition
(E) confuses economic reasons for selecting a treatment with medical reasons

18. Which one of the following principles, if established, would most help to justify a doctor's decision to use drug Z rather than drug Y when treating a patient?

(A) Only patients to whom the cost of an expensive treatment will not be a financial hardship should receive that treatment rather than a less expensive alternative one.
(B) Doctors who are willing to assist in research on the relative effectiveness of drugs by participating in clinical trials deserve fair remuneration for that participation.
(C) The decision to use a particular drug when treating a patient should not be influenced by the marketing practices employed by the company manufacturing that drug.
(D) A drug company's criticism of studies of its product that do not report favorably on that product is unavoidably biased and therefore invalid.
(E) Where alternative treatments exist and there is a chance that one is more effective than the other, the possibly more effective one should be employed, regardless of cost.

GO ON TO THE NEXT PAGE.

19. Jane: According to an article in this newsmagazine, children's hand-eye coordination suffers when they spend a great amount of time watching television. Therefore, we must restrict the amount of time Jacqueline and Mildred are allowed to watch television.

    Alan: Rubbish! The article says that only children under three are affected in that way. Jacqueline is ten and Mildred is eight. Therefore, we need not restrict their television viewing.

    Alan's argument against Jane's conclusion makes which one of the following errors in reasoning?

    (A) It relies on the same source that Jane cited in support of her conclusion.
    (B) It confuses undermining an argument in support of a given conclusion with showing that the conclusion itself is false.
    (C) It does not address the main point of Jane's argument and focuses instead on a side issue.
    (D) It makes an irrelevant appeal to an authority.
    (E) It fails to distinguish the consequences of a certain practice from the causes of the practice.

20. A new gardening rake with an S-shaped handle reduces compression stress on the spine during the pull stroke to about one-fifth of what it is with a straight-handled rake. During the push stroke, however, compression stress is five times more with the new rake than with a straight-handled rake. Neither the push stroke nor the pull stroke with a straight-handled rake produces enough compression stress to cause injury, but compression stress during the push stroke with the new rake is above the danger level. Therefore, straight-handled rakes are better than the new rakes for minimizing risk of spinal injury.

    The conclusion above is properly drawn from the premises given if which one of the following is true?

    (A) Compression stress resulting from pushing is the only cause of injuries to the spine that occur as a result of raking.
    (B) Raking is a frequent cause of spinal injury among gardeners.
    (C) The redesign of a tool rarely results in a net gain of efficiency, since gains tend to be counterbalanced by losses.
    (D) A garden rake can never be used in such a way that all the strokes with that rake are push strokes.
    (E) It is not possible to design a garden rake with a handle that is other than straight or S-shaped.

21. Some people fear that global warming will cause the large ice formations in the polar seas to melt, thereby warming the waters of those seas and threatening the plankton that is crucial to the marine food chain. Some scientists contend that it is unlikely that the melting process has begun, since water temperatures in the polar seas are the same today as they were a century ago.

    Which one of the following, if true, most seriously undermines the scientists' contention?

    (A) Much of the marine plant life that flourishes in the polar seas will die in the event that the water temperatures rise above their present levels.
    (B) The overall effect of the melting process will be an increase in global sea levels.
    (C) The mean air temperature above both land and water in the polar regions has not varied significantly over the past 100 years.
    (D) The temperature of water that contains melting ice tends to remain constant until all of the ice in the ice-and-water mixture has melted.
    (E) The mean temperature of ocean waters near the equator has remained constant over the past 100 years.

22. A long-term health study that followed a group of people who were age 35 in 1950 found that those whose weight increased by approximately half a kilogram or one pound per year after the age of 35 tended, on the whole, to live longer than those who maintained the weight they had at age 35. This finding seems at variance with other studies that have associated weight gain with a host of health problems that tend to lower life expectancy.

    Which one of the following, if true, most helps to resolve the apparently conflicting findings?

    (A) As people age, muscle and bone tissue tends to make up a smaller and smaller proportion of total body weight.
    (B) Individuals who reduce their cholesterol levels by losing weight can thereby also reduce their risk of dying from heart attacks or strokes.
    (C) Smokers, who tend to be leaner than nonsmokers, tend to have shorter life spans than nonsmokers.
    (D) The normal deterioration of the human immune system with age can be slowed down by a reduction in the number of calories consumed.
    (E) Diets that tend to lead to weight gain often contain not only excess fat but also unhealthful concentrations of sugar and sodium.

GO ON TO THE NEXT PAGE.

23. Insurance industry statistics demonstrate that cars with alarms or other antitheft devices are more likely to be stolen or broken into than cars without such devices or alarms. Therefore antitheft devices do not protect cars against thieves.

The pattern of flawed reasoning in the argument above is most similar to that in which one of the following?

(A) Since surveys reveal that communities with flourishing public libraries have, on average, better-educated citizens, it follows that good schools are typically found in communities with public libraries.

(B) Most public libraries are obviously intended to serve the interests of the casual reader, because most public libraries contain large collections of fiction and relatively small reference collections.

(C) Studies reveal that people who are regular users of libraries purchase more books per year than do people who do not use libraries regularly. Hence using libraries regularly does not reduce the number of books that library patrons purchase.

(D) Since youngsters who read voraciously are more likely to have defective vision than youngsters who do not read very much, it follows that children who do not like to read usually have perfect vision.

(E) Societies that support free public libraries are more likely to support free public universities than are societies without free public libraries. Hence a society that wishes to establish a free public university should first establish a free public library.

24. The problem that environmental economics aims to remedy is the following: people making economic decisions cannot readily compare environmental factors, such as clean air and the survival of endangered species, with other costs and benefits. As environmental economists recognize, solving this problem requires assigning monetary values to environmental factors. But monetary values result from people comparing costs and benefits in order to arrive at economic decisions. Thus, environmental economics is stymied by what motivates it.

If the considerations advanced in its support are true, the passage's conclusion is supported

(A) strongly, on the assumption that monetary values for environmental factors cannot be assigned unless people make economic decisions about these factors

(B) strongly, unless economic decision-making has not yet had any effect on the things categorized as environmental factors

(C) at best weakly, because the passage fails to establish that economic decision-makers do not by and large take adequate account of environmental factors

(D) at best weakly, because the argument assumes that pollution and other effects on environmental factors rarely result from economic decision-making

(E) not at all, since the argument is circular, taking that conclusion as one of its premises

S T O P

IF YOU FINISH BEFORE TIME IS CALLED, YOU MAY CHECK YOUR WORK ON THIS SECTION ONLY.
DO NOT WORK ON ANY OTHER SECTION IN THE TEST.

SIGNATURE_____ / /
DATE

LSAT WRITING SAMPLE TOPIC

Sea Coast University is hiring new faculty for its science program and has narrowed its selection to Louise Park or the team of Joe Echevarria and Jeanne Myrdal. Assuming the cost of hiring Park alone or the team is comparable, write an argument supporting one choice over the other based on the following considerations:

- Sea Coast University wants to develop a science program that will attract more undergraduate science majors.
- Sea Coast University wants to increase private and public support for its scientific research.

Louise Park, an internationally recognized scientist, plans to retire in three to five years. The recipient of numerous prizes for several key discoveries, Dr. Park has published extensively in scientific journals. While many of her graduate students have become influential scientists, undergraduates often find her inaccessible. Dr. Park is eager to leave her current university for Sea Coast's warmer climate, and she will bring a large, well-equipped laboratory if she comes to Sea Coast. This year, as usual, Dr. Park has secured grants from public and private sources to support her research.

Joe Echevarria and Jeanne Myrdal number among the most promising young scientists in the country. They have begun to publish in respected scientific journals and have received research grants from major foundations. Last year, their team-teaching approach won them a national teaching award. They recently published an article detailing their groundbreaking research on commercial uses of biotechnology; this research has attracted the attention of major corporations, several of whom are eager to fund their future work

Directions:

1. Use the Answer Key on the next page to check your answers.

2. Use the Scoring Worksheet below to compute your raw score.

3. Use the Score Conversion Chart to convert your raw score into the 120-180 scale.

Scoring Worksheet

1. Enter the number of questions you answered correctly in each section.

Number Correct

SECTION I . . . . . . _____
SECTION II . . . . . _____
SECTION III . . . . . _____
SECTION IV . . . . . _____

2. Enter the sum here: _____
This is your Raw Score.

Conversion Chart

For Converting Raw Score to the 120-180 LSAT Scaled Score
LSAT Form 4LSS26

Reported Score	Raw Score Lowest	Raw Score Highest
180	100	101
179	99	99
178	98	98
177	—*	—*
176	97	97
175	96	96
174	—*	—*
173	95	95
172	94	94
171	93	93
170	92	92
169	90	91
168	89	89
167	88	88
166	86	87
165	84	85
164	83	83
163	81	82
162	79	80
161	77	78
160	75	76
159	73	74
158	72	72
157	70	71
156	68	69
155	66	67
154	64	65
153	62	63
152	60	61
151	58	59
150	56	57
149	54	55
148	52	53
147	51	51
146	49	50
145	47	48
144	45	46
143	44	44
142	42	43
141	41	41
140	39	40
139	37	38
138	36	36
137	34	35
136	33	33
135	32	32
134	30	31
133	29	29
132	28	28
131	27	27
130	26	26
129	25	25
128	24	24
127	23	23
126	22	22
125	21	21
124	20	20
123	—*	—*
122	19	19
121	18	18
120	0	17

*There is no raw score that will produce this scaled score for this form.

SECTION I

1.	D	8.	C	15.	B	22.	C
2.	C	9.	E	16.	B	23.	C
3.	E	10.	B	17.	C	24.	A
4.	B	11.	D	18.	A	25.	B
5.	D	12.	D	19.	B	26.	E
6.	A	13.	D	20.	D		
7.	B	14.	D	21.	C		

SECTION II

1.	E	8.	A	15.	A	22.	E
2.	B	9.	E	16.	C	23.	E
3.	C	10.	D	17.	C	24.	D
4.	B	11.	B	18.	D		
5.	C	12.	D	19.	C		
6.	D	13.	B	20.	B		
7.	E	14.	B	21.	A		

SECTION III

1.	D	8.	E	15.	E	22.	A
2.	E	9.	C	16.	E	23.	B
3.	B	10.	D	17.	D	24.	A
4.	C	11.	E	18.	A	25.	E
5.	B	12.	A	19.	C	26.	C
6.	E	13.	A	20.	A	27.	E
7.	E	14.	C	21.	D		

SECTION IV

1.	D	8.	C	15.	B	22.	C
2.	E	9.	D	16.	E	23.	C
3.	E	10.	A	17.	C	24.	A
4.	B	11.	A	18.	E		
5.	A	12.	A	19.	B		
6.	B	13.	C	20.	A		
7.	D	14.	D	21.	D		

■ **The Official**

LSAT

PrepTest™ XIII

The sample test that follows consists of
four sections corresponding to the four
scored sections of the December 1994 LSAT.

December 1994
Form 5LSS28

General Directions for the LSAT Answer Sheet

The actual testing time for this portion of the test will be 2 hours 55 minutes. There are five sections, each with a time limit of 35 minutes. The supervisor will tell you when to begin and end each section. If you finish a section before time is called, you may check your work on that section <u>only</u>; do not turn to any other section of the test book and do not work on any other section either in the test book or on the answer sheet.

There are several different types of questions on the test, and each question type has its own directions. <u>Be sure you understand the directions for each question type before attempting to answer any questions in that section.</u>

Not everyone will finish all the questions in the time allowed. Do not hurry, but work steadily and as quickly as you can without sacrificing accuracy. You are advised to use your time effectively. If a question seems too difficult, go on to the next one and return to the difficult question after completing the section. MARK THE BEST ANSWER YOU CAN FOR EVERY QUESTION. NO DEDUCTIONS WILL BE MADE FOR WRONG ANSWERS. YOUR SCORE WILL BE BASED ONLY ON THE NUMBER OF QUESTIONS YOU ANSWER CORRECTLY.

ALL YOUR ANSWERS MUST BE MARKED ON THE ANSWER SHEET. Answer spaces for each question are lettered to correspond with the letters of the potential answers to each question in the test book. After you have decided which of the answers is correct, blacken the corresponding space on the answer sheet. BE SURE THAT EACH MARK IS BLACK AND COMPLETELY FILLS THE ANSWER SPACE. Give only one answer to each question. If you change an answer, be sure that all previous marks are <u>erased completely</u>. Since the answer sheet is machine scored, incomplete erasures may be interpreted as intended answers. ANSWERS RECORDED IN THE TEST BOOK WILL NOT BE SCORED.

There may be more questions noted on this answer sheet than there are questions in a section. Do not be concerned but be certain that the section and number of the question you are answering matches the answer sheet section and question number. Additional answer spaces in any answer sheet section should be left blank. Begin your next section in the number one answer space for that section.

Score Cancellation

Complete this section only if you are absolutely certain you want to cancel your score. A CANCELLATION REQUEST CANNOT BE RESCINDED. IF YOU ARE AT ALL UNCERTAIN, YOU SHOULD NOT COMPLETE THIS SECTION; INSTEAD, YOU SHOULD USE THE TIME ALLOWED AFTER THE TEST (UP TO 5 DAYS) TO FULLY CONSIDER YOUR DECISION.

To cancel your score from this administration, you must:

A.   fill in the ovals here........ ◯ ◯

B.   read the following statement. Then sign your name and enter the date.

I certify that I wish to cancel my test score from this administration. I understand that my request is irreversible and that my score will not be sent to me or to the law schools to which I apply.

_____
Sign your name in full

_____
Date

HOW DID YOU PREPARE FOR THE LSAT?
(Select all that apply.)

Responses to this item are voluntary and will be used for statistical research purposes only.

- ◯ By studying the sample questions in the *LSAT/LSDAS Registration and Information Book*.
- ◯ By taking the free sample LSAT.
- ◯ By working through *The Official LSAT PrepTest(s), PrepBook, Workbooks, or PrepKit*.
- ◯ By using a book on how to prepare for the LSAT **not** published by Law Services.
- ◯ By attending a commercial test preparation or coaching course.
- ◯ By attending a test preparation or coaching course offered through an undergraduate institution.
- ◯ Self study.
- ◯ Other preparation.
- ◯ No preparation.

CERTIFYING STATEMENT

Please write (DO NOT PRINT) the following statement. Sign and date.

I certify that I am the examinee whose name appears on this answer sheet and that I am here to take the LSAT for the sole purpose of being considered for admission to law school. I further certify that I will neither assist nor receive assistance from any other candidate, and I agree not to copy or retain examination questions or to transmit them in any form to any other person.

_____
_____
_____
_____
_____
_____
_____
_____
_____

SIGNATURE: _____   TODAY'S DATE: ___/___/___
                                                                          MONTH DAY YEAR

INSTRUCTIONS FOR COMPLETING THE BIOGRAPHICAL AREA ARE ON THE BACK COVER OF YOUR TEST BOOKLET.
USE ONLY A NO. 2 OR HB PENCIL TO COMPLETE THIS ANSWER SHEET. DO NOT USE INK.

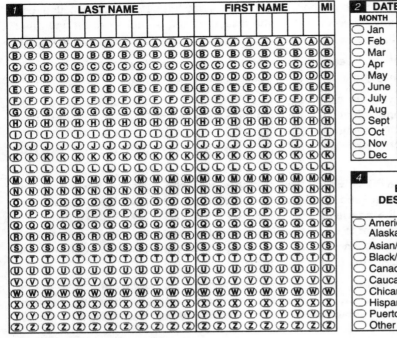

1 LAST NAME / FIRST NAME / MI (bubble grid A–Z)

2 DATE OF BIRTH

MONTH	DAY	YEAR
○ Jan		
○ Feb		
○ Mar		
○ Apr		
○ May		
○ June		
○ July		
○ Aug		
○ Sept		
○ Oct		
○ Nov		
○ Dec		

3 SOCIAL SECURITY NO.

Right Mark: ●
Wrong Marks: ⊘ ⊗ ⊙

4 ETHNIC DESCRIPTION
- ○ American Indian/Alaskan Native
- ○ Asian/Pacific Islander
- ○ Black/African Amer.
- ○ Canadian Aboriginal
- ○ Caucasian/White
- ○ Chicano/Mex. Amer.
- ○ Hispanic
- ○ Puerto Rican
- ○ Other

5 GENDER
- ○ Male
- ○ Female

6 DOMINANT LANGUAGE
- ○ English
- ○ Other

7 ENGLISH FLUENCY
- ○ Yes
- ○ No

8 CENTER NUMBER (bubble grid 0–9)

9 TEST FORM CODE (bubble grid 0–9)

10 TEST BOOK SERIAL NO.

11 TEST FORM

12 TEST DATE

MONTH / DAY / YEAR

13 PLEASE PRINT ALL INFORMATION

LAST NAME   FIRST

MAILING ADDRESS

SOCIAL SECURITY/SOCIAL INSURANCE NO.

NOTE: If you have a new address, you must write Law Services at Box 2000-C, Newtown, PA 18940 or call (215) 968-1001. We cannot guarantee that all address changes will be processed before scores are mailed, so be sure to notify your post office of your forwarding address.

LAW SCHOOL ADMISSION TEST

MARK ONE AND ONLY ONE ANSWER TO EACH QUESTION. BE SURE TO FILL IN COMPLETELY THE SPACE FOR YOUR INTENDED ANSWER CHOICE. IF YOU ERASE, DO SO COMPLETELY. MAKE NO STRAY MARKS.

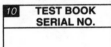
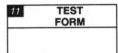

SECTION 1	SECTION 2	SECTION 3	SECTION 4	SECTION 5
1 A B C D E	1 A B C D E	1 A B C D E	1 A B C D E	1 A B C D E
2 A B C D E	2 A B C D E	2 A B C D E	2 A B C D E	2 A B C D E
3 A B C D E	3 A B C D E	3 A B C D E	3 A B C D E	3 A B C D E
4 A B C D E	4 A B C D E	4 A B C D E	4 A B C D E	4 A B C D E
5 A B C D E	5 A B C D E	5 A B C D E	5 A B C D E	5 A B C D E
6 A B C D E	6 A B C D E	6 A B C D E	6 A B C D E	6 A B C D E
7 A B C D E	7 A B C D E	7 A B C D E	7 A B C D E	7 A B C D E
8 A B C D E	8 A B C D E	8 A B C D E	8 A B C D E	8 A B C D E
9 A B C D E	9 A B C D E	9 A B C D E	9 A B C D E	9 A B C D E
10 A B C D E	10 A B C D E	10 A B C D E	10 A B C D E	10 A B C D E
11 A B C D E	11 A B C D E	11 A B C D E	11 A B C D E	11 A B C D E
12 A B C D E	12 A B C D E	12 A B C D E	12 A B C D E	12 A B C D E
13 A B C D E	13 A B C D E	13 A B C D E	13 A B C D E	13 A B C D E
14 A B C D E	14 A B C D E	14 A B C D E	14 A B C D E	14 A B C D E
15 A B C D E	15 A B C D E	15 A B C D E	15 A B C D E	15 A B C D E
16 A B C D E	16 A B C D E	16 A B C D E	16 A B C D E	16 A B C D E
17 A B C D E	17 A B C D E	17 A B C D E	17 A B C D E	17 A B C D E
18 A B C D E	18 A B C D E	18 A B C D E	18 A B C D E	18 A B C D E
19 A B C D E	19 A B C D E	19 A B C D E	19 A B C D E	19 A B C D E
20 A B C D E	20 A B C D E	20 A B C D E	20 A B C D E	20 A B C D E
21 A B C D E	21 A B C D E	21 A B C D E	21 A B C D E	21 A B C D E
22 A B C D E	22 A B C D E	22 A B C D E	22 A B C D E	22 A B C D E
23 A B C D E	23 A B C D E	23 A B C D E	23 A B C D E	23 A B C D E
24 A B C D E	24 A B C D E	24 A B C D E	24 A B C D E	24 A B C D E
25 A B C D E	25 A B C D E	25 A B C D E	25 A B C D E	25 A B C D E
26 A B C D E	26 A B C D E	26 A B C D E	26 A B C D E	26 A B C D E
27 A B C D E	27 A B C D E	27 A B C D E	27 A B C D E	27 A B C D E
28 A B C D E	28 A B C D E	28 A B C D E	28 A B C D E	28 A B C D E
29 A B C D E	29 A B C D E	29 A B C D E	29 A B C D E	29 A B C D E
30 A B C D E	30 A B C D E	30 A B C D E	30 A B C D E	30 A B C D E

FOR LAW SERVICES USE ONLY	
LR	
LW	
LCS	

SECTION I

Time—35 minutes

24 Questions

Directions: Each group of questions in this section is based on a set of conditions. In answering some of the questions, it may be useful to draw a rough diagram. Choose the response that most accurately and completely answers each question and blacken the corresponding space on your answer sheet.

Questions 1–6

Exactly eight consumers—F, G, H, J, K, L, M, and N—will be interviewed by market researchers. The eight will be divided into exactly two 4-person groups—group 1 and group 2—before interviews begin. Each person is assigned to exactly one of the two groups according to the following conditions:

F must be in the same group as J.
G must be in a different group from M.
If H is in group 1, then L must be in group 1.
If N is in group 2, then G must be in group 1.

1. Group 1 could consist of

    (A) F, G, H, and J
    (B) F, H, L, and M
    (C) F, J, K, and L
    (D) G, H, L, and N
    (E) G, K, M, and N

2. If K is in the same group as N, which one of the following must be true?

    (A) G is in group 1.
    (B) H is in group 2.
    (C) J is in group 1.
    (D) K is in group 2.
    (E) M is in group 1.

3. If F is in the same group as H, which one of the following must be true?

    (A) G is in group 2.
    (B) J is in group 1.
    (C) K is in group 1.
    (D) L is in group 2.
    (E) M is in group 2.

4. If L and M are in group 2, then a person who could be assigned either to group 1 or, alternatively, to group 2 is

    (A) F
    (B) G
    (C) H
    (D) J
    (E) K

5. Each of the following is a pair of people who could be in group 1 together EXCEPT

    (A) F and G
    (B) F and H
    (C) F and L
    (D) H and G
    (E) H and N

6. If L is in group 2, then each of the following is a pair of people who could be in group 1 together EXCEPT

    (A) F and M
    (B) G and N
    (C) J and N
    (D) K and M
    (E) M and N

GO ON TO THE NEXT PAGE.

Questions 7–11

Five people—Harry, Iris, Kate, Nancy, and Victor—are to be scheduled as contestants on a television show, one contestant per day, for five consecutive days from Monday through Friday. The following restrictions governing the scheduling of contestants must be observed:

Nancy is not scheduled for Monday.

If Harry is scheduled for Monday, Nancy is scheduled for Friday.

If Nancy is scheduled for Tuesday, Iris is scheduled for Monday.

Kate is scheduled for the next day after the day for which Victor is scheduled.

7. Victor can be scheduled for any day EXCEPT

(A) Monday
(B) Tuesday
(C) Wednesday
(D) Thursday
(E) Friday

8. If Iris is scheduled for the next day after Harry, which one of the following lists all those days any one of which could be the day for which Harry is scheduled?

(A) Monday, Tuesday
(B) Monday, Wednesday
(C) Monday, Thursday
(D) Monday, Tuesday, Wednesday
(E) Monday, Wednesday, Thursday

9. If Kate is scheduled for Wednesday, which one of the following could be true?

(A) Iris is scheduled for Friday.
(B) Nancy is scheduled for Tuesday.
(C) Nancy is scheduled for an earlier day than the day for which Harry is scheduled.
(D) Nancy is scheduled for an earlier day than the day for which Iris is scheduled.
(E) Nancy is scheduled for an earlier day than the day for which Kate is scheduled.

10. If Kate is scheduled for Friday, which one of the following must be true?

(A) Harry is scheduled for Tuesday.
(B) Harry is scheduled for Wednesday.
(C) Iris is scheduled for Monday.
(D) Iris is scheduled for Wednesday.
(E) Nancy is scheduled for Wednesday.

11. If Iris is scheduled for Wednesday, which one of the following must be true?

(A) Harry is scheduled for an earlier day than the day for which Nancy is scheduled.
(B) Harry is scheduled for an earlier day than the day for which Kate is scheduled.
(C) Kate is scheduled for an earlier day than the day for which Harry is scheduled.
(D) Nancy is scheduled for an earlier day than the day for which Kate is scheduled.
(E) Nancy is scheduled for an earlier day than the day for which Iris is scheduled.

GO ON TO THE NEXT PAGE.

Questions 12–17

An art teacher will schedule exactly six of eight lectures—fresco, history, lithography, naturalism, oils, pastels, sculpture, and watercolors—for three days—1, 2, and 3. There will be exactly two lectures each day—morning and afternoon. Scheduling is governed by the following conditions:

Day 2 is the only day for which oils can be scheduled.
Neither sculpture nor watercolors can be scheduled for the afternoon.
Neither oils nor pastels can be scheduled for the same day as lithography.
If pastels is scheduled for day 1 or day 2, then the lectures scheduled for the day immediately following pastels must be fresco and history, not necessarily in that order.

12. Which one of the following is an acceptable schedule of lectures for days 1, 2, and 3, respectively?

(A) Morning: lithography, history, sculpture
Afternoon: pastels, fresco, naturalism
(B) Morning: naturalism, oils, fresco
Afternoon: lithography, pastels, history
(C) Morning: oils, history, naturalism
Afternoon: pastels, fresco, lithography
(D) Morning: sculpture, lithography, naturalism
Afternoon: watercolors, fresco, pastels
(E) Morning: sculpture, pastels, fresco
Afternoon: lithography, history, naturalism

13. If lithography and fresco are scheduled for the afternoons of day 2 and day 3, respectively, which one of the following is a lecture that could be scheduled for the afternoon of day 1 ?

(A) history
(B) oils
(C) pastels
(D) sculpture
(E) watercolors

14. If lithography and history are scheduled for the mornings of day 2 and day 3, respectively, which one of the following lectures could be scheduled for the morning of day 1 ?

(A) fresco
(B) naturalism
(C) oils
(D) pastels
(E) sculpture

15. If oils and lithography are scheduled for the mornings of day 2 and day 3, respectively, which one of the following CANNOT be scheduled for any day?

(A) fresco
(B) history
(C) naturalism
(D) pastels
(E) sculpture

16. If neither fresco nor naturalism is scheduled for any day, which one of the following must be scheduled for day 1 ?

(A) history
(B) lithography
(C) oils
(D) pastels
(E) sculpture

17. If the lectures scheduled for the mornings are fresco, history, and lithography, not necessarily in that order, which one of the following could be true?

(A) Lithography is scheduled for day 3.
(B) Naturalism is scheduled for day 2.
(C) Fresco is scheduled for the same day as naturalism.
(D) History is scheduled for the same day as naturalism.
(E) History is scheduled for the same day as oils.

GO ON TO THE NEXT PAGE.

Questions 18–24

The population of a small country is organized into five clans—N, O, P, S, and T. Each year exactly three of the five clans participate in the annual harvest ceremonies. The rules specifying the order of participation of the clans in the ceremonies are as follows:

Each clan must participate at least once in any two consecutive years.

No clan participates for three consecutive years.

Participation takes place in cycles, with each cycle ending when each of the five clans has participated three times. Only then does a new cycle begin.

No clan participates more than three times within any cycle.

18. If the clans participating in the first year of a given cycle are N, O, and P, which one of the following could be the clans participating in the second year of that cycle?

(A) N, O, S
(B) N, O, T
(C) N, P, S
(D) O, P, T
(E) O, S, T

19. Which one of the following can be true about the clans' participation in the ceremonies?

(A) N participates in the first, second, and third years.
(B) N participates in the second, third, and fourth years.
(C) Both O and S participate in the first and third years.
(D) Both N and S participate in the first, third, and fifth years.
(E) Both S and T participate in the second, third, and fifth years.

20. Any cycle for the clans' participation in the ceremonies must be completed at the end of exactly how many years?

(A) five
(B) six
(C) seven
(D) eight
(E) nine

21. Which one of the following must be true about the three clans that participate in the ceremonies in the first year?

(A) At most two of them participate together in the third year.
(B) At least two of them participate together in the second year.
(C) All three of them participate together in the fourth year.
(D) All three of them participate together in the fifth year.
(E) None of them participates in the third year.

22. If, in a particular cycle, N, O, and S participate in the ceremonies in the first year, which one of the following must be true?

(A) N participates in the second and third years.
(B) O participates in the third and fourth years.
(C) N and O both participate in the third year.
(D) P and T both participate in the fifth year.
(E) S and T both participate in the fifth year.

23. If, in a particular cycle, N, O, and T participate in the first year and if O and P participate in the fourth year, any of the following could be a clan that participates in the third year EXCEPT

(A) N
(B) O
(C) P
(D) S
(E) T

24. If, in a particular cycle, N, O, and S participate in the ceremonies in the first year and O, S, and T participate in the third year, then which one of the following could be the clans that participate in the fifth year?

(A) N, O, P
(B) N, O, S
(C) N, P, S
(D) O, P, S
(E) P, S, T

S T O P

IF YOU FINISH BEFORE TIME IS CALLED, YOU MAY CHECK YOUR WORK ON THIS SECTION ONLY.
DO NOT WORK ON ANY OTHER SECTION IN THE TEST.

SECTION II
Time—35 minutes
26 Questions

<u>Directions:</u> The questions in this section are based on the reasoning contained in brief statements or passages. For some questions, more than one of the choices could conceivably answer the question. However, you are to choose the <u>best</u> answer; that is, the response that most accurately and completely answers the question. You should not make assumptions that are by commonsense standards implausible, superfluous, or incompatible with the passage. After you have chosen the best answer, blacken the corresponding space on your answer sheet.

1. Paperback books wear out more quickly than hardcover books do, but paperback books cost much less. Therefore, users of public libraries would be better served if public libraries bought only paperback books, since by so doing these libraries could increase the number of new book titles added to their collections without increasing their budgets.

   Which one of the following, if true, most seriously weakens the argument?

   (A) If a public library's overall budget is cut, the budget for new acquisitions is usually cut back more than is that for day-to-day operations.
   (B) Paperback books can very inexpensively have their covers reinforced in order to make them last longer.
   (C) Many paperback books are never published in hardcover.
   (D) Library users as a group depend on their public library for access to a wide variety of up-to-date reference books that are published in hardcover only.
   (E) People are more likely to buy for themselves a copy of a book they had previously borrowed from the public library if that book is available in paperback.

2. Garbage in this neighborhood probably will not be collected until Thursday this week. Garbage is usually collected here on Wednesdays, and the garbage collectors in this city are extremely reliable. However, Monday was a public holiday, and after a public holiday that falls on a Monday, garbage throughout the city is supposed to be collected one day later than usual.

   The argument proceeds by

   (A) treating several pieces of irrelevant evidence as though they provide support for the conclusion
   (B) indirectly establishing that one thing is likely to occur by directly ruling out all of the alternative possibilities
   (C) providing information that allows application of a general rule to a specific case
   (D) generalizing about all actions of a certain kind on the basis of a description of one such action
   (E) treating something that is probable as though it were inevitable

3. When compact discs first entered the market, they were priced significantly higher than vinyl records. Manufacturers attributed the difference in price to the difference in production costs, saying that compact disc production was expensive because the technology was new and unfamiliar. As the technology became more efficient, the price of the discs did indeed come down. But vinyl records, whose production technology has long been established, then went up in price to approach that of compact discs.

   Which one of the following most helps to explain why the price of vinyl records went up?

   (A) Consumers were so enthusiastic about the improved sound quality offered by compact disc technology that they were willing to pay a higher price to obtain it.
   (B) Some consumers who continued to buy vinyl records instead of compact discs did so because they were unwilling to pay a higher price for compact discs.
   (C) As consumers bought compact discs instead of vinyl records, the number of vinyl records produced decreased, making their production less cost-efficient.
   (D) Compact disc player technology continued to change and develop even after compact discs first entered the market.
   (E) When compact discs first entered the market, many consumers continued to buy vinyl records rather than buying the equipment necessary to play compact discs.

GO ON TO THE NEXT PAGE.

4. Conservationists have established land reserves to preserve the last remaining habitat for certain species whose survival depends on the existence of such habitat. A grove of trees in Mexico that provide habitat for North American monarch butterflies in winter is a typical example of such a land reserve. If global warming occurs as predicted, however, the temperature bands within which various types of vegetation can grow will shift into regions that are currently cooler.

If the statements above are true, they provide the most support for which one of the following?

(A) If global warming occurs as predicted, the conservation land reserves will cease to serve their purpose.
(B) Monarch butterflies will succeed in adapting to climatic change by shortening their migration.
(C) If global warming occurs, it will melt polar ice and so will cause the sea level to rise so high that many coastal plants and animals will become extinct.
(D) The natural world has adapted many times in the past to drastic global warming and cooling.
(E) If global warming occurs rapidly, species of plants and animals now protected in conservation land reserves will move to inhabit areas that are currently used for agriculture.

5. Financial success does not guarantee happiness. This claim is not mere proverbial wisdom but a fact verified by statistics. In a recently concluded survey, only one-third of the respondents who claimed to have achieved financial success reported that they were happy.

Which one of the following, if true, most strongly supports the conclusion drawn from the survey results?

(A) The respondents who reported financial success were, for the most part, financially successful.
(B) Financial success was once thought to be necessary for happiness but is no longer considered a prerequisite for happiness.
(C) Many of the respondents who claimed not to have achieved financial success reported that they were happy five years ago.
(D) Many of the respondents who failed to report financial success were in fact financially successful.
(E) Most of the respondents who reported they were unhappy were in fact happy.

6. The distance that animals travel each day and the size of the groups in which they live are highly correlated with their diets. And diet itself depends in large part on the sizes and shapes of animals' teeth and faces.

The statements above provide the most support for which one of the following?

(A) Animals that eat meat travel in relatively small groups and across relatively small ranges compared to animals that eat plants.
(B) Animals that have varied diets can be expected to be larger and more robust than animals that eat only one or two kinds of food.
(C) When individual herd animals lose their teeth through age or injury, those animals are likely to travel at the rear of their herd.
(D) Information about the size and shape of an animal's face is all that is needed to identify the species to which that animal belongs.
(E) Information about the size and shape of an extinct animal's teeth and face can establish whether that animal is likely to have been a herd animal.

7. It is not correct that the people of the United States, relative to comparable countries, are the most lightly taxed. True, the United States has the lowest tax, as percent of gross domestic product, of the Western industrialized countries, but tax rates alone do not tell the whole story. People in the United States pay out of pocket for many goods and services provided from tax revenues elsewhere. Consider universal health care, which is an entitlement supported by tax revenues in every other Western industrialized country. United States government health-care expenditures are equivalent to about 5 percent of the gross domestic product, but private health-care expenditures represent another 7 percent. This 7 percent, then, amounts to a tax.

The argument concerning whether the people of the United States are the most lightly taxed is most vulnerable to which one of the following criticisms?

(A) It bases a comparison on percentages rather than on absolute numbers.
(B) It unreasonably extends the application of a key term.
(C) It uses negatively charged language instead of attempting to give a reason.
(D) It generalizes from only a few instances.
(E) It sets up a dichotomy between alternatives that are not exclusive.

GO ON TO THE NEXT PAGE.

8. Various mid-fourteenth-century European writers show an interest in games, but no writer of this period mentions the playing of cards. Nor do any of the mid-fourteenth-century statutes that proscribe or limit the play of games mention cards, though they do mention dice, chess, and other games. It is therefore likely that, contrary to what is sometimes claimed, at that time playing cards was not yet common in Europe.

The pattern of reasoning in which one of the following is most similar to that in the argument above?

(A) Neither today's newspapers nor this evening's television news mentioned a huge fire that was rumored to have happened in the port last night. Therefore, there probably was no such fire.

(B) This evening's television news reported that the cruise ship was only damaged in the fire last night, whereas the newspaper reported that it was destroyed. The television news is based on more recent information, so probably the ship was not destroyed.

(C) Among the buildings that are near the port is the newspaper's printing plant. Early editions of this morning's paper were very late. Therefore, the fire at the port probably affected areas beyond the port itself.

(D) The newspaper does not explicitly say that the port reopened after the fire, but in its listing of newly arrived ships it mentions some arrival times after the fire. Therefore, the port was probably not closed for long.

(E) The newspaper is generally more reliable than the television news, and the newspaper reported that the damage from last night's fire in the port was not severe. Therefore, the damage probably was not severe.

9. In a mature tourist market such as Bellaria there are only two ways hotel owners can increase profits: by building more rooms or by improving what is already there. Rigid land-use laws in Bellaria rule out construction of new hotels or, indeed, any expansion of hotel capacity. It follows that hotel owners cannot increase their profits in Bellaria since Bellarian hotels _____.

Which one of the following logically completes the argument?

(A) are already operating at an occupancy rate approaching 100 percent year-round

(B) could not have been sited any more attractively than they are even in the absence of land-use laws

(C) have to contend with upward pressures on the cost of labor which stem from an incipient shortage of trained personnel

(D) already provide a level of luxury that is at the limits of what even wealthy patrons are prepared to pay for

(E) have shifted from serving mainly Bellarian tourists to serving foreign tourists traveling in organized tour groups

10. Every political philosopher of the early twentieth century who was either a socialist or a communist was influenced by Rosa Luxemburg. No one who was influenced by Rosa Luxemburg advocated a totalitarian state.

If the statements above are true, which one of the following must on the basis of them also be true?

(A) No early-twentieth-century socialist political philosopher advocated a totalitarian state.

(B) Every early-twentieth-century political philosopher who did not advocate a totalitarian state was influenced by Rosa Luxemburg.

(C) Rosa Luxemburg was the only person to influence every early-twentieth-century political philosopher who was either socialist or communist.

(D) Every early-twentieth-century political philosopher who was influenced by Rosa Luxemburg and was not a socialist was a communist.

(E) Every early-twentieth-century political philosopher who did not advocate a totalitarian state was either socialist or communist.

GO ON TO THE NEXT PAGE.

Questions 11–12

Harris: Currently, hybrid animals are not protected by international endangered-species regulations. But new techniques in genetic research suggest that the red wolf, long thought to be an independent species, is a hybrid of the coyote and the gray wolf. Hence, since the red wolf clearly deserves protection, these regulations should be changed to admit the protection of hybrids.

Vogel: Yet hybrids do not need protection. Since a breeding population that arises through hybridization descends from independent species, if any such population were to die out, it could easily be revived by interbreeding members of the species from which the hybrid is descended.

11. Which one of the following is a point at issue between Harris and Vogel?

(A) whether the red wolf descends from the gray wolf and the coyote
(B) whether there are some species that are currently considered endangered that are not in fact in any danger
(C) whether the packs of red wolves that currently exist are in danger of dying out
(D) whether there are some hybrids that ought to be protected by endangered-species regulations
(E) whether new techniques in genetic research should be used to determine which groups of animals constitute species and which constitute hybrids

12. Which one of the following is an assumption on which Vogel's argument relies?

(A) The techniques currently being used to determine whether a population of animals is a hybrid of other species have proven to be reliable.
(B) The international regulations that protect endangered species and subspecies are being enforced successfully.
(C) The gray wolf has been successfully bred in captivity.
(D) All hybrids are the descendants of species that are currently extant.
(E) The coyote and the red wolf are not related genetically.

13. From an analysis of broken pottery and statuary, archaeologists have estimated that an ancient settlement in southwestern Arabia was established around 1000 B.C. However, new evidence suggests that the settlement is considerably older: tests show that a piece of building timber recently uncovered at the site is substantially older than the pottery and statuary.

Which one of the following, if true, most seriously undermines the conclusion drawn from the new evidence?

(A) The building timber bore marks suggesting that it had been salvaged from an earlier settlement.
(B) The pieces of pottery and fragments of statues that were analyzed come from several parts of the site.
(C) The tests used to determine the age of the pottery and statuary had been devised more recently than those used to determine the age of the building timber.
(D) The site has yielded many more samples of pottery and statuary than of building timber.
(E) The type of pottery found at the site is similar to a type of pottery associated with civilizations that existed before 1000 B.C.

14. The book *To Save the Earth* is so persuasive that no one who reads it can fail to heed its environmentalist message. Members of the Earth Association have given away 2,000 copies in the last month. Thus the Earth Association can justly claim credit for at least 2,000 people in one month converted to the environmentalist cause.

Which one of the following is an assumption on which the argument depends?

(A) No other environmental organization gave away copies of *To Save the Earth* during the month in which the Earth Association gave away its 2,000 copies.
(B) The people to whom the Earth Association gave copies of *To Save the Earth* would not have been willing to pay to receive it from the Earth Association.
(C) The copies of *To Save the Earth* given away by members of the Earth Association were printed on recycled paper.
(D) None of those who received *To Save the Earth* from a member of the Earth Association were already committed to the environmentalist cause when they received this book.
(E) Every recipient of *To Save the Earth* will embrace the environmental program advocated by the Earth Association.

GO ON TO THE NEXT PAGE.

15. Smokers of pipes or cigars run a distinctly lower risk to their health than do cigarette smokers. However, whereas cigarette smokers who quit smoking altogether sharply reduce their risk of smoking-related health problems, those who give up cigarettes and take up pipes or cigars remain in as much danger as before.

Which one of the following, if true, offers the best prospects for an explanation of why the two changes in smoking habits do not both result in reduced health risks?

(A) Smokers of pipes or cigars who quit smoking thereby reduce their risk of smoking-related health problems.

(B) Cigarette smokers who quit smoking for a time and who then resume cigarette smoking do not necessarily reduce their risk of smoking-related health problems.

(C) The kinds of illnesses that smokers run an increased risk of contracting develop no earlier in cigarette smokers than they do in smokers of pipes or cigars.

(D) At any given period in their lives, virtually all smokers smoke either cigarettes exclusively or cigars exclusively or pipes exclusively, rather than alternating freely among various ways of smoking.

(E) People who switch from cigarette smoking to smoking pipes or cigars inhale smoke in a way that those who have never smoked cigarettes do not.

Questions 16–17

Production manager: The building materials that we produce meet industry safety codes but pose some safety risk. Since we have recently developed the technology to make a safer version of our product, we should stop producing our current product and sell only the safer version in order to protect public safety.

Sales manager: If we stop selling our current product, we will have no money to develop and promote the safer product. We need to continue to sell the less-safe product in order to be in a position to market the safer product successfully.

16. Which one of the following principles, if established, most helps to justify the production manager's conclusion?

(A) Companies should be required to develop safer products if such development can be funded from sales of existing products.

(B) That a product does not meet industry safety codes should be taken as sufficient indication that the product poses some safety risks.

(C) Companies should not sell a product that poses safety risks if they are technologically capable of producing a safer version of that product.

(D) Product safety codes should be reviewed whenever an industry replaces one version of a product with a technologically more advanced version of that product.

(E) In order to make building materials safer, companies should continually research new technologies whether or not they are required to do so in order to comply with safety codes.

17. The sales manager counters the production manager's argument by

(A) pointing out that one part of the production manager's proposal would have consequences that would prevent successful execution of another part

(B) challenging the production manager's authority to dictate company policy

(C) questioning the product manager's assumption that a product is necessarily safe just because it is safer than another product

(D) proposing a change in the standards by which product safety is judged

(E) presenting evidence to show that the production manager has overestimated the potential impact of the new technology

GO ON TO THE NEXT PAGE.

Questions 18–19

Each year, an official estimate of the stock of cod in the Grand Banks is announced. This estimate is obtained by averaging two separate estimates of how many cod are available, one based on the number of cod caught by research vessels during a once-yearly sampling of the area and the other on the average number of tons of cod caught by various commercial vessels per unit of fishing effort expended there in the past year—a unit of fishing effort being one kilometer of net set out in the water for one hour. In previous decades, the two estimates usually agreed closely. However, for the last decade the estimate based on commercial tonnage has been increasing markedly, by about the same amount as the sampling-based estimate has been decreasing.

18. If the statements in the passage are true, which one of the following is most strongly supported by them?

   (A) Last year's official estimate was probably not much different from the official estimate ten years ago.
   (B) The number of commercial vessels fishing for cod in the Grand Banks has increased substantially over the past decade.
   (C) The sampling-based estimate is more accurate than the estimate based on commercial tonnage in that the data on which it relies is less likely to be inaccurate.
   (D) The once-yearly sampling by research vessels should be used as the sole basis for arriving at the official estimate of the stock of cod.
   (E) Twenty years ago, the overall stock of cod in the Grand Banks was officially estimated to be much larger than it is estimated to be today.

19. Which one of the following, if true, most helps to account for the growing discrepancy between the estimate based on commercial tonnage and the research-based estimate?

   (A) Fishing vessels often exceed their fishing quotas for cod and therefore often underreport the number of tons of cod that they catch.
   (B) More survey vessels are now involved in the yearly sampling effort than were involved 10 years ago.
   (C) Improvements in technology over the last 10 years have allowed commercial fishing vessels to locate and catch large schools of cod more easily.
   (D) Survey vessels count only those cod caught during a 30-day survey period, whereas commercial fishing vessels report all cod caught during the course of a year.
   (E) Because of past overfishing of cod, fewer fishing vessels now catch the maximum tonnage of cod each vessel is allowed by law to catch.

20. Pretzels can cause cavities. Interestingly, the longer that a pretzel remains in contact with the teeth when it is being eaten, the greater the likelihood that a cavity will result. What is true of pretzels in this regard is also true of caramels. Therefore, since caramels dissolve more quickly in the mouth than pretzels do, eating a caramel is less likely to result in a cavity than eating a pretzel is.

The reasoning in the argument is vulnerable to criticism on the grounds that the argument

   (A) treats a correlation that holds within individual categories as thereby holding across categories as well
   (B) relies on the ambiguous use of a key term
   (C) makes a general claim based on particular examples that do not adequately represent the respective classes that they are each intended to represent
   (D) mistakes the cause of a particular phenomenon for the effect of that phenomenon
   (E) is based on premises that cannot all be true

GO ON TO THE NEXT PAGE.

Questions 21–22

Mark: Plastic-foam cups, which contain environmentally harmful chlorofluorocarbons, should no longer be used; paper cups are preferable. Styrene, a carcinogenic by-product, is generated in foam production, and foam cups, once used, persist indefinitely in the environment.

Tina: You overlook the environmental effects of paper cups. A study done 5 years ago showed that making paper for their production burned more petroleum than was used for foam cups and used 12 times as much steam, 36 times as much electricity, and twice as much cooling water. Because paper cups weigh more, their transportation takes more energy. Paper mills produce water pollution, and when the cups decay they produce methane, a gas that contributes to harmful global warming. So they are a worse choice.

21. Which one of the following, if true, could Mark cite to counter evidence offered by Tina?

(A)   The use of energy for chain saws that cut down trees and for trucks that haul logs is part of the environmental cost of manufacturing paper.

(B)   Foam cups are somewhat more acceptable to consumers than paper cups because of their better insulating qualities.

(C)   The production and transportation of petroleum occasions serious environmental pollution, but the energy that runs paper mills now comes from burning waste wood rather than petroleum.

(D)   The amount of styrene escaping into the environment or remaining in foam cups after their manufacture is negligible.

(E)   Acre for acre, tree farms for the production of wood for paper have fewer beneficial effects on the environment than do natural forests that remain uncut.

22. To decide the issue between Mark and Tina, it would first be most important to decide

(A)   how soon each of the kinds of harm cited by Mark and Tina would be likely to be at its maximum level

(B)   whether members of some societies use, on average, more disposable goods than do members of other societies

(C)   whether it is necessary to seek a third alternative that has none of the negative consequences cited with respect to the two products

(D)   how much of the chains of causation involved in the production, marketing, and disposal of the products should be considered in analyzing their environmental impact

(E)   whether paper and foam cups, in their most popular sizes, hold the same quantities of liquid

23. When people experience throbbing in their teeth or gums, they have serious dental problems, and if a dental problem is serious, it will be a problem either of tooth decay or of gum disease. Therefore, since throbbing in the teeth or gums is a sign of serious dental problems, and neither Sabina's teeth nor her gums are throbbing, Sabina can be suffering from neither tooth decay nor gum disease.

Which one of the following contains an error of reasoning most similar to that made in the argument above?

(A)   People who drink a lot of coffee are said to have jittery nerves. Therefore, medical students who drink a lot of coffee should not become neonatologists or surgeons since neither neonatology nor surgery should be practiced by people with jittery nerves.

(B)   A legally practicing psychiatrist must have both a medical degree and psychiatric training. Thus, since Emmett has not undergone psychiatric training, if he is practicing as a psychiatrist, he is not doing so legally.

(C)   Someone with severe nasal congestion has a sinus infection or else is suffering from an allergy. Therefore, if Barton does not have a sinus infection, Barton probably does not have severe nasal congestion.

(D)   If a person is interested in either physics or chemistry, then that person would be wise to consider a career in medicine. Yolanda, however, is interested in neither physics nor chemistry, so it would not be wise for her to consider a career in medicine.

(E)   Someone who is neither an ophthalmologist nor an optometrist lacks specialized training for diagnosing defects of the eye. Therefore, Kim must have been trained in ophthalmology or optometry, given that she accurately diagnosed John's eye defect.

GO ON TO THE NEXT PAGE.

24. A certain airport security scanner designed to detect explosives in luggage will alert the scanner's operator whenever the piece of luggage passing under the scanner contains an explosive. The scanner will erroneously alert the operator for only one percent of the pieces of luggage that contain no explosives. Thus in ninety-nine out of a hundred alerts explosives will actually be present.

The reasoning in the argument is flawed because the argument

(A) ignores the possibility of the scanner's failing to signal an alert when the luggage does contain an explosive
(B) draws a general conclusion about reliability on the basis of a sample that is likely to be biased
(C) ignores the possibility of human error on the part of the scanner's operator once the scanner has alerted him or her
(D) fails to acknowledge the possibility that the scanner will not be equally sensitive to all kinds of explosives
(E) substitutes one group for a different group in the statement of a percentage

25. Unless negotiations begin soon, the cease-fire will be violated by one of the two sides to the dispute. Negotiations will be held only if other countries have pressured the two sides to negotiate; an agreement will emerge only if other countries continue such pressure throughout the negotiations. But no negotiations will be held until international troops enforcing the cease-fire have demonstrated their ability to counter any aggression from either side, thus suppressing a major incentive for the two sides to resume fighting.

If the statements above are true, and if negotiations between the two sides do begin soon, at the time those negotiations begin each of the following must also be true EXCEPT:

(A) The cease-fire has not been violated by either of the two sides.
(B) International troops enforcing the cease-fire have demonstrated that they can counter aggression from either of the two sides.
(C) A major incentive for the two sides to resume hostilities has been suppressed.
(D) Other countries have exerted pressure on the two sides to the dispute.
(E) The negotiations' reaching an agreement depends in part on the actions of other countries.

26. If Blankenship Enterprises has to switch suppliers in the middle of a large production run, the company will not show a profit for the year. Therefore, if Blankenship Enterprises in fact turns out to show no profit for the year, it will also turn out to be true that the company had to switch suppliers during a large production run.

The reasoning in the argument is most vulnerable to criticism on which one of the following grounds?

(A) The argument is a circular argument made up of an opening claim followed by a conclusion that merely paraphrases that claim.
(B) The argument fails to establish that a condition under which a phenomenon is said to occur is the only condition under which that phenomenon occurs.
(C) The argument involves an equivocation, in that the word "profit" is allowed to shift its meaning during the course of the argument.
(D) The argument erroneously uses an exceptional, isolated case to support a universal conclusion.
(E) The argument explains one event as being caused by another event, even though both events must actually have been caused by some third, unidentified event.

S T O P

IF YOU FINISH BEFORE TIME IS CALLED, YOU MAY CHECK YOUR WORK ON THIS SECTION ONLY.
DO NOT WORK ON ANY OTHER SECTION IN THE TEST.

SECTION III

Time—35 minutes

27 Questions

Directions: Each passage in this section is followed by a group of questions to be answered on the basis of what is stated or implied in the passage. For some of the questions, more than one of the choices could conceivably answer the question. However, you are to choose the best answer; that is, the response that most accurately and completely answers the question, and blacken the corresponding space on your answer sheet.

A major tenet of the neurosciences has been that all neurons (nerve cells) in the brains of vertebrate animals are formed early in development. An adult vertebrate, it was believed, must make do with a
(5) fixed number of neurons: those lost through disease or injury are not replaced, and adult learning takes place not through generation of new cells but through modification of connections among existing ones.
(10) However, new evidence for neurogenesis (the birth of new neurons) has come from the study of canary song. Young canaries and other songbirds learn to sing much as humans learn to speak, by imitating models provided by their elders. Several
(15) weeks after birth, a young bird produces its first rudimentary attempts at singing; over the next few months the song becomes more structured and stable, reaching a fully developed state by the time the bird approaches its first breeding season. But
(20) this repertoire of song is not permanently learned. After each breeding season, during late summer and fall, the bird loses mastery of its developed "vocabulary," and its song becomes as unstable as that of a juvenile bird. During the following winter
(25) and spring, however, the canary acquires new songs, and by the next breeding season it has developed an entirely new repertoire.
Recent neurological research into this learning and relearning process has shown that the two most
(30) important regions of the canary's brain related to the learning of songs actually vary in size at different times of the year. In the spring, when the bird's song is highly developed and uniform, the regions are roughly twice as large as they are in the
(35) fall. Further experiments tracing individual nerve cells within these regions have shown that the number of neurons drops by about 38 percent after the breeding season, but by the following breeding season, new ones have been generated to replace
(40) them. A possible explanation for this continual replacement of nerve cells may have to do with the canary's relatively long life span and the requirements of flight. Its brain would have to be substantially larger and heavier than might be
(45) feasible for flying if it had to carry all the brain cells needed to process and retain all the information gathered over a lifetime.
Although the idea of neurogenesis in the adult mammalian brain is still not generally accepted,
(50) these findings might help uncover a mechanism that would enable the human brain to repair itself through neurogenesis. Whether such replacement of neurons would disrupt complex learning processes or long-term memory is not known, but
(55) songbird research challenges scientists to identify the genes or hormones that orchestrate neurogenesis in the young human brain and to learn how to activate them in the adult brain.

1. Which one of the following best expresses the main idea of the passage?

(A) New evidence of neurogenesis in canaries challenges an established neurological theory concerning brain cells in vertebrates and suggests the possibility that human brains may repair themselves.

(B) The brains of canaries differ from the brains of other vertebrate animals in that the brains of adult canaries are able to generate neurons.

(C) Recent studies of neurogenesis in canaries, building on established theories of vertebrate neurology, provide important clues as to why researchers are not likely to discover neurogenesis in adult humans.

(D) Recent research into neurogenesis in canaries refutes a long-held belief about the limited supply of brain cells and provides new information about neurogenesis in the adult human brain.

(E) New information about neurogenesis in canaries challenges older hypotheses and clarifies the importance of the yearly cycle in learning processes and neurological replacement among vertebrates.

GO ON TO THE NEXT PAGE.

2. According to the passage, which one of the following is true of the typical adult canary during the late summer and fall?

(A) The canary's song repertoire takes on a fully structured and stable quality.

(B) A process of neurogenesis replaces the song-learning neurons that were lost during the preceding months.

(C) The canary begins to learn an entirely new repertoire of songs based on the models of other canaries.

(D) The regions in the canary's brain that are central to the learning of song decrease in size.

(E) The canary performs slightly modified versions of the songs it learned during the preceding breeding season.

3. Information in the passage suggests that the author would most likely regard which one of the following as LEAST important in future research on neurogenesis in humans?

(A) research on possible similarities between the neurological structures of humans and canaries

(B) studies that compare the ratio of brain weight to body weight in canaries to that in humans

(C) neurological research on the genes or hormones that activate neurogenesis in the brain of human infants

(D) studies about the ways in which long-term memory functions in the human brain

(E) research concerning the processes by which humans learn complicated tasks

4. Which one of the following, if true, would most seriously undermine the explanation proposed by the author in the third paragraph?

(A) A number of songbird species related to the canary have a shorter life span than the canary and do not experience neurogenesis.

(B) The brain size of several types of airborne birds with life spans similar to those of canaries has been shown to vary according to a two-year cycle of neurogenesis.

(C) Several species of airborne birds similar to canaries in size are known to have brains that are substantially heavier than the canary's brain.

(D) Individual canaries that have larger-than-average repertoires of songs tend to have better developed muscles for flying.

(E) Individual canaries with smaller and lighter brains than the average tend to retain a smaller-than-average repertoire of songs.

5. The use of the word "vocabulary" (line 23) serves primarily to

(A) demonstrate the presence of a rudimentary grammatical structure in canary song

(B) point out a similarity between the patterned groupings of sounds in a canary's song and the syllabic structures of words

(C) stress the stability and uniformity of the canary's song throughout its lifetime

(D) suggest a similarity between the possession of a repertoire of words among humans and a repertoire of songs among canaries

(E) imply that the complexity of the canary's song repertoire is equal to that of human language

6. According to the passage, which one of the following factors may help account for the occurrence of neurogenesis in canaries?

(A) the life span of the average canary

(B) the process by which canaries learn songs

(C) the frequency of canary breeding seasons

(D) the number of regions in the canary brain related to song learning

(E) the amount of time an average canary needs to learn a repertoire of songs

7. Which one of the following best describes the organization of the third paragraph?

(A) A theory is presented, analyzed, and modified, and a justification for the modification is offered.

(B) Research results are advanced and reconciled with results from other studies, and a shared principle is described.

(C) Research results are presented, further details are provided, and a hypothesis is offered to explain the results.

(D) Research findings are described, their implications are explained, and an application to a related field is proposed.

(E) Research results are reported, their significance is clarified, and they are reconciled with previously established neurological tenets.

8. It can be inferred from the passage that the author would most likely describe the current understanding of neurogenesis as

(A) exhaustive
(B) progressive
(C) incomplete
(D) antiquated
(E) incorrect

GO ON TO THE NEXT PAGE.

For too many years scholars of African American history focused on the harm done by slaveholders and by the institution of slavery, rather than on what Africans in the United States were
(5) able to accomplish despite the effects of that institution. In *Myne Owne Ground*, T. H. Breen and Stephen Innes contribute significantly to a recent, welcome shift from a white-centered to a black-centered inquiry into the role of African Americans
(10) in the American colonial period. Breen and Innes focus not on slaves, but on a small group of freed indentured servants in Northampton County (in the Chesapeake Bay region of Virginia) who, according to the authors, maintained their freedom, secured
(15) property, and interacted with persons of different races and economic standing from 1620 through the 1670s. African Americans living on the Chesapeake were to some extent disadvantaged, say Breen and Innes, but this did not preclude the attainment of
(20) status roughly equal to that of certain white planters of the area. Continuously acting within black social networks, and forming economic relationships with white planters, local Native Americans, indentured servants, and white settlers outside the gentry class,
(25) the free African Americans of Northampton County held their own in the rough-hewn world of Chesapeake Bay.

The authors emphasize that in this early period, when the percentage of African Americans in any
(30) given Chesapeake county was still no more than 10 percent of the population, very little was predetermined so far as racial status or race relations were concerned. By schooling themselves in the local legal process and by working
(35) prodigiously on the land, African Americans acquired property, established families, and warded off contentious white neighbors. Breen and Innes do acknowledge that political power on the Chesapeake was asymmetrically distributed among
(40) black and white residents. However, they underemphasize much evidence that customary law, only gradually embodied in statutory law, was closing in on free African Americans well before the 1670s: during the 1660s, when the proportion
(45) of African Americans in Virginia increased dramatically, Virginia tightened a law regulating interracial relations (1662) and enacted a statute prohibiting baptism from altering slave status (1667). Anthony Johnson, a leader in the
(50) community of free African Americans in the Chesapeake Bay region, sold the land he had cultivated for more than twenty years and moved north with his family around 1665, an action that the authors attribute to a search for "fresh, more
(55) productive land." But the answer to why the Johnsons left that area where they had labored so long may lie in their realization that their white neighbors were already beginning the transition from a largely white indentured labor force to
(60) reliance on a largely black slave labor force, and that the institution of slavery was threatening their descendants' chances for freedom and success in Virginia.

9. The author of the passage objects to many scholarly studies of African American history for which one of the following reasons?

(A) Their emphases have been on statutory law rather than on customary law.
(B) They have ignored specific historical situations and personages in favor of broad interpretations.
(C) They have focused on the least eventful periods in African American history.
(D) They have underemphasized the economic system that was the basis of the institution of slavery.
(E) They have failed to focus to a sufficient extent on the achievements of African Americans.

10. Which one of the following can be inferred from the passage concerning the relationship between the African American population and the law in the Chesapeake Bay region of Virginia between 1650 and 1670 ?

(A) The laws affecting black citizens were embodied in statutes much more gradually than were laws affecting white citizens.
(B) As the percentage of black citizens in the population grew, the legal restrictions placed on them also increased.
(C) Because of discriminatory laws, black farmers suffered more economic setbacks than did white farmers.
(D) Because of legal constraints on hiring indentured servants, black farmers faced a chronic labor shortage on their farms.
(E) The adherence to customary law was more rigid in regions with relatively large numbers of free black citizens.

GO ON TO THE NEXT PAGE.

11. The author of the passage most probably refers to Anthony Johnson and his family in order to

(A) provide a specific example of the potential shortcomings of Breen and Innes's interpretation of historical events

(B) provide a specific example of relevant data overlooked by Breen and Innes in their discussion of historical events

(C) provide a specific example of data that Breen and Innes might profitably have used in proving their thesis

(D) argue that the standard interpretation of historical events is superior to Breen and Innes's revisionist interpretation

(E) argue that a new historiographical method is needed to provide a full and coherent reading of historical events

12. The attitude of the author of the passage toward Breen and Innes's study can best be described as one of

(A) condescending dismissal
(B) wholehearted acceptance
(C) contentious challenge
(D) qualified approval
(E) sincere puzzlement

13. The primary purpose of the passage is to

(A) summarize previous interpretations
(B) advocate a new approach
(C) propose and then illustrate a thesis
(D) present and evaluate an interpretation
(E) describe a historical event

GO ON TO THE NEXT PAGE.

Late-nineteenth-century books about the French artist Watteau (1684–1721) betray a curious blind spot: more than any single artist before or since, Watteau provided his age with an influential image

(5) of itself, and nineteenth-century writers accepted this image as genuine. This was largely due to the enterprise of Watteau's friends who, soon after his death, organized the printing of engraved reproductions of the great bulk of his work—both

(10) his paintings and his drawings—so that Watteau's total artistic output became and continued to be more accessible than that of any other artist until the twentieth-century advent of art monographs illustrated with photographs. These engravings

(15) presented aristocratic (and would-be aristocratic) eighteenth-century French society with an image of itself that was highly acceptable and widely imitated by other artists, however little relationship that image bore to reality. By 1884, the bicentenary of

(20) Watteau's birth, it was standard practice for biographers to refer to him as "the personification of the witty and amiable eighteenth century."

In fact, Watteau saw little enough of that "witty and amiable" century for which so much nostalgia

(25) was generally felt between about 1870 and 1920, a period during which enthusiasm for the artist reached its peak. The eighteenth century's first decades, the period of his artistic activity, were fairly calamitous ones. During his short life, France

(30) was almost continually at war: his native region was overrun with foreign troops, and Paris was threatened by siege and by a rampaging army rabble. The dreadful winter of 1709, the year of Watteau's first Paris successes, was marked by

(35) military defeat and a disastrous famine.

Most of Watteau's nineteenth-century admirers simply ignored the grim background of the works they found so lyrical and charming. Those who took the inconvenient historical facts into consideration

(40) did so only in order to refute the widely held deterministic view that the content and style of an artist's work were absolutely dictated by heredity and environment. (For Watteau admirers, such determinism was unthinkable: the artist was born

(45) in a Flemish town only six years after it first became part of France, yet Watteau was quintessentially French. As one patriotic French biographer put it, "In Dresden, Potsdam, and Berlin I have never come across a Watteau without feeling refreshed by

(50) a breath of native air.") Even such writers, however, persisted in according Watteau's canvases a privileged status as representative "personifications" of the eighteenth century. The discrepancy between historical fact and artistic

(55) vision, useful in refuting the extreme deterministic position, merely forced these writers to seek a new formula that allowed them to preserve the desired identity between image and reality, this time a rather suspiciously psychic one: Watteau did not

(60) record the society he knew, but rather "foresaw" a society that developed shortly after his death.

14. Which one of the following best describes the overall organization of the passage?

(A) A particular phenomenon is discussed, the reasons that it is atypical are put forward, and these reasons are evaluated and refined.

(B) An assumption is made, results deriving from it are compared with what is known to be true, and the assumption is finally rejected as counterfactual.

(C) A point of view is described, one hypothesis accounting for it is introduced and rejected, and a better hypothesis is offered for consideration.

(D) A general characterization is offered, examples supporting it are introduced, and its special applicability to a particular group is asserted.

(E) A particular viewpoint is explained, its shortcomings are discussed, and its persistence in the face of these is noted.

15. The passage suggests that late-nineteenth-century biographers of Watteau considered the eighteenth century to be "witty and amiable" in large part because of

(A) what they saw as Watteau's typical eighteenth-century talent for transcending reality through art

(B) their opposition to the determinism that dominated late-nineteenth-century French thought

(C) a lack of access to historical source material concerning the early eighteenth century in France

(D) the nature of the image conveyed by the works of Watteau and his many imitators

(E) their political bias in favor of aristocratic regimes and societies

GO ON TO THE NEXT PAGE.

16. According to the passage, explanations of artistic production based on determinism were unthinkable to Watteau admirers for which one of the following reasons?

(A) If such explanations were widely accepted, too many people who would otherwise have admired Watteau would cease to appreciate Watteau's works.

(B) If such explanations were adopted, they would make it difficult for Watteau admirers to explain why Watteau's works were purchased and admired by foreigners.

(C) If such explanations were correct, many artists who, like Watteau, considered themselves French would have to be excluded from histories of French art.

(D) If such simple explanations were offered, other more complex arguments concerning what made Watteau's works especially charming would go unexplored.

(E) If such explanations were true, Watteau's works would reflect a "Flemish" sensibility rather than the especially "French" one these admirers saw in them.

17. The phrase "curious blind spot" (lines 2–3) can best be interpreted as referring to which one of the following?

(A) some biographers' persistent inability to appreciate what the author considers a particularly admirable quality

(B) certain writers' surprising lack of awareness of what the author considers an obvious discrepancy

(C) some writers' willful refusal to evaluate properly what the author considers a valuable source of information about the past

(D) an inexplicable tendency on the part of some writers to undervalue an artist whom the author considers extremely influential

(E) a marked bias in favor of a certain painter and a concomitant prejudice against contemporaries the author considers equally talented

18. It can be inferred from the passage that the author's view of Watteau's works differs most significantly from that of most late-nineteenth-century Watteau admirers in which one of the following ways?

(A) Unlike most late-nineteenth-century Watteau admirers, the author appreciates the importance of Watteau's artistic accomplishment.

(B) The author finds Watteau's works to be much less lyrical and charming than did most late-nineteenth-century admirers of the works.

(C) In contrast to most late-nineteenth-century Watteau admirers, the author finds it misleading to see Watteau's works as accurately reflecting social reality.

(D) The author is much more willing to entertain deterministic explanations of the origins of Watteau's works than were most late-nineteenth-century Watteau admirers.

(E) Unlike most late-nineteenth-century admirers of Watteau, the author considers it impossible for any work of art to personify or represent a particular historical period.

19. The author asserts that during the period of Watteau's artistic activity French society was experiencing which one of the following?

(A) widespread social upheaval caused by war

(B) a pervasive sense of nostalgia for an idealized past

(C) increased domination of public affairs by a powerful aristocracy

(D) rapid adoption by the middle classes of aristocratic manners and life-styles

(E) a need to reconcile the French self-image with French social realities

20. The information given in the passage suggests that which one of the following principles accurately characterizes the relationship between an artist's work and the impact it is likely to have on a society?

(A) An artist's recognition by a society is most directly determined by the degree to which his or her works are perceived as lyrical and charming.

(B) An artist will have the greatest influence on a society that values art particularly highly.

(C) The works of an artist who captures the true and essential nature of a given society will probably have a great impact on that society.

(D) The degree of influence an artist's vision will have on a society is conditional on the visibility of the artist's work.

(E) An artist who is much imitated by contemporaries will usually fail to have an impact on a society unless the imitators are talented.

GO ON TO THE NEXT PAGE.

Faced with the problems of insufficient evidence, of conflicting evidence, and of evidence relayed through the flawed perceptual, retentive, and narrative abilities of witnesses, a jury is forced to
(5) draw inferences in its attempt to ascertain the truth. By applying the same cognitive tools they have developed and used over a lifetime, jurors engage in the inferential exercise that lawyers call fact-finding. In certain decision-making contexts that are
(10) relevant to the trial of lawsuits, however, these normally reliable cognitive tools may cause jurors to commit inferential errors that distort rather than reveal the truth.

Although juries can make a variety of inferential
(15) errors, most of these mistakes in judgment involve the drawing of an unwarranted conclusion from the evidence, that is, deciding that the evidence proves something that, in reality, it does not prove. For example, evidence that the defendant in a criminal
(20) prosecution has a prior conviction may encourage jurors to presume the defendant's guilt, because of their preconception that a person previously convicted of a crime must be inclined toward repeated criminal behavior. That commonly held
(25) belief is at least a partial distortion of reality; not all former convicts engage in repeated criminal behavior. Also, a jury may give more probative weight than objective analysis would allow to vivid photographic evidence depicting a shooting victim's
(30) wounds, or may underestimate the weight of defense testimony that is not delivered in a sufficiently forceful or persuasive manner. Finally, complex or voluminous evidence might be so confusing to a jury that its members would draw
(35) totally unwarranted conclusions or even ignore the evidence entirely.

Recent empirical research in cognitive psychology suggests that people tend to commit inferential errors like these under certain
(40) predictable circumstances. By examining the available information, the situation, and the type of decision being made, cognitive psychologists can describe the kinds of inferential errors a person or group is likely to make. These patterns of human
(45) decision-making may provide the courts with a guide to evaluating the effect of evidence on the reliability of the jury's inferential processes in certain situations.

The notion that juries can commit inferential
(50) errors that jeopardize the accuracy of the fact-finding process is not unknown to the courts. In fact, one of a presiding judge's duties is to minimize jury inferential error through explanation and clarification. Nonetheless, most judges now employ
(55) only a limited and primitive concept of jury inferential error: limited because it fails to recognize the potential for error outside certain traditional situations, primitive because it ignores the research and conclusions of psychologists in
(60) favor of notions about human cognition held by lawyers.

21. Which one of the following best expresses the main idea of the passage?

(A) When making decisions in certain predictable situations, juries may commit inferential errors that obscure rather than reveal the truth.

(B) The views of human cognition taken by cognitive psychologists on the one hand and by the legal profession on the other are demonstrably dissimilar.

(C) When confronting powerful preconceptions, particularly shocking evidence, or complex situations, jurors make errors in judgment.

(D) The problem of inferential error by juries is typical of the difficulties with cognitive processes that people face in their everyday lives.

(E) Juries would probably make more reliable decisions if cognitive psychologists, rather than judges, instructed them about the problems inherent in drawing unwarranted conclusions.

22. Of the following hypothetical reforms in trial procedure, which one would the author be most likely to support as the best way to address the problem of jury inferential error?

(A) a move away from jury trials
(B) the institution of minimum formal educational requirements for jurors
(C) the development of strict guidelines for defense testimony
(D) specific training for judges in the area of jury instruction
(E) restrictions on lawyers' use of psychological research

23. In the second paragraph, the author's primary purpose is to

(A) refute the idea that the fact-finding process is a complicated exercise
(B) emphasize how carefully evidence must be presented in order to avoid jury inferential error
(C) explain how commonly held beliefs affect the jury's ability to ascertain the truth
(D) provide examples of situations that may precipitate jury errors
(E) recommend a method for minimizing mistakes by juries

GO ON TO THE NEXT PAGE.

24. Which one of the following best describes the author's attitude toward the majority of judges today?

(A) apprehensive about whether they are consistent in their instruction of juries
(B) doubtful of their ability to draw consistently correct conclusions based on the evidence
(C) critical of their failure to take into account potentially helpful research
(D) pessimistic about their willingness to make significant changes in trial procedure
(E) concerned about their allowing the presentation of complex and voluminous evidence in the courtroom

25. Which one of the following statements, if true, would most seriously undermine the author's suggestion about the use of current psychological research in the courtroom?

(A) All guidelines about human behavior must take account of variations in the patterns of human decision-making.
(B) Current models of how humans make decisions apply reliably to individuals but do not hold for decisions made by groups.
(C) The current conception of jury inferential error employed by judges has been in use for nearly a century.
(D) Inferential errors can be more easily predicted in controlled situations such as the trial of lawsuits than in other kinds of decision-making processes.
(E) In certain predictable circumstances, juries are less susceptible to inferential errors than they are in other circumstances.

26. It can be inferred from the passage that the author would be most likely to agree with which one of the following generalizations about lawyers?

(A) They have a less sophisticated understanding of human cognition than do psychologists.
(B) They often present complex or voluminous information merely in order to confuse a jury.
(C) They are no better at making logical inferences from the testimony at a trial than are most judges.
(D) They have worked to help judges minimize jury inferential error.
(E) They are unrealistic about the ability of jurors to ascertain the truth.

27. The author would be most likely to agree with which one of the following generalizations about a jury's decision-making process?

(A) The more evidence that a jury has, the more likely it is that the jury will reach a reliable verdict.
(B) Juries usually overestimate the value of visual evidence such as photographs.
(C) Jurors have preconceptions about the behavior of defendants that prevent them from making an objective analysis of the evidence in a criminal trial.
(D) Most of the jurors who make inferential errors during a trial do so because they are unaccustomed to having to make difficult decisions based on inferences.
(E) The manner in which evidence is presented to a jury may influence the jury either to overestimate or to underestimate the value of that evidence.

S T O P

IF YOU FINISH BEFORE TIME IS CALLED, YOU MAY CHECK YOUR WORK ON THIS SECTION ONLY.
DO NOT WORK ON ANY OTHER SECTION IN THE TEST.

SECTION IV

Time—35 minutes

24 Questions

Directions: The questions in this section are based on the reasoning contained in brief statements or passages. For some questions, more than one of the choices could conceivably answer the question. However, you are to choose the best answer; that is, the response that most accurately and completely answers the question. You should not make assumptions that are by commonsense standards implausible, superfluous, or incompatible with the passage. After you have chosen the best answer, blacken the corresponding space on your answer sheet.

1. James: In my own house, I do what I want. In banning smoking on passenger airlines during domestic flights, the government has ignored the airlines' right to set smoking policies on their own property.

   Eileen: Your house is for your own use. Because a passenger airline offers a service to the public, the passengers' health must come first.

   The basic step in Eileen's method of attacking James' argument is to

   (A)   draw a distinction
   (B)   offer a definition
   (C)   establish an analogy
   (D)   derive a contradiction from it
   (E)   question its motivation

2. The company that produces XYZ, a computer spreadsheet program, estimates that millions of illegally reproduced copies of XYZ are being used. If legally purchased, this number of copies would have generated millions of dollars in sales for the company, yet despite a company-wide effort to boost sales, the company has not taken available legal measures to prosecute those who have copied the program illegally.

   Which one of the following, if true, most helps to explain why the company has not taken available legal measures?

   (A)   XYZ is very difficult to copy illegally, because a sophisticated anticopying mechanism in the program must first be disabled.
   (B)   The legal measures that the company that produces XYZ could take against those who have copied its product became available several years before XYZ came on the market.
   (C)   Many people who purchase a software program like XYZ are willing to purchase that program only after they have already used it.
   (D)   The number of illegally reproduced copies of XYZ currently in use exceeds the number of legally reproduced copies currently in use.
   (E)   The company that produces ABC, the spreadsheet program that is XYZ's main rival in the marketplace, is well known for taking legal action against people who have copied ABC illegally.

Questions 3–4

Kim: Some people claim that the battery-powered electric car represents a potential solution to the problem of air pollution. But they forget that it takes electricity to recharge batteries and that most of our electricity is generated by burning polluting fossil fuels. Increasing the number of electric cars on the road would require building more generating facilities since current facilities are operating at maximum capacity. So even if all of the gasoline-powered cars on the roads today were replaced by electric cars, it would at best be an exchange of one source of fossil-fuel pollution for another.

3. The main point made in Kim's argument is that

   (A)   replacing gasoline-powered cars with battery-powered electric cars will require building more generating facilities
   (B)   a significant reduction in air pollution cannot be achieved unless people drive less
   (C)   all forms of automobile transportation are equally harmful to the environment in terms of the air pollution they produce
   (D)   battery-powered electric cars are not a viable solution to the air-pollution problem
   (E)   gasoline-powered cars will probably remain a common means of transportation for the foreseeable future

4. Which one of the following is an assumption on which Kim's argument depends?

   (A)   Replacing gasoline-powered cars with battery-powered electric cars will not lead to a net increase in the total number of cars on the road.
   (B)   Gasoline-powered cars are currently not the most significant source of fossil-fuel pollution.
   (C)   Replacing gasoline-powered cars with battery-powered electric cars is justified only if electric cars produce less air pollution.
   (D)   While it is being operated, a battery-powered electric car does not cause any significant air pollution.
   (E)   At least some of the generating facilities built to meet the demand for electricity for battery-powered electric cars would be of a type that burns fossil fuel.

GO ON TO THE NEXT PAGE.

5. Planetary bodies differ from one another in their composition, but most of those in the Solar System have solid surfaces. Unless the core of such a planetary body generates enough heat to cause volcanic action, the surface of the body will not be renewed for millions of years. Any planetary body with a solid surface whose surface is not renewed for millions of years becomes heavily pockmarked by meteorite craters, just like the Earth's Moon. Some old planetary bodies in the Solar System, such as Europa, a very cold moon belonging to Jupiter, have solid icy surfaces with very few meteorite craters.

If the claims above are true, which one of the following must, on the basis of them, be true?

(A) The Earth's Moon does not have an icy surface.
(B) If a planetary body does not have a heavily pockmarked surface, its core does not generate enough heat to cause volcanic action.
(C) Some planetary bodies whose cores generate enough heat to cause volcanic action do not have solid icy surfaces.
(D) Some of Jupiter's moons are heavily pockmarked by meteorite craters.
(E) Some very cold planetary bodies have cores that generate enough heat to cause volcanic action.

6. Patient: Pharmacists maintain that doctors should not be permitted to sell the medicine that they prescribe because doctors would then be tempted to prescribe unnecessary medicines in order to earn extra income. But pharmacists have a financial interest in having a monopoly on the sale of prescription medicines, so their objection to the sale of medicines by doctors cannot be taken seriously.

The patient's argument proceeds by

(A) pointing out an unstated assumption on which the pharmacists' argument relies and then refuting it
(B) attempting to discredit a position by questioning the motives of the proponents of that position
(C) undermining the pharmacists' conclusion by demonstrating that one of the statements used to support the conclusion is false
(D) rejecting a questionable position on the grounds that the general public does not support that position
(E) asserting that pharmacists lack the appropriate knowledge to have informed opinions on the subject under discussion

7. Murray: You claim Senator Brandon has accepted gifts from lobbyists. You are wrong to make this criticism. That it is motivated by personal dislike is shown by the fact that you deliberately avoid criticizing other politicians who have done what you accuse Senator Brandon of doing.

Jane: You are right that I dislike Senator Brandon, but just because I have not criticized the same failing in others doesn't mean you can excuse the senator's offense.

If Murray and Jane are both sincere in what they say, then it can properly be concluded that they agree that

(A) Senator Brandon has accepted gifts from lobbyists
(B) it is wrong for politicians to accept gifts from lobbyists
(C) Jane's criticism of Senator Brandon is motivated only by personal dislike
(D) Senator Brandon should be criticized for accepting gifts from lobbyists
(E) one or more politicians have accepted gifts from lobbyists

GO ON TO THE NEXT PAGE.

Questions 8–9

Oscar: Emerging information technologies will soon make speed of information processing the single most important factor in the creation of individual, corporate, and national wealth. Consequently, the division of the world into northern countries—in general rich—and southern countries—in general poor—will soon be obsolete. Instead, there simply will be fast countries and slow countries, and thus a country's economic well-being will not be a function of its geographical position but just a matter of its relative success in incorporating those new technologies.

Sylvia: But the poor countries of the south lack the economic resources to acquire those technologies and will therefore remain poor. The technologies will thus only widen the existing economic gap between north and south.

8. Sylvia's reasoning depends on the assumption that

(A)   the prosperity of the rich countries of the north depends, at least in part, on the natural resources of the poor countries of the south

(B)   the emergence of new information technologies will not result in a significant net increase in the total amount of global wealth

(C)   there are technologies other than information technologies whose development could help narrow the existing economic gap between north and south

(D)   at least some of the rich countries of the north will be effective in incorporating new information technologies into their economies

(E)   the speed at which information processing takes place will continue to increase indefinitely

9. The reasoning that Oscar uses in supporting his prediction is vulnerable to criticism on the ground that it

(A)   overlooks the possibility that the ability of countries to acquire new technologies at some time in the future will depend on factors other than those countries' present economic status

(B)   fails to establish that the division of the world into rich countries and poor countries is the single most important problem that will confront the world economy in the future

(C)   ignores the possibility that, in determining a country's future wealth, the country's incorporation of information-processing technologies might be outweighed by a combination of other factors

(D)   provides no reason to believe that faster information processing will have only beneficial effects on countries that successfully incorporate new information technologies into their economies

(E)   makes no distinction between those of the world's rich countries that are the wealthiest and those that are less wealthy

10. At the beginning of each month, companies report to the federal government their net loss or gain in jobs over the past month. These reports are then consolidated by the government and reported as the total gain or loss for the past month. Despite accurate reporting by companies and correct tallying by the government, the number of jobs lost was significantly underestimated in the recent recession.

Which one of the following, if true, contributes most to a resolution of the apparent discrepancy described?

(A)   More jobs are lost in a recession than in a period of growth.

(B)   The expenses of collecting and reporting employment data have steadily increased.

(C)   Many people who lose their jobs start up their own businesses.

(D)   In the recent recession a large number of failing companies abruptly ceased all operations.

(E)   The recent recession contributed to the growing preponderance of service jobs over manufacturing jobs.

GO ON TO THE NEXT PAGE.

Questions 11–12

Beverage company representative: The plastic rings that hold six-packs of beverage cans together pose a threat to wild animals, which often become entangled in the discarded rings and suffocate as a result. Following our lead, all beverage companies will soon use only those rings consisting of a new plastic that disintegrates after only three days' exposure to sunlight. Once we all complete the switchover from the old to the new plastic rings, therefore, the threat of suffocation that plastic rings pose to wild animals will be eliminated.

11. The argument depends on which one of the following assumptions?

(A)   None of the new plastic rings can disintegrate after only two days' exposure to sunlight.
(B)   The switchover to the new plastic rings can be completed without causing significant financial hardship to the beverage companies.
(C)   Wild animals will not become entangled in the new plastic rings before the rings have had sufficient exposure to sunlight to disintegrate.
(D)   Use of the old plastic rings poses no substantial threat to wild animals other than that of suffocation.
(E)   Any wild animal that becomes entangled in the old plastic rings will suffocate as a result.

12. Which one of the following, if true, most seriously weakens the representative's argument?

(A)   The switchover to the new plastic rings will take at least two more years to complete.
(B)   After the beverage companies have switched over to the new plastic rings, a substantial number of the old plastic rings will persist in most aquatic and woodland environments.
(C)   The new plastic rings are slightly less expensive than the old rings.
(D)   The new plastic rings rarely disintegrate during shipping of beverage six-packs because most trucks that transport canned beverages protect their cargo from sunlight.
(E)   The new plastic rings disintegrate into substances that are harmful to aquatic animals when ingested in substantial quantities by them.

13. Alcohol consumption has been clearly linked to high blood pressure, which increases the likelihood of developing heart disease. Yet in a study of the effects of alcohol consumption, the incidence of heart disease was lower among participants who drank moderate quantities of alcohol every day than it was among participants identified as nondrinkers.

Which one of the following, if true, most helps to resolve the apparent discrepancy in the information above?

(A)   Because many people who do not drink alcohol are conscious of their health habits, they are likely to engage in regular exercise and to eat nutritionally well-balanced meals.
(B)   Many of the participants identified as nondrinkers were people who had been heavy drinkers but had stopped drinking alcohol prior to participating in the study.
(C)   Some of the participants who drank moderate quantities of alcohol every day said that they occasionally drank large quantities of alcohol.
(D)   Some of the participants who drank moderate quantities of alcohol every day had high blood pressure.
(E)   The two groups of participants were similar to each other with respect to the participants' age, sex, geographical origin, and economic background.

14. Some of the world's most beautiful cats are Persian cats. However, it must be acknowledged that all Persian cats are pompous, and pompous cats are invariably irritating.

If the statements above are true, each of the following must also be true on the basis of them EXCEPT:

(A)   Some of the world's most beautiful cats are irritating.
(B)   Some irritating cats are among the world's most beautiful cats.
(C)   Any cat that is not irritating is not a Persian cat.
(D)   Some pompous cats are among the world's most beautiful cats.
(E)   Some irritating and beautiful cats are not Persian cats.

GO ON TO THE NEXT PAGE.

15. At Flordyce University any student who wants to participate in a certain archaeological dig is eligible to do so but only if the student has taken at least one archaeology course and has shown an interest in the field. Many students who have shown an interest in archaeology never take even one archaeology course. Therefore, many students who want to participate in the dig will be ineligible to do so.

The flawed reasoning of which one of the following arguments is most similar to that of the argument above?

(A) Theoretically, any jar is worth saving regardless of its size, but only if it has a lid. Therefore, since some jars are sure not to have lids, there are certain sizes of jar that are actually not worth saving.

(B) For a horse that is well schooled to be ideal for beginning riders that horse must also be surefooted and gentle. Many horses that are surefooted are not gentle. Therefore many well-schooled horses are not ideal for beginning riders.

(C) If an author's first novel has a romantic setting and a suspenseful plot, it will become a best-seller. Since many authors' first novels have neither, not many first novels become best-sellers.

(D) Any automobile that is more than a few years old is eventually sure to need repairs if it is not regularly maintained. Many automobiles are more than a few years old, but still do not need repairs. Therefore, many automobiles are regularly maintained.

(E) An expensive new building will prove to be a good investment only if it is aesthetically pleasing or provides lots of office space. However, since many expensive new buildings are not aesthetically pleasing, few expensive new buildings will prove to be good investments.

16. From the observation that each member of a group could possess a characteristic, it is fallacious to conclude immediately that it is possible for all the group's members to possess the characteristic. An example in which the fallacy is obvious: arguing that because each of the players entering a tennis tournament has a possibility of winning it, there is therefore a possibility that all will win the tournament.

Which one of the following commits the fallacy described above?

(A) You can fool some of the people all of the time and all of the people some of the time, but you cannot fool all of the people all of the time.

(B) Each of the candidates for mayor appears at first glance to possess the necessary qualifications. It would therefore be a mistake to rule out any of them without more careful examination.

(C) Each of the many nominees could be appointed to any one of the three openings on the committee. Therefore it is possible for all of the nominees to be appointed to the openings on the committee.

(D) If a fair coin is tossed five times, then on each toss the chance of heads being the result is half. Therefore the chance of heads being the result on all five tosses is also half.

(E) It is estimated that ten million planets capable of supporting life exist in our galaxy. Thus to rule out the possibility of life on worlds other than Earth, ten million planetary explorations would be needed.

GO ON TO THE NEXT PAGE.

17. Recent research shows that hesitation, shifting posture, and failure to maintain eye contact are not reliable indicators in discriminating between those who are lying and those who are telling the truth. The research indicates that behavior that cannot be controlled is a much better clue, at least when the lie is important to the liar. Such behavior includes the dilation of eye pupils, which indicates emotional arousal, and small movements of facial muscles, which indicate distress, fear, or anger.

Which one of the following provides the strongest reason for exercising caution when relying on the "better" clues mentioned above in order to discover whether someone is lying?

(A) A person who is lying might be aware that he or she is being closely observed for indications of lying.
(B) Someone who is telling the truth might nevertheless have a past history of lying.
(C) A practiced liar might have achieved great control over body posture and eye contact.
(D) A person telling the truth might be affected emotionally by being suspected of lying or by some other aspect of the situation.
(E) Someone who is lying might exhibit hesitation and shifting posture as well as dilated pupils.

Questions 18–19

Orthodox medicine is ineffective at both ends of the spectrum of ailments. At the more trivial end, orthodox medicine is largely ineffective in treating aches, pains, and allergies, and, at the other extreme, it has yet to produce a cure for serious, life-threatening diseases such as advanced cancer and lupus. People turn to alternative medicine when orthodox medicine fails to help them and when it produces side effects that are unacceptable to them. One of the reasons alternative medicine is free of such side effects is that it does not have any effects at all.

18. If the statements above are true, which one of the following can be properly inferred from them?

(A) Practitioners of alternative medicine are acting in bad faith.
(B) There are some medical conditions for which no orthodox or alternative treatment is effective.
(C) There are some trivial illnesses that can be treated effectively by the methods of alternative medicine.
(D) There are no effective medical treatments that are free from unacceptable side effects.
(E) Orthodox medicine will eventually produce a solution for the diseases that are currently incurable.

19. The charge made above against alternative medicine is most seriously weakened if it is true that

(A) predictions based on orthodox medicine have sometimes failed, as when a patient has recovered despite the judgment of doctors that an illness is fatal
(B) alternative medicine relies on concepts of the body and of the nature of healing that differ from those on which orthodox medicine is based
(C) alternative medicine provides hope to those for whom orthodox medicine offers no cure
(D) a patient's belief in the medical treatment the patient is receiving can release the body's own chemical painkillers, diminish allergic reactions, and promote healing
(E) many treatments used for a time by orthodox medicine have later been found to be totally ineffective

GO ON TO THE NEXT PAGE.

20. Humans began to spread across North America around 12,000 years ago, as the climate became warmer. During the same period the large mammals that were once abundant in North America, such as the mastodon, the woolly mammoth, and the saber-toothed tiger, became extinct. Thus, contrary to the myth that humans formerly lived in harmony with the rest of nature, it is clear that even 12,000 years ago human activity was causing the extinction of animal species.

The argument is most vulnerable to the criticism that

(A) it adopts without question a view of the world in which humans are seen as not included in nature

(B) in calling the idea that humans once lived in harmony with nature a myth the argument presupposes what it attempts to prove

(C) for early inhabitants of North America the destruction of mastodons, woolly mammoths, and saber-toothed tigers might have had very different significance than the extinction of mammal species does for modern humans

(D) there might have been many other species of animals, besides mastodons, woolly mammoths, and saber-toothed tigers, that became extinct as the result of the spread of humans across North America

(E) the evidence it cites is consistent with the alternative hypothesis that the large mammals' extinction was a direct result of the same change in climate that allowed humans to spread across North America

21. The town of Greenfield recently instituted a substantial supplementary tax on all households, whereby each household is taxed in proportion to the volume of the trash that it puts out for trash collectors to pick up, as measured by the number of standard-sized garbage bags put out. In order to reduce the volume of the trash on which their tax bill is based, Greenfield households can deliver their recyclable trash to a conveniently located local commercial recycling center, where such trash is accepted free of charge.

The supplementary tax provides some financial incentive to Greenfield households to do each of the following EXCEPT

(A) sort out recyclable trash thoroughly from their other trash

(B) dump nonrecyclable trash illegally at parks and roadsides

(C) compress and nest items of nonrecyclable trash before putting them out for pickup

(D) deliver recyclable materials to the recycling center instead of passing them on to neighbors who want to reuse them

(E) buy products without packaging or with recyclable rather than nonrecyclable packaging

22. In a survey of consumers in an Eastern European nation, respondents were asked two questions about each of 400 famous Western brands: whether or not they recognized the brand name and whether or not they thought the products bearing that name were of high quality. The results of the survey were a rating and corresponding rank order for each brand based on recognition, and a second rating-plus-ranking based on approval. The brands ranked in the top 27 for recognition were those actually available in that nation. The approval rankings of these 27 brands often differed sharply from their recognition rankings. By contrast, most of the other brands had ratings, and thus rankings, that were essentially the same for recognition as for approval.

Which one of the following, if each is a principle about consumer surveys, is violated by the survey described?

(A) Never ask all respondents a question if it cannot reasonably be answered by respondents who make a particular response to another question in the same survey.

(B) Never ask a question that is likely to generate a large variety of responses that are difficult to group into a manageable number of categories.

(C) Never ask all respondents a question that respondents cannot answer without giving up their anonymity.

(D) It is better to ask the same question about ten different products than to ask ten different questions about a single product.

(E) It is best to ask questions that a respondent can answer without fear of having gotten the answer wrong.

GO ON TO THE NEXT PAGE.

23. A certain species of bird has two basic varieties, crested and noncrested. The birds, which generally live in flocks that contain only crested or only noncrested birds, tend to select mates of the same variety as themselves. However, if a bird that is raised in a flock in which all other members are crested is later moved to a mixed flock, then that bird—whether crested or noncrested—is likely to select a crested mate. This fact indicates that the birds' preference for crested or noncrested mates is learned rather than genetically determined.

Which one of the following, if true, provides the most support for the argument?

(A) Birds of other species also tend to show preferences for mates that have one or another specific physical feature.

(B) In general there are few behavioral differences between the crested and noncrested birds of the species.

(C) Both the crested and noncrested birds of the species tend to select mates that are similar to themselves in size and age.

(D) If a crested bird of the species is raised in captivity apart from other birds and is later moved to a mixed flock, that bird is likely to select a crested mate.

(E) If a bird of the species is raised in a flock that contains both crested and noncrested birds, that bird shows no preference for one variety or the other in its selection of a mate.

24. Plant species differ in that renewed growth in spring can be triggered by day length or by temperature or else by a combination of both. Day length is the same, year after year, for any given date. Therefore, any plant species that starts to grow again on widely different dates in different years resumes growth at least in part in response to temperature.

Which one of the following arguments is most similar in its pattern of reasoning to the argument above?

(A) In Xandia, medical assistant trainees must either complete a formal training course or work for one year under the close supervision of a physician. Since few physicians are willing to act as supervisors, it must be true that most medical assistant trainees in Xandia take the training course.

(B) In the Crawford area, easterly winds mean rain will come and westerly winds mean dry weather will come; winds from other directions do not occur. Therefore, since it is currently raining in Crawford, there must be an easterly wind blowing there now.

(C) Some landfills charge garbage companies by volume only, some charge by weight only, and all others use a formula sensitive to both volume and weight. So if at a particular landfill the charges for two particular loads of equal volume dumped on the same day are different, weight must determine, or help determine, charges at that landfill.

(D) Depending on volume of business, either one or two or three store detectives are needed for adequate protection against shoplifting. Therefore, if on any particular day store management has decided that three detectives will be needed, it must be because business that day is expected to be heavy.

(E) A call is more likely to be heard if it is loud rather than soft, if it is high-pitched rather than low-pitched, and especially if it is both loud and high-pitched. Therefore, anyone whose call goes unheard in spite of being at maximum loudness should try to raise the pitch of the call.

S T O P

IF YOU FINISH BEFORE TIME IS CALLED, YOU MAY CHECK YOUR WORK ON THIS SECTION ONLY.
DO NOT WORK ON ANY OTHER SECTION IN THE TEST.

SIGNATURE_____ __/__/__
DATE

139

LSAT WRITING SAMPLE TOPIC

Sea Coast University is hiring new faculty for its science program and has narrowed its selection to Louise Park or the team of Joe Echevarria and Jeanne Myrdal. Assuming the cost of hiring Park alone or the team is comparable, write an argument supporting one choice over the other based on the following considerations:

- Sea Coast University wants to develop a science program that will attract more undergraduate science majors.
- Sea Coast University wants to increase private and public support for its scientific research.

Louise Park, an internationally recognized scientist, plans to retire in three to five years. The recipient of numerous prizes for several key discoveries, Dr. Park has published extensively in scientific journals. While many of her graduate students have become influential scientists, undergraduates often find her inaccessible. Dr. Park is eager to leave her current university for Sea Coast's warmer climate, and she will bring a large, well-equipped laboratory if she comes to Sea Coast. This year, as usual, Dr. Park has secured grants from public and private sources to support her research.

Joe Echevarria and Jeanne Myrdal number among the most promising young scientists in the country. They have begun to publish in respected scientific journals and have received research grants from major foundations. Last year, their team-teaching approach won them a national teaching award. They recently published an article detailing their groundbreaking research on commercial uses of biotechnology; this research has attracted the attention of major corporations, several of whom are eager to fund their future work

Directions:

1. Use the Answer Key on the next page to check your answers.

2. Use the Scoring Worksheet below to compute your raw score.

3. Use the Score Conversion Chart to convert your raw score into the 120-180 scale.

Scoring Worksheet

1. Enter the number of questions you answered correctly in each section.

	Number Correct
SECTION I	_____
SECTION II	_____
SECTION III	_____
SECTION IV	_____

2. Enter the sum here: _____
   This is your Raw Score.

Conversion Chart

For Converting Raw Score to the 120-180 LSAT Scaled Score
LSAT Form 5LSS28

Reported Score	Raw Score Lowest	Raw Score Highest
180	98	101
179	97	97
178	96	96
177	95	95
176	94	94
175	93	93
174	91	92
173	90	90
172	89	89
171	88	88
170	87	87
169	86	86
168	84	85
167	83	83
166	81	82
165	80	80
164	78	79
163	77	77
162	75	76
161	74	74
160	72	73
159	71	71
158	69	70
157	67	68
156	66	66
155	64	65
154	62	63
153	60	61
152	59	59
151	57	58
150	55	56
149	53	54
148	52	52
147	50	51
146	48	49
145	47	47
144	45	46
143	43	44
142	42	42
141	40	41
140	39	39
139	37	38
138	35	36
137	34	34
136	32	33
135	31	31
134	30	30
133	28	29
132	27	27
131	26	26
130	24	25
129	23	23
128	22	22
127	21	21
126	20	20
125	18	19
124	17	17
123	16	16
122	15	15
121	14	14
120	0	13

SECTION I

1.	D	8.	E	15.	D	22.	D
2.	B	9.	C	16.	B	23.	C
3.	C	10.	C	17.	E	24.	E
4.	E	11.	C	18.	E		
5.	B	12.	B	19.	C		
6.	D	13.	A	20.	A		
7.	E	14.	E	21.	A		

SECTION II

1.	D	8.	A	15.	E	22.	D
2.	C	9.	D	16.	C	23.	D
3.	C	10.	A	17.	A	24.	E
4.	A	11.	D	18.	A	25.	A
5.	A	12.	D	19.	C	26.	B
6.	E	13.	A	20.	A		
7.	B	14.	D	21.	C		

SECTION III

1.	A	8.	C	15.	D	22.	D
2.	D	9.	E	16.	E	23.	D
3.	B	10.	B	17.	B	24.	C
4.	C	11.	A	18.	C	25.	B
5.	D	12.	D	19.	A	26.	A
6.	A	13.	D	20.	D	27.	E
7.	C	14.	E	21.	A		

SECTION IV

1.	A	8.	D	15.	B	22.	A
2.	C	9.	C	16.	C	23.	E
3.	D	10.	D	17.	D	24.	C
4.	E	11.	C	18.	B		
5.	E	12.	B	19.	D		
6.	B	13.	B	20.	E		
7.	E	14.	E	21.	D		

The following prompts are provided to help acquaint you with the type of prompt you are likely to encounter in an actual LSAT. An additional prompt can be found at the end of each of the three PrepTests in this book.

The program director of a television station must select the guest for the first edition of *Timewaves*, a new talk show. Write an argument in favor of selecting one of the guests over the other, with the following considerations in mind:
- *Timewaves* must have enough appeal to attract a significant viewing audience in a competitive time slot.
- *Timewaves* must continue the station's tradition of providing serious commentary on current topics.

Jeanne Josephs, a popular writer, is known for her sharp analysis of contemporary issues. Her most recent article, published in a widely read newsmagazine, was entitled "Success: Who's Got It and Why." In the article, Josephs interviews celebrities in various fields, including sports, business, and the arts, about their views on success and how they achieve it. Josephs has not appeared on a television talk show in several years. Last year, however, she won a prestigious journalism award for "The Private Pain of Politics," a series of articles on the toll public office has taken on the family lives of prominent politicians. At that time reports about Josephs and her work appeared in many major newspapers.

Dr. Kingston Evans, a prominent criminologist, recently led an expert panel in a study investigating the theory and practice of prisons. The panel's controversial final report, "Rethinking Incarceration" is to be published as a book soon after the first edition of Timewaves is shown. The report calls into question the effectiveness of incarceration and argues for alternative models of rehabilitation. The study has received media attention after certain victim's rights groups questioned the panel's methodology. Other critics have charged that the panel is composed entirely of members of the academic community and is out of touch with the realities of crime and punishment. Dr. Evans, however, is not only a distinguished professor but has considerable practical experience in the corrections field.

Karen works in the personnel division of a large company, and has decided to make a career change. She has narrowed her choices to the following possibilities. Write an argument in favor of choosing one over the other, based on the following considerations:
- To cover future educational expenses for her children, Karen needs to increase her income substantially within five years.
- Karen is bored with her present job and wants more creative, challenging employment.

One possibility is for Karen to return to school to earn a master's degree. With a master's, Karen would be a strong candidate for promotion to an executive management position with her company. Such a promotion would require Karen to move to the company's headquarters in another city, but she is reluctant to disrupt her children's lives in this way. Because of her successful record, her company has offered her time off to return to school and will pay for half of her educational expenses. If she returns to school as a part-time student while she is working, she can finish the degree in three years. Karen's company is in the process of improving the benefits it offers employees. The idea of reimbursing employees for money spent on their children's educational expenses has been discussed, but no final decisions have been made.

Karen's other option is to quit her job to go into business with her friend Bob. Three years ago, he and Karen published a book on job recruitment and placement. They made a modest amount in sales, but favorable reviews in several high-profile publications brought numerous requests from many different companies for assistance and advice in their recruitment efforts. As a result, Bob, who left his job and opened his own consulting business a year ago, has more work than he can handle. Based on inquiries from individuals, he believes a profitable market exists in employment counseling. Karen could not expect to make even her current salary until she developed the new market, but the market is potentially unlimited.

An oil tanker has spilled its cargo near the economically depressed town of Gull Point, which is situated near a pristine coastal area. The local government is selecting an environmental contractor to clean up the spill; the oil company will underwrite the cost. Write an argument supporting one contractor over the other based on the following criteria:
- The government wants to provide income to Gull Point residents whose livelihoods were affected by the spill.
- The government needs a fast and effective cleanup of the oil spill to protect the coastline and its wildlife.

BayTech, a local biotechnology company with 50 full-time employees, has developed a chemical product that in laboratory tests rapidly consumes crude oil. These tests predict that this product would be 90 percent effective in eliminating oil from salt water and would minimize oil reaching the shore, but the product is too new to have been tested on an actual oil spill in the open ocean. BayTech promises to use as many town residents as possible to assist in the cleanup, which it estimates will take four to six months. If BayTech's chemical product proves effective in the ocean, the scientific community believes it will be a significant advance in environmental technology.

Clear Waters is a international environmental consulting firm with a solid reputation for environmental cleanup work. Clear Waters proposes to contain and absorb the offshore spill using technology of booms and suction that it developed 20 years ago. The Clear Waters technology is 70 percent effective in eliminating oil from the open ocean. This contractor claims that the cleanup can be accomplished in four months and would employ 100 town residents full time to mop up oil from the shore and clean oil from affected wildlife.

Multivision Studios, an independent studio devoted to promoting education through film, is deciding between two directors for an upcoming film on the life of painter Jane Ogden. Write an argument supporting one director over the other based on the following considerations:

- Multivision wants the film to promote a deeper understanding of Ogden's work.
- Multivision, which has a modest amount of money to spend on the film, needs to make a substantial profit to fund future projects.

The legendary Geary Curtis has been making popular films for years. His most recent films—an adventure, <u>Racers</u>, and a horror film, <u>Night Schooner</u>—have made hundreds of millions of dollars. However, his exacting production standards have resulted in several films being unable to recover their high production costs. Curtis wants the film to be both a tribute to Ogden and a new direction for documentary films. He envisions using state-of-the-art technology to re-create the collage effect of her paintings as he tells her life story through her works. He also plans to interweave actual tapes of Ogden's voice with current interviews with persons who knew her in order to create "a conversation between past and present."

Paul Walbert, a documentary filmmaker, won several prestigious awards two years ago for his moving portrait of a World War II resistance leader. His most recent films—one about a Latin American dance troupe and another about the life of a famous jazz drummer—have made modest profits. A disciplined director, Walbert is known for producing fine films on a limited budget. He proposes a chronological account of Ogden's life, focusing on the influences that affected her work. A personal friend of Ogden's for many years, Walbert will feature in the film his private collection of early Ogden drawings, most of which have never before been shown to the public. A famous actress with a strong interest in Ogden's work has agreed to play the lead if Walbert directs.

The city of Stockville must choose an event to inaugurate its new auditorium, an open-air stage with seats for about 15,000 people and a surrounding lawn with room for 30,000 more. Write an argument in favor of hiring either of the following performers with these considerations in mind.

- The city hopes the inaugural performance will raise as much money as possible to pay off the auditorium's construction loans.
- The city wants to obtain considerable positive publicity for the new auditorium.

Astrani, one of the legends of popular music, is giving a farewell concert tour before retiring. He has proposed holding the final three concerts in Stockville; because of his elaborate sets and costumes, tickets would be sold only for the auditorium's seats and no lawn seating would be available. Astrani never allows souvenirs to be sold at his concerts, but the city will receive 20 percent of the proceeds from ticket sales. If the tour ends in Stockville, a well-known director will film the historic event and plans to release a full-length feature which will share the final shows with fans around the world.

A number of prominent bands have organized "Animal-Aid" to raise money for endangered species. The concern has already generated significant attention in the press and a number of important arenas competed for the privilege of hosting the event. Stockville's new auditorium is the organizer's first choice as the site for the all-day concert and the city would be allowed to design and sell souvenirs commemorating the event. While tickets would be available for both the seats and surrounding lawn, all of the proceeds from ticket sales would go to "Animal-Aid." The auditorium's security expert is concerned that the facility's novice staff may not yet have the experience to handle a large crowd during an all-day event.

Dorchester University has a vacancy for a fine arts librarian. Write an argument in support of hiring one of the two candidates described below, taking into account the following considerations:

- Dorchester wants to publicize in the community at large its collection of early Asian musical instruments and its recently donated collection of related artwork.
- Dorchester needs to raise money to improve and update its entire fine arts program, including its museum.

Xiang Chen, who holds an undergraduate degree in music, was born and raised in China; he speaks fluent Mandarin, Cantonese, Hindi, and Japanese and has lived throughout Asia. He has been translating ancient Chinese texts for a major library over the past year. Two years ago, Mr. Chen served as art consultant to the Japanese consulate as it began its collection of contemporary Asian sculpture. An accomplished musician, he has studied piano with the well-known Chinese composer Mei-Ying Liang. Mr. Chen, who often performs in benefit concerts, suggests a chamber music series, featuring Gilman's collection of early instruments, to raise funds.

Elise Bogart received a master's degree in library science ten years ago. She has completed the coursework for a master's degree in ethnomusicology and is finishing her thesis, which analyzes the work of four Asian composers. Ms. Bogart worked as assistant fine arts librarian for two years at the Museum of Contemporary Art and before that, was the head librarian for six years at Connor & Doud, a major law firm. After persuading the firm to begin an art collection, she organized a gala opening exhibit, which featured contemporary local artists. Four years ago, during her tenure as president of a community service organization. Ms. Bogart organized about fifty other volunteers and ran a successful scholarship fund-raising drive.

The English department at a university must choose a text for its first-year composition course. Write an argument in favor of selecting either of the following texts with these considerations in mind:

- The department has a strong commitment to teaching basic writing skills, such as grammar and essay organization.
- The department wants to increase the students' enthusiasm for and interest in writing.

During the three years that the department has used *The Standard Textbook of English*, instructors in other departments have reported significant improvement in students' writing skills. Nicknamed "The Best and the Dullest" the text contains classic essays from both ancient and modern authors and is organized to illustrate the various forms of the essay—such as narration, exposition, and persuasion. The essays average more than 10 pages, and almost all are written in a formal style. While students find some of the subjects foreign, they feel the materials covered are often useful in their other coursework.

A new text, *The Modern Writer*, contains both an introduction describing the basics of grammar and a number of journalistic essays by contemporary authors. The pieces are typically short (only 2 to 3 pages) and explore topics of interest to most college students, such as popular music and career planning. The style of the essays tends to be informal, even colloquial. Each chapter contains several essays on a given topic and exercises designed to aid students in developing essays of their own. Although the introduction provides an adequate overview of basic grammar, the text does not discuss the essay form.

Valerie, a first-year graduate student in mathematics, needs a part-time job, and competition for jobs in the small town where her university is located is keen. With the following considerations in mind, write an argument supporting one of Valerie's two job offers over the other:

- Valerie wants the income from her job to minimize the money she must borrow for living expenses.
- Valerie wants the job to interfere with her graduate program as little as possible.

The university's Undergraduate Learning Center has offered Valerie a job tutoring groups of students taking introductory mathematics courses. Valerie has been assigned five 1:00 PM to 5:00 PM sessions, for which she will receive $160 per week. The ULC also provides free individual tutoring for students in advanced mathematics courses who request it. As a graduate student employee, Valerie would be eligible to serve as an individual tutor, in addition to her regular sessions, for which she would receive $15 per hour. The schedule of this job will require her to make changes in the courses she had planned to take this semester. She will also miss the afternoon office hours that most professors set aside to work individually with graduate students.

Milano's, a local restaurant has offered Valerie a job as a food server. She will work Tuesday, Thursday, Friday, and Saturday nights each week, starting at 5:00 PM. The salary is $130 per week plus tips, which can range anywhere from $80 to $140 for four nights of work. Milano's is often crowded on Friday and Saturday nights but rarely during the week. A server at Milano's told Valerie that although the restaurant's kitchen closes at 11:00 PM, servers must stay until all customers have left, which can be midnight or later. Valerie's most demanding class meets at 8:00 AM. Wednesdays and Fridays and cannot be rescheduled. Taking this job also means that she must give up the evening meetings of her study group.

The president of a university has sufficient funds to hire one of the following professors. Argue in support of hiring one rather than the other based on the following criteria:

- The president wants to enhance the university's reputation by attracting science faculty who can compete successfully for research funds.
- The president is committed to enrolling more local applicants, some of whom are underprepared for university-level work.

Dr. Jackson is currently a chemistry professor at a well-respected university. She has published widely and earned a considerable number of research grants. A dynamic lecturer, Dr. Jackson keeps office hours sporadically and occasionally cancels classes to present scholarly papers at conferences. She advises several large corporations on environmental issues and regulations. Recently, she established a "Science Scholars" program with three of these corporations to assist students at her university with their educational expenses; the program promotes high-technology careers. Dr. Jackson has persuaded the university to fund a summer institute for entering students whose academic credentials fall below the usual admission standards.

Dr. Calder is a biology professor at a nearby university well-known for its strong science programs. She has published two biology textbooks and frequently consults with primary and secondary schools throughout the region on ways to improve their science programs. Recipient of her university's most prestigious teaching award two years ago, Dr. Calder is particularly interested in developing methods for teaching basic sciences to beginning students and nonscience majors. Recently, Dr. Calder was chosen as one of ten professors to receive a grant to direct a three-year research study on the effectiveness of innovative science teaching techniques. Dr. Calder is also in the process of organizing an interdisciplinary research team to pursue an ongoing investigation of the biological, chemical, and psychological bases of human learning.

An accounting firm providing services in small retail stores has sufficient resources to develop one new project. Two project proposals are being considered—a newsletter and a software package. Write an argument for developing one project rather than the other, based on these considerations:

- The firm wants the new project to generate a significant profit.
- The firm wants its primary business to continue to be accounting.

A by-product of the firm's accounting service is the accumulation of information on trends in the local retail market. Clients frequently ask the firm's opinion on market conditions, and several have suggested that the firm start a newsletter. Starting costs would be $15,000. After the first year, the newsletter would earn a $5,000 profit annually, if 10 percent of the firm's current clients subscribe, but could earn much more if more subscriptions are sold. A successful newsletter could also lead to additional accounting work. The firm has sufficient staff at present to begin the newsletter, though more people would have to be hired to work on it if the newsletter turns out to be very successful.

The firm has developed its own computer software which it uses to manage the financial records of its largest client. Other clients have complained that there is no easy-to-use financial management software on the market and have asked about the firm's system. The firm's software specialists say that it would take them six months and cost $20,000 to package the software for use by non-accountants. If half the current clients purchased it, the firm would recapture only $10,000. However, if the firm can demonstrate that clients use and like it, a well-known software company has expressed an interest in purchasing the rights to the software package for $25,000. The accounting firm would then receive a royalty on all sales; annual royalties on similar products range from $2,000 to as much as $15,000.

The town of Ralston is planning its 100th anniversary celebration, which will end with speeches in front of City Hall. The town is considering including a theatrical performance. Write an argument favoring one of the following two productions over the other, with two considerations guiding your decision:

- The town wants to promote significant out-of-town interest in the event.
- The town wants to encourage as much community participation as possible.

A Voice for All, a serious drama, was written by a local author who is also a community leader in Ralston. It is the story of Ada Jeffers, the controversial, outspoken proponent of women's suffrage. Jeffers' unceasing, uncompromising stance against various forms of oppression was the subject of a television special last year. Theresa Alan, a native of Ralston and famous film actor, will play the lead. She has promised to recruit a small professional cast to perform the parts of the main characters in the play, and all other roles will be filled by area residents. The town's newspaper, the *Ralston Times Daily*, in conjunction with the town historical society, will publish a special anniversary edition featuring Jeffers' many activities.

Ralston Redux is a musical revue based on a fictionalized account of the colorful life and exploits of Herbert Ralston, the town founder and confidence man. Two of the region's leading satirists adapted the script from a popular play. The show includes a children's chorus and a number of crowd scenes, all to be played by community members. Leading roles will be filled through auditions. The director of a successful summer stock company has offered her assistance and the services of her professional technical crew. The Ralston High School Band, which has won the regional competition for the past three years, will provide the music. Local merchants have contributed money for a fireworks extravaganza that will be part of the play's finale.

The port city of Cedarville is considering two offers for the purchase of a large waterfront tract just within the city limits. Write an argument for one offer over the other with the following considerations in mind:

- Cedarville wants to reverse recent declines in both employment and population.
- Cedarville wants to boost its dwindling tourist industry.

Excel Glassware Company proposes to build a three-story factory on the site. It will employ 150 people and include a research laboratory. The company, part of an international conglomerate, is known for its extensive training programs and other employee benefits. Excel manufactures glassware for private and commercial use, including a world-famous line of crystal. The offer includes a promise to bring an award-winning crystal collection to be housed in a specially designed gallery built as part of a park next to the factory. Excel promises an advertising campaign promoting guided tours of the gallery and demonstrations of glassblowers at work.

Nature Life, a national conservation organization, wants to turn the site into a wildflower and animal sanctuary. The organization plans a tourist area, complete with slide shows, nature paths, and guided tours. The facility would employ a small staff of naturalists and would include a restaurant and a lodge with accommodations for 100 guests. The organization also plans to use the site as a training center and summer school for high school and university students considering a career in conservation. Since the river contains an extensive variety of marine life, including some rare and endangered species, the local university has expressed an interest in locating a branch of its research facility nearby if the sanctuary is built.

Green Earth, an organization devoted to preserving the environment, has decided to expand its activities into the field of publishing. Write an argument in favor of selecting one or the other of the following manuscripts as the organization's inaugural publication. Consider the following when making your decision:
- Green Earth wishes to develop a reputation as a publishing house for scholarly and influential works on the environment.
- Green Earth is financially dependent on the voluntary contributions of its supporters and hopes to raise significant funds through proceeds from the book.

John Dailey, a journalist who has spent most of his career travelling the world in order to gain first-hand knowledge of environmental issues, has submitted a collection of essays discussing both his experiences and a variety of environmental problems. Dailey's work has always been extremely popular, and his book would likely prove one of the few accessible texts addressing the difficult scientific issues underlying many of today's environmental questions. Despite his extensive experience and careful research, several scholars have recently expressed concern about the scientific accuracy of some of Dailey's reports. Dailey, currently researching a new article on herbal medicines obtained from endangered plant species in the Amazon rain forest, has not yet had time to prepare a response.

Ginny Fredericks, a professor and author of several well-known scientific studies of environmental issues, has submitted a manuscript proposing a sweeping plan of action for preserving the environment. Dr. Fredericks' reputation as a scientist guarantees that the book, the crowning achievement of her long and distinguished career will receive a significant amount of media attention. However, those accustomed to her impartial approach to environmental questions may be taken aback and perhaps outraged by her impassioned argument for a very radical program of action. Dr. Fredericks has volunteered to donate a percentage of the proceeds from a lecture tour she plans in conjunction with her book to the book's publisher, but William Stone, a noted philanthropist and long-time supporter of Green Earth, has expressed concern over the organization's support of such a potentially controversial figure.

The town of Rosedale has recommended that the community support efforts to raise the academic achievement of its students by setting up a neighborhood study center. Write an argument for one of the following two proposals for the location of the study center. The following criteria should guide your decision:
- The study center must be inviting and convenient enough that students will voluntarily come to do schoolwork.
- The study center should provide a supervised environment conducive to studying.

The first plan is to locate the study center in the largest of Rosedale's apartment complexes, which is home to 25 percent of the students who attend the Rosedale school and can be easily reached by the remainder. The Rosedale Community Association has been concerned about the unsupervised congregation of young people in the recreation areas of the complex and is eager to convert one of them into a study center. The Association has volunteered to fix up the room, including painting it and providing used furniture. Public funding is available to purchase some reference materials, including dictionaries and a set of encyclopedias. Although funding is not available to hire monitors, a group of students from a local university has volunteered to help with the supervision, as well as to provide some tutoring for the center.

The second plan calls for converting a storage area in the Rosedale public library into a study center. The Rosedale library has an excellent selection of reference materials, as well as thorough collections of recorded music and periodicals. The library, located next to the Rosedale school, is open from 10 AM to 9 PM daily except Sunday. The proposed study center, adjacent to the reference room, is a relatively small space that will be furnished by the library with tables and a few individual desks. Several computers will be provided for use as study aids. The library board, which has approved funds to complete the conversion of the storage area, has also agreed to have regular staff periodically monitor the room.

Increased traffic has made it almost impossible to drive on Main Street in the historic town of Winfield. The town council has been presented with two proposals for remedying the problem. Write an essay supporting one proposal over the other with the following in mind:
- The council wants to facilitate the flow of traffic on Main Street.
- The council wants to preserve and improve the town's attractiveness as a historic site.

The first plan would prohibit parking on Main Street and construct a four-story concrete garage on what is now an empty lot at one end of Main Street. The garage could be built in less than a year, and buses would shuttle people up and down Main Street. The garage would be significantly taller than any other building in town. If parking fees were set at the level currently charged on Main Street, the garage would pay for itself in five years; thereafter income could be used to renovate several historic buildings that have fallen into disrepair and to maintain the historic district along Main Street.

Proponents of the second plan point out that much of the traffic on Main Street is merely passing through Winfield on its way to various surrounding towns. They propose building a bypass around the town and continuing to allow parking on Main Street. The local government, eager to speed traffic between the surrounding towns, will provide funds for the project, but three years would be required to build the four-lane highway and the only available route separates Winfield from a local battlefield that is an important element in the area's history. However, the highway will provide access to the original, but later abandoned, site of the town of Winfield. If the highway is built, a nearby museum plans a historically accurate restoration of the settlement.

After a four-year break, Denise is returning to the nursing profession. She has recently received two job offers, write an argument in favor of her accepting one or the other with the following in mind:
- Denise wants to develop an area of expertise that will advance her career.
- Denise is committed to balancing the requirements of her job with her desire to spend time with her husband and two children.

One offer is with City Hospital, a 40-minute bus ride from Denise's home. With her degree and three years' experience, Denise qualifies to participate in the hospital's innovative management program. This program provides training in management through classroom lectures and individual instruction from professionals in the field. Nurses who complete the training, a management program, and a year of employment are qualified to become managers of a team of health care professionals responsible for a patient's total care. City Hospital offers a flexible system of shifts, including the option to work three twelve-hour days instead of five eight-hour days. Weekends and nights are optional, though nurses who accumulate extra hours on these shifts can earn up to an additional twenty percent of their annual salaries.

Bethune Medical Center, a teaching hospital, has offered Denise a starting salary which is 20 percent higher than that offered by City Hospital. The medical center offers a benefits package that includes paid time off to study at the local university and free day care for children of employees. The medical center is located near the university, which has a program offering advanced degrees in nursing education, administration, and various clinical specialties. As Denise completes the appropriate coursework, she will be eligible for placement in the medical center's specialty units. The job requires Denise to work a variety of shifts, though as her seniority increases, she can minimize night and weekend work. The medical center is a 20-minute subway ride from Denise's home.

The city of Midport has agreed to allow the developer of a retail store/office complex to extend its project beyond standard limitations in return for a public improvement. Write an argument supporting one of the developer's proposals over the other, using these two criteria to guide your decision:
- Midport wants to enhance a sense of community in the commercial center where the complex is located.
- Midport hopes to encourage professionals to move into the area.

One proposal is for the developer to help plan, build, and operate a day care center. It will be built three blocks from the complex on a vacant lot owned by the city. The facility, which will accommodate up to fifty children and will operate from 7:00 AM to 6:30 PM weekdays, will serve employees in the complex as well as those who work or live nearby. The developer will operate the center for five years and be responsible for a share of the costs—including the director's salary, which will be set high enough to attract someone with excellent qualifications. The center's tuition charges are expected to cover additional staff salaries. At the end of five years, a neighborhood nonprofit association will buy and operate the center.

The developer's second proposal is to restore a badly deteriorated theater located adjacent to the complex. The theater, owned by the city, will be refurbished to accommodate theatrical productions as well as movies, and will be run by the Fine Arts Committee of the City Council. The developer has agreed to subsidize all entertainment presented by the theater for the first five years of its operation. These subsidies will cover part of the cost of professional productions booked by the Fine Arts Council, locally produced shows, and any classic and current films rented by the Council. Because the theater will offer a variety of entertainment, it is expected to appeal to a broad audience with a variety of cultural interests.

The Johnson's car has just broken down, and they must decide whether to repair it or purchase a new one. Write an argument supporting one of these options, using the following two considerations to guide your decision:
- Maria and Larry want to conserve what is left of their savings after recently purchasing their first home.
- Larry needs a reliable car because there is no public transportation to his place of employment about an hour's drive to the east of their home.

When Maria's parents bought a new car four years ago, they gave their old one to Maria and Larry as a gift. A station wagon, it is bigger than the Johnsons need, and both the air-conditioning and the radio work sporadically. The couple has been careful to monitor the ordinary maintenance of the car. While the car is eight years old and gets lower than average gas mileage, until now it has required only one major repair—a costly brake job. The current problem is a faulty transmission. Although the repair estimate amounts to 20 percent of the Johnson's savings, the mechanic who has worked regularly on the car believes that with the transmission repaired, the car should last another three or four years.

After studying the new car market, the Johnsons have identified a small compact model as one that could meet their needs. This car is advertised as getting exceptional gas mileage and is available with many features, including a five-year warranty against major repairs. The car has a reputation for low maintenance costs, though the only dealership in the Johnson's area that works on this make of car is a busy one an hour's drive north of their home. The salesperson assures them that they qualify for a loan through the dealership. If the Johnson's trade-in their old car and make a down payment amounting to 60 percent of their savings, their monthly payments for the basic model with no extra features will be a manageable strain on their budget.

The Citizens' Association of Winchester is deciding whether to renovate the town's original Park and Shop shopping center or to demolish and replace it. Write an argument favoring one plan over the other based on the following guidelines:

- The association wants to increase the variety of shops and services in the neighborhood by attracting new merchants to the area.
- The association wants the building to remain a center of community-oriented activity for residents of the neighborhood.

One proposal calls for renovating the Park and Shop by adding two stories to the existing structure for additional shops and a restaurant. The original two-story structure, surrounded by parking spaces, currently houses family-owned businesses, including a gift shop, a bakery, a hardware store, and a small clothing boutique. The building also houses the offices of a doctor, a lawyer, and a dental group. It is architecturally undistinguished, but it blends well with the neighborhood, and every Saturday morning, a section of the parking lot is used for a flea market where people from the neighborhood come to buy crafts and fresh produce. The current shop-owners are not likely to be able to afford the rent if the center is demolished and a new building is constructed.

The other proposal is to demolish the existing Park and Shop and replace it with a six-story building that features a dramatic forty-foot atrium and an underground parking garage. The top two floors of the new structure will be used for offices, the ground floor will house a four-screen movie theater, and the remaining floors will be used for clothing and jewelry stores, and specialty boutiques. Three open-air restaurants, each with an ethnic theme, will surround the atrium on the first floor. The developer has agreed to provide a large room on the ground floor rent-free for years for community artwork and projects.

The large publishing firm that owns financially troubled Westerly Books has allocated $50,000 to the small company in one major effort to save it. Write an argument for spending the money on one of the following plans. The publishing firm has set the following conditions for keeping Westerly in business:

- Westerly must show a profit within one year by significantly increasing total sales.
- Westerly must change its image from an elite literary press to one with a broader audience appeal.

The Series Plan calls for contracting with a commercial artist who designs covers and book jackets. Westerly primarily publishes fiction by young and little-known writers whose names are recognized by only a small reading audience. This artist successfully launched a series of biographies for another small press by designing distinctive covers that became a trademark for the series. She believes that she can do something similar for Westerly by developing individual cover designs that will also become recognized trademarks. Book stores have told Westerly that its covers lack visual appeal and estimate that sales of its twenty current titles could jump at least 50 percent with better designs. The artist wants a $50,000 contract to undertake this project.

The Star Plan calls for spending the money on promotion of one promising novel. Westerly's books are generally well received by the critics but rarely sell more than five thousand copies. Westerly usually does not have the resources for extensive advertising. As a result, young writers who start out with Westerly usually sign with larger publishing houses once they achieve some success. Westerly has published two novels by a writer whose popularity has grown steadily. He is about to complete his third novel and claims that, with the right promotion, sales of this novel alone will exceed those of Westerly's entire line. Though optimistic, Westerly's staff has a more conservative estimate of expected sales. To remain with Westerly, the author wants a promotional campaign costing the entire $50,000.

Corinne Dunne, a microbiologist at a prestigious university, gained international attention through a series of articles she wrote about an oil spill off the coast of Chile. Dr. Dunne has decided to leave the academic setting. Write an argument in favor of her accepting one of the following job offers over the other. Keep two guidelines in mind:

- Dr. Dunne is committed to fighting industrial pollution.
- Dr. Dunne wants to continue her promising research to develop a potent strain of oil-devouring bacteria.

The Zero Pollution Task Force wants Dr. Dunne to assist with its international efforts to gain passage of legislation requiring polluters to assume greater financial responsibility for cleanups. Her responsibilities would include writing documents and articles to make technical information accessible to a nonspecialist audience. She will testify as an expert before various government committees and lobby on behalf of proposed legislation. The Task Force asks that she make a three-year commitment for 75 percent of her time, since they anticipate a prolonged fight with powerful corporate interests. Dr. Dunne could remain involved with her research during the remaining part of her time by collaborating with a colleague who is working at a research institution located in the same city as the Task Force.

At Broad River Chemical Company, Dr. Dunne will assume the directorship of the Research and Development Division. She will oversee a staff of ten scientists who are working on pollution prevention projects. Broad River wants her to take the lead in reporting to the public on the company's recent voluntary cleanup of a river that was polluted by a pesticide the company manufactures. This project is important to Broad River because it is trying to overcome an image of unconcern about the environment. Completion of existing projects will be Dr. Dunne's first priority, but she has also been assured of staff and facilities for her own research, which Broad River hopes to use in its own cleanup efforts and to sell to other chemical companies.

The city of Truron has received funding to build one hundred units of housing for elderly persons and has narrowed its decision about the placement of the project to two locations. Write an argument in support of one over the other, using the following guidelines:
- The town wants to maximize opportunities for elderly persons to be productive members of the community.
- The housing project must be located to give elderly residents access to needed services.

The first location is in an older, densely populated community on the fringes of the city's downtown area. Many of the city's elderly poor have spent their entire lives within this area. Some of them still work part time in area stores and restaurants as a result of a community action effort to hire retirees. The shops and services have deteriorated along with the housing and crime is increasing. The neighborhood Citizens' Association is lobbying the city to commit funds to improve these conditions. The Truron Hospital and several houses of worship can be accessed by bus services that crisscross this neighborhood.

The second location is on the southern edge of the city in a less densely populated residential neighborhood made up primarily of rowhouses. Due to the recently opened subway running through the neighborhood, it is in the early stages of revitalization and is beginning to attract young families. There is a new shopping mall that includes a bank and supermarket. Plans are underway to build a community center, including an adult day care center. The city's botanical gardens located in one corner of this neighborhood has tree garden plots for residents' use. In an effort to improve student achievement, two elementary schools in the neighborhood are initiating foster-grandparent programs to help staff after-school activities.

Broadhurst, faced with a substantial decrease in the city budget, must cut services in one area. Write an argument in favor of making the cuts in one of the following two areas, keeping in mind two guidelines:
- Broadhurst wants the cuts to defer spending in a way that will have minimal impact on the quality of services delivered.
- Broadhurst wants to avoid any negative publicity that could undermine the city government's reputation for effective management.

One way to cope with the budget cuts is to deny funding for the proposed plan to improve Broadhurst's emergency services. This plan was created after an article in the local newspaper charged that outdated equipment was causing problems and suggested that in one instance slow ambulance response may have been responsible for a person's death. A new director with a record of successfully improving services in another town was brought in to take over the emergency services. She has proposed a plan that calls for hiring three paramedics who are specially trained in using the most advanced equipment. The centerpiece of the plan is the purchase of a computerized dispatching system to improve response time, and a package to train existing staff to use the system.

The alternative is to make cuts in the public library's budget. This would require the library to reduce its staff by twenty percent, freeze salaries at their current level, and cut back evening and weekend hours substantially. Library officials fear that without salary increases some of their best employees are likely to leave. They are also concerned that these cuts would have a negative impact on the library's popularity, and so might undermine volunteer support for the library. Without the assistance of volunteers, the library would have to scale back some of its community outreach programs, such as the Books on Wheels program that serves residents unable to travel to the library.

The Clarksville school board is considering two plans to better its schools. Write an argument in favor of one of these plans over the other, keeping the following criteria in mind:
- Clarksville wants to improve the quality of instruction in its schools.
- Clarksville wants to reverse the growing trend of losing its best teachers to higher paying jobs in the private sector.

The Mentor Plan will be a cooperative project between Clarksville and the local university. School principals will identify their best teachers to serve as mentors to less experienced colleagues or those who have received poor evaluations from the principal. As preparation, the mentors will be paid to participate in a two-week summer institute under the direction of university faculty. Once assigned, the mentors will assist colleagues with approaches to teaching and the design of lesson plans, and will routinely observe classes. Mentors, who may serve for up to ten years, will receive a bonus of 5 percent of their annual salary and a reduced class load for each year they serve. In addition, each year mentors will lead faculty development workshops, some offering college credit, in conjunction with university faculty.

The Merit Plan centers on a pay system that includes merit pay rewards for successful teachers. Under this plan, all teachers, including new ones, will be observed and evaluated annually by members of the administration and a team of teachers from outside schools. A cash award of 10 percent of their yearly salary will be given to teachers who receive "outstanding" ratings. In addition, a series of in-service courses, designed to develop skills that reflect the criteria used to evaluate teachers, will be offered at no charge to participating teachers. Teachers who receive ratings of "excellent" or "outstanding" for three consecutive years will be offered more highly paid administrative positions with the school system.

Two million bottles of a popular medicine were labeled and priced to contain one hundred tablets but, in fact, contained only eighty tablets. The pharmaceutical manufacturer is considering two plans to rectify this error. Write an argument for one of them over the other, keeping the following guidelines in mind:
- The company wants to minimize its financial risks.
- The company wants to maintain its strong public image of dependability.

Under the Business Plan, the manufacturer will handle the matter through distributors and retail stores. The company will inform all distributors of the serial numbers on affected bottles. Distributors will be asked to instruct retail stores to return the defective bottles for credit and to place unobtrusive signs on the shelves where the pills are displayed stating that consumers may receive a full bottle from the store where the original was purchased by presenting the label with the serial number from the defective bottle. Store clerks will ask those making returns to fill out a form with their names and addresses, and the manufacturer will send a letter thanking them for their cooperation. Marketing analysts expect this plan to yield a low return rate.

The Public Awareness Plan calls for incorporating the packaging error into the manufacturer's existing television advertisement time slots. The new ad will open with a well-known personality who has an image of trustworthiness acknowledging the error and emphasizing that all companies make mistakes. This "public service announcement" stresses that the manufacturer is publicly admitting the error to reassure customers that the number of tablets in bottles currently available is now accurate. The ad ends with the company's guarantee of complete customer satisfaction. Consumers will be urged to send labels from defective bottles back to the manufacturer and will receive store coupons redeemable for a full bottle. Advertising will be costly, and the return rate is expected to be double that under the Business Plan.

Bill Benson, a single parent, must find a day care provider for his only child, two-year-old Rebecca. Bill works in a downtown office from 9:00 AM to 5:00 PM, though he is sometimes asked to work overtime. Write an argument in favor of one of the following two choices over the other. Two considerations guide your decision.
- The day care provider must be convenient to Bill's home or job and have hours that can accommodate Bill's work schedule.
- The day care provider must offer a stimulating and nurturing environment for Rebecca.

The Sunny Day Care Center is located in the basement of the building where Bill works, which is a thirty-minute commute from his apartment. The Center is directed by Leslie Hyde, an expert in child development, and generally has between fifteen and twenty preschool children of diverse backgrounds who are divided into three classes by age group. Sunny Day provides an elaborate array of art supplies, educational toys, and innovative playground equipment. The staff is composed of three recent graduates with degrees in early childhood education. Additionally each age group has a teacher's aide. Lunch is planned and prepared by a nutritionist. Sunny Day's hours are 8:30 AM to 5:30 PM.

Rachel Tepper, a thirty-five-year-old mother of two preschool children, runs a day care center in her home, which is a block from Bill's apartment. Author of several children's books, Ms. Tepper offers services for five neighborhood children, aged six months to five years, with the help of her sixty-year-old mother. She is licensed as a day care provider. Ms. Tepper's large backyard is filled with children's toys, many of them those her children share with the others, and a swing set. She and her mother prepare daily snacks and lunches for the five children. Her monthly fee is the same as Sunny Day's and includes a flexible range of hours between 7:00 AM and 7:00 PM.

Neil Jefferson, who is starting medical school in a large urban center, has found the search for affordable housing a difficult one. He has narrowed his choices to the following two. Write an argument for one of them over the other, keeping in mind these guidelines:
- Neil must keep his living expenses as low as possible, since he must take a part-time job to pay for them.
- Neil wants his living arrangements to be conducive to the studying that he anticipates will be required for success in medical school.

Two second-year medical students have invited Neil to be the fifth person in their group house. They now share the house with two people who work full-time, day jobs. A furnished rowhouse right in the city, it has two large bedrooms, one small bedroom, kitchen, living room, and dining room; the residents have fixed up part of the basement as a spare room. Neil will share a bedroom with one of the medical students. Rent is high, but split five ways it is manageable for Neil. The house is near a subway stop that is a fifteen-minute ride to the medical school. Neil thinks he can get a well-paying part-time job in City Hospital's emergency room, which is four blocks away.

Neil has found a two-bedroom, unfurnished apartment in a suburb outside the city. If he finds a roommate, his portion of the rent will be $150 per month less than what he would pay in the group house. The apartment has a small kitchen and living-dining area and is in the only apartment complex in a quiet, residential neighborhood. Neil could drive to medical school, but he has an old car that he wants to use as little as possible because it breaks down frequently. If he drives to the nearest subway stop and rides into the city, he will have about a one-hour commute each way. Part-time jobs are plentiful in area restaurants and stores, though they usually pay minimum wage.

Sam, a young jazz pianist, is deciding between two jobs. Write an argument for one over the other, keeping in mind the following criteria:
- Sam's long-term goal is to make a lasting contribution to the field of jazz.
- Sam wants to build up a following of dedicated listeners as quickly as possible.

One job offer is to play three nights per week in a hotel in the city where Sam lives. He will be providing background music in the lounge. Although he will be expected to take requests from the patrons; he will be free to develop his own repertoire and program. Sam will initially perform during a two-month trial period; if response is favorable, he will receive a one-year contract. This luxurious hotel, which has guests from all over the world, is well known among musicians because of a famous pianist who got his start there in the 1950s. With this job, Sam will be able to continue his teaching: he has a number of private students and is a part-time faculty member at a local university. The teaching and performing income will enable Sam to live comfortably.

The other job is a one-year contract to go on the road as part of a jazz trio. The group, known for its jazz interpretations of popular songs, has recorded two albums. The other two members of this group have been together for six years and recently lost their piano player when she left to try a solo career. The group will play in a variety of settings—some private parties for individuals and professional organizations, some at fund-raising benefits, and others at small nightclubs. To work with the group, Sam must be familiar with a wide range of music and styles, many new to him. As the junior member, he might be called upon to do some local promotional work and to serve as emcee during performances. The wages for this job are high enough to support Sam.

The Norton Community Travel Club is considering two travel packages for its annual summer vacation trip. Write an argument for selecting one trip over the other, keeping two guidelines in mind:
- The club is committed to serving the needs and interests of its membership, drawn from a retirement community and a subdivision of moderately priced homes.
- Club members are eager to keep costs down as much as possible.

Worldwide Travel Agency has offered a two-week guided tour of three South American countries. The group will travel together in an air-conditioned bus and stop at major attractions. All members will be expected to be packed and ready to leave each morning at a designated time. Round-trip airfare, meals, and accommodations are included in the price of the trip. While serviceable, the accommodations are not first-class; first-class accommodations are available to those who pay an additional fee. Worldwide is an experienced travel agency that has been running this particular tour for fifteen years. The agency has a reputation for knowledgeable, personable tour guides.

For the same price, Leisure Tours has offered a three-week trip to three major South American cities. Included in the fee will be round-trip airfare, airfare to each of the three cities, and a shared room in highly rated hotels; the cost of meals is not included in the price. On the first day of each stop, Leisure Tours schedules a guided tour of the city, and provides brochures and maps and offers suggestions for those wishing to take side trips. Otherwise, there are no planned activities. Leisure Tours, a relatively new company, recently received an award for superior service from the Association of Business Executives. Leisure Tour's president is a well-known travel writer.

The Adamsville School Board recently voted to establish a health education center for adolescents. Write an argument supporting one of the two plans, which are comparable in cost, over the other. Two criteria influence your decision:
- The center must offer health education to the town's teenage population.
- The center must be able to attract a student clientele large enough to justify its cost.

The school plan calls for locating the center in the basement of the town's high school. The school system will hire a nurse practitioner to staff the center during its regular weekday hours: two hours each morning, one hour during lunch break, and another hour after school. One of the school's guidance counselors proposes to lead small group discussions one afternoon per week on a variety of topics of interest to adolescents and to enlist medical professionals to volunteer at the center. So far, two physicians from the community, who direct a successful drug and alcohol awareness program, will lead a series of workshops at the center.

In the community plan, the school system will rent space in the downtown Community Activities Building, a twenty-minute bus ride from the high school. Two professionals will be available to staff the center's regular hours, after school on Tuesday and Thursday and all day Saturday. The first professional is a social worker who plans to offer weekly workshops on teenagers and sexuality. He will also train teenage volunteers as peer counselors and develop a teen hotline run from the Activities Building on weekends. The second professional will be a medical resident assigned as part of the physician training program at City Hospital.

Joe and Janet Wilson want to open a restaurant in Clearmont, a city of about a million people. The restaurant would feature country French cooking. The Wilsons are considering the two locations described below. Using the following guidelines, write an argument in favor of one of the locations:

- The Wilsons have only a modest amount of capital to start their restaurant and therefore need to generate income fairly quickly.
- The Wilsons want the restaurant to be distinctive enough to attract a steady clientele.

The Wilsons could take a five-year lease, at $1,200 per month, on a storefront property on Main Street in Clearmont's theater district. Within ten blocks are four theaters, three movie houses, and ten other restaurants. Only one of the ten restaurants serves French food. The Wilsons have spoken with the owner of the French restaurant and it appears to be doing well financially. The space they are considering has an exterior like any other plate-glass storefront and an interior of one large room. The Wilsons would like to have an outdoor cafe, and the sidewalk is wide enough to accommodate a dozen outside tables. Parking is a problem, but there is plenty of public transportation. Because of its downtown location, the restaurant should have no trouble attracting a first-class kitchen and serving staff.

The Wilsons could also take a three-year lease, at $900 per month, on a charming farmhouse fifteen kilometers from downtown Clearmont, with an option to buy the property. There are lovely views and adequate parking, but no area available for outdoor tables. During peak rush hours, getting from Clearmont to the expressway that goes near the farmhouse can be slow, but at other times it is a quick and direct drive to this location. The area around the farmhouse is largely undeveloped, but it is beginning to attract antique and specialty craft shops. There is only one other nearby restaurant and it caters to vegetarians. The Wilsons could have a large garden and grow their own herbs, vegetables, and flowers. If the Wilsons choose this site, a local food critic, who writes a weekly column in the newspaper, is interested in joining them in a partnership.

A law school in the town of Brighton plans to offer an elective course on insurance liability. Write an argument for the selection of one of the following candidates to teach the course. The following two considerations provide the context for your decision:

- The school wants to maintain its reputation for an impressive faculty of teacher-practitioners.
- The school placement office is trying to develop stronger ties with the local business community in order to assist the large number of graduates who want to secure jobs in Brighton.

Joseph Heath is a partner in Brighton's small but prestigious firm of Barrow, Heath, and Harriman. He has taught at three law schools over the past 25 years. He has written extensively in his major field of labor law. While he has never taught a course on insurance, he has long had an interest in the subject and, during the last year, he has worked on two medical malpractice suits for his firm. Heath is a member of the city council and is active in the local bar association.

George Cole has run his own insurance agency in Brighton for 20 years. He is a very successful businessman and known to be an expert in liability insurance. Cole has never taught in an academic setting, but he is often invited to speak at professional conferences. Recently, he delivered a popular series of consumer education workshops on liability insurance. Cole is known by those who have done business with him as an excellent communicator. Once a mayoral candidate, he is the past president of the Better Business Bureau and a popular leader in community activities.

The Krypton Corporation, an international computer company, has agreed to fund a ten-week course intended to improve the writing skills of its midlevel managers. There are two proposals for this course under consideration. You are to write an argument supporting one of them. The following factors should be taken into consideration:

- Krypton Corporation expects a final report on the course with a demonstration of measurable improvements in each participant's writing.
- Krypton Corporation wants the course to be conducted in the spirit of its Employee Continuing Education Program which is committed "not just to the worker, but to the whole person."

Springville University's Graduate College has proposed a course that will combine traditional expository writing with applications specific to business. The theme will be "Managers as Communicators." Working with consultants from the University's business school, professors of English will focus on practice in writing memoranda, abstracts, reports, and customer letters, as well as practice in other standard forms and formats of business writing. Class time will be divided between lecture and discussion. The course will use a popular textbook on business and technical writing that includes examples of various types of writing from actual business situations. The professors will write critiques of the four or five writing assignments that each student submits during the course.

The Writers' Cooperative of Springville has proposed a course that will be taught by published fiction writers. At each meeting, participants in the course will write an assignment addressing three specific techniques of fiction: detailed description, characterization, and scene setting. The emphasis will be on style and presentation and their effects on readers. A textbook of short stories and interviews with the authors of those stories about their writing will encourage each student to analyze his or her own process of writing and to compare it with that of his or her colleagues. Class time will be spent in group discussions of each student's work, with the instructor acting as collaborator and respondent. Throughout the course, students will be drafting an original short story and sharing parts of it with others in the class. The instructor will write critiques on the finished stories submitted at the end of the course.

Write an argument for the selection of one of the proposed sites for the Makefield Public Library. An allocation of $2 million has been provided for this project with the stipulation that any funds remaining after purchase and preparation of the building will be used to expand the library's limited services. The following factors should also be taken into consideration:
- The library is expected to support Makefield's efforts to upgrade the education of its citizenry.
- The library building should serve as a community meeting place.

The Sutter Avenue site is a three-story building two blocks from the current library. It once housed the city's first bank, the oldest banking facility in the region, and it has been recognized as an architectural and historical landmark. The site is in the heart of the business district. Parking facilities are few and expensive during the day and only slightly better after 7 P.M. Public transportation does, however, make the site accessible to suburban and downtown neighborhoods, including Makefield's Center for Adult Literacy. The building has nearly twice the floor space of the current library, making it sufficiently large to accommodate expansion of the current collection and to have both classrooms and meeting rooms. Since the building is in serious disrepair, the estimated cost for purchase and renovation is $2 million.

The Hillside Mall site, two miles from the current library, was formerly occupied by Bell's Department Store. It is convenient by car to all suburban neighborhoods and has abundant parking. A stop for buses serving the downtown and outlying residential areas is four blocks away; this stop also serves a popular suburban campus of the area community college, which has a continuing education program. The building has only slightly more floor space than the current library. A modular design is proposed to convert the large basement storage area into a space that can be arranged and rearranged into classrooms, study carrels, or two large meeting rooms. The estimated cost to purchase the building, install shelving and modular dividers, and buy library furnishings is $1.8 million. The remaining $200,000 will be used at the discretion of the library board.

Napier University must decide to grant tenure to one of two candidates in the economics department. Write an argument supporting one over the other. Two considerations guide your decision:
- The tenure committee has traditionally granted tenure on the basis of scholarship and service to the academic community.
- The tenure committee must take into account the administration's recent recommendation that teaching ability be weighed heavily in tenure decisions.

Professor Morgan is widely respected as a scholar and has published five books and many scholarly articles on a variety of topics, though her area of specialization is the domestic impact of economic globalization. She also writes a monthly column for a prominent business magazine. The applications to Napier's graduate program in economics have increased since Morgan joined the faculty four years ago. Morgan is a familiar figure on the academic lecture circuit and spends about three months per year at other campuses throughout the world. A large part of her teaching consists of directing the independent research studies of graduate students. These graduate students do most of the teaching in her undergraduate courses, though she makes a point of lecturing to each undergraduate class several times a term.

Professor Lewis, a member of the economics department for five years, teaches year-round and meets informally with students several times a week. He has published five scholarly articles, and his manuscript for a book on the pension system was well-received by members of the department and has been accepted for publication by an academic press. He is one of the few members of his department who volunteers to teach the introductory economics course; he says that he enjoys devising ways to present the rather difficult material to a general audience. At Napier, his dynamic presentations draw crowds of students. He has won the teacher-of-the-year award for two consecutive years. His colleagues respect him as a "talented individual who is committed to his students."

Gail has inherited $50,000 from her uncle. This money is a windfall to Gail, who has worked as an assistant photographer in the graphics department of a retail store for the past three years. She is considering two plans for the money. Write an essay in support of one plan over the other. Two considerations should guide your decision:
- Gail wants to use the $50,000 for her long-term benefit.
- The $50,000 must cover the entire cost of the plan she chooses since Gail has no appreciable savings of her own.

Gail is considering buying a house in a changing part of town. Fashionable 25 years ago, this area, near the downtown business district, has been in decline for some time. In the past few years, however, a prominent developer has turned several apartment houses into condominiums, and private owners have begun restoring some of the larger old homes to their former elegance. More modest townhouses are still within Gail's price range, and she has found one she likes. With the inheritance, she can afford a down payment that would leave her monthly mortgage payments only slightly higher than the rent on her current apartment. Although it is livable, the house needs considerable work. Gail can do much of the carpentry herself, and she can generate sufficient income to pay for plumbing and electrical repairs by renting out the second bedroom. Should interest rates remain stable and the neighborhood redevelopment continue, the value of the house will increase substantially in the next five years.

Gail is also considering using the inheritance to realize her dream of opening her own commercial photography business. The inheritance would be adequate to cover her living expenses for nearly one year, to cover the cost of renting space for a darkroom and small office, and to pay for basic equipment. She believes she can count on her present employer for some freelance work, and she has enough contacts to provide sufficient work to sustain her for another six months. In addition to her current job experience, Gail has exhibited her photographs in local galleries. She wants to work for advertising firms or private businesses, although she is willing to do weddings or portraits to earn extra income at the outset. Her ultimate goal is to build up a clientele that will support a profitable five- or six-person business.

The Spann Foundation has been named executor of the estate of Morgan Brody, a famous novelist. Two persons have petitioned for sole access to all of Brody's manuscripts and personal papers in order to write his biography. Write an argument in favor of one of the two writers based on the following guidelines:
- The Foundation expects to balance its precarious budget by realizing a quarter of the profits from the biography's sales.
- The Foundation, proud of its reputation for authorizing serious and scholarly work, wants to encourage other artists to will their personal papers to the Spann Foundation.

Maribelle Hartness, professor of literature at a highly prestigious university, has written two books: a critical study of modern poetry and a biography of an obscure novelist. Although the biography won a critics' award fifteen years ago, it is now out of print. An academic press has already agreed to publish Hartness's biography of Brody, if she gets access to the manuscripts and papers. Hartness envisions the book as the definitive Brody biography (approximately 800 pages), including a thorough record of the novelist's life as well as critical interpretations of his novels. Hartness's previous books sold respectably for books of their type, although none was issued in paperback. Since Brody was a famous and colorful literary figure, Hartness expects her biography of Brody to be a popular success.

Felton Seltzer is a best selling author of historical novels. Although the covers of his books can be described as "sensational," Seltzer maintains their historical authenticity by using the standard research methods he learned while earning his M.A. in history from a prestigious university. His Master's thesis, the only nonfiction Seltzer has written, was published by a small press and sold well. He maintains that writing biographies and constructing historical novels call upon the same skills. He promises to tone down his somewhat flamboyant style while still retaining his masterful storytelling techniques. Seltzer may have more than a professional interest in the project because of his twenty-year marriage to Brody's daughter.

Susan, a 26-year-old bank teller, wants to return to school for an undergraduate degree in business. She must decide whether to enter the university in her city immediately or to begin at a nearby community college. She must keep her job to cover tuition costs, which are comparable at the two schools. Both schools are an easy commute from Susan's home and work. Write an argument for the choice you think Susan should make. Two considerations should influence your decision:
- Susan, who went to work as soon as she finished high school, will need some help adjusting to her new role as a student.
- Susan wants the degree in business to be a direct route to career advancement.

The community college is a two-year school known for its small, informal classes where students and teachers get to know one another. While the community college has a full-time faculty, many instructors are practitioners from the community; for example, a partner in one of the area's largest accounting firms teaches *Principles of Accounting*. The average student age at the community college is 28. Since the majority of students work between 25 and 30 hours a week, the school offers a flexible class schedule including many evening and several weekend courses. Susan can earn a degree with an area of concentration in business. While most of the credits from her general requirement courses can be transferred to the university, she will be able to transfer only a few of those from business courses.

The university serves the large metropolitan area where Susan lives. The majority of the entering students are recent high school graduates, and they are full-time students. Classes for most of the general requirement courses are large. The university boasts a faculty of well-respected scholars. To increase enrollment, two years ago the school initiated an adult continuing education program. At the start of each semester, this program offers noncredit workshops in time management and effective study habits. The degree in business at the university stresses executive management. All business majors participate in a one semester internship program with a local business during the year.

Township School District has received a grant to fund an introductory course in computer training for high school students. Write an argument for selecting one of the proposals over the other. Two considerations influence your decision:
- The introductory course should prepare students for university level computer courses.
- The introductory course should provide students with skills to enter the community's growing job market in data and word processing.

Proposal A, open to all students, would provide an introduction to the computer system used at the regional medical complex. Students would learn how the medical complex uses the computer system as a problem-solving tool in everything from admissions to personnel to management planning. As part of the course, each student would spend one day working with one of the data-entry operators in the billing department. When the medical complex completes the expansion of its computer systems, there will be many entry-level openings for computer operators. A professor in the data-processing department at the local community college has agreed to team-teach this course with the director of the computer system at the medical complex.

Proposal B would be open to only 60% of the students because it would require completion of two years of algebra. Proposal B would introduce students to the computer programming curriculum at the local community college and would provide one credit toward the community college's two-year course of study in data processing. It would include sessions on such topics as data-filing systems and computer graphics. Students would write simple programs in a state-of-the-art computer language, and they would have the opportunity to use several popular word processing programs. Two faculty members from Township School District, who have taken graduate courses in computer programming, would teach the course.

Ellen Houlihan must choose between two job offers. Write an argument in favor of one of the two, taking into account the following guidelines:
- Ellen, a recent graduate of journalism school, is concerned about repaying her student loans.
- Ellen's career goal is to have a column in a major newspaper.

The Herald, the only daily paper in a small town, has offered Ellen a job as a reporter. According to its editor, her initial responsibility would be writing about local politics, including school board activities, city elections, and tax assessments. Ellen would have sole responsibility for the focus of her assigned stories and would have the opportunity to develop other stories on her own. Because of its small staff, journalists for *The Herald* are expected to move into positions of responsibility quickly. The editor of *The Herald* was formerly London Bureau Chief of the Associated Press and has gone into semiretirement to run this small town newspaper. *The Herald* can pay Ellen only a modest salary, but the cost of living in the town is low and a modest salary will be more than enough to cover her living expenses.

The Sun Journal, one of two daily newspapers in a major city, has offered Ellen a job on its metropolitan desk. The entry-level job involves more fact checking and research than actual reporting. Promotion to staff writer, which usually takes 12 to 18 months, is a reward for hard work and perseverance. At the staff writer level, there are many reporters and competition for the best assignments is fierce. Ellen's first assignment at that level would likely be to the police beat, covering local crime. It would probably be five years or so before she would be covering stories that are picked up by the news services, such as profiles of prominent people in business and government. The cost of living in the city is high and Ellen will have to budget carefully if she is to cover her living expenses.

A bank in a small farming town is deciding which of the following loan requests for $20,000 to grant. Both applicants can meet the bank's repayment terms. Write an argument supporting one of the requests. Two considerations guide your decision:
- The bank is committed to maintaining the agricultural base of the community.
- The bank wants to make loans to stabilize the depressed economy of the town.

The first applicant is Ed Welch, a young farmer who lives on the outskirts of town. Several years ago, Welch inherited his father's prosperous farm. He and his family now raise wheat, barley, and some livestock. Poor market conditions have made it difficult for Welch to make a profit, and consequently, the farm has become rundown. He wants the loan to purchase some new equipment and to repair his barn. Without the loan, he must lower his level of production to bare subsistence. Welch was recently elected to the town council on a campaign centered on the importance of supporting the small farmer. He has called attention to himself as an example of the sturdy tradition that built the community but that is now threatened.

The second applicant, Eli Hinton, wants to open a low-cost day care center. His business plan points out that the day care center not only will allow parents from farm families with small children to take on needed part-time jobs, but will also encourage new industry in town by freeing up a significant labor force. Hinton proposes a center that would accept toddlers and would offer an after-school program for elementary school children. There is another day care center in a church basement, open only in the mornings and with fairly high fees. Hinton, a retired schoolteacher, has located a building and identified two people interested in working in the center. By proposing a high-volume operation and taking advantage of some government grants, he intends to keep the rates within reach of the salaries his clients are likely to earn.

A committee in the town of Stony Creek has decided to commission a sculpture to commemorate 20 miners who died in a mining cave-in. Two designs for a sculpture have been submitted. Write an argument in favor of either the Hadley or the Peters sculpture based on the following information. Two criteria are relevant to your decision:
- The committee wants the townspeople to feel a special affinity for the sculpture.
- The committee would like the artistic merit of the sculpture to attract national attention.

Anne Hadley is a sculptor who has lived in Paris for the past 15 years. She grew up in Stony Creek, where both her grandfathers were miners, and she continues to visit her family there once or twice a year. Hadley's abstract sculptures have been purchased by museums throughout the world. The design she has submitted to Stony Creek consists of several intersecting and twisting arcs of steel. Hadley states that the sculpture will "suggest open spaces versus entrapment." The sculpture will be constructed to double as climbing bars and slides for children in order to show, according to Hadley, "that joy exists alongside tragedy."

Toni Peters has no personal ties to Stony Creek or to mining. She is not as well-known among art critics as Hadley, but she has sold several sculptures for display in public spaces. All the sculptures have been well received by the public. Recently, the local chapter of a labor union bought one of her works for the lobby of its headquarters building. That particular work is part of a series she is planning called "People at Work." Peters wants the sculpture she has proposed for Stony Creek to be an important part of that series. The design she has submitted calls for a sculpture of two miners chiseled in rough stone to suggest the harsh realities of life in the mines.

Despite being identified by school psychologists as a "gifted child," Angie Harrison has been experiencing problems in the fifth grade. After meeting with school staff, Angie's parents are considering the two courses of action described below. Write an argument explaining why you would advise them to choose one over the other. The following two points should guide you:

- Angie's parents want her to have the opportunity to achieve her full potential.
- Angie's parents want her to develop a healthy self-image that reflects her understanding of her role and responsibilities in her school community.

One option is for Angie to skip the sixth grade and go directly into Whitman Junior High School. Angie's grades have been poor the last two years. Her fifth grade teachers report that she has many friends, is an enthusiastic player on the school's softball team, and is an active participant in the school theater club. Yet she rarely participates in class, frequently neglects assignments, and generally seems bored by her courses. Whitman is considered a good school and has a special program for gifted children. Class sizes range from 30 to 40 students. Whitman places a premium on achievement and reinforces this value with scholastic and extracurricular awards. A"C" average in the core curriculum courses is required for participation in sports and other activities.

The other option is for Angie to enter the sixth grade at Spark Academy, a school for grades 6 through 8. It is located in another community, and Angie would have to commute on the school's bus. With a total student body of 300, Spark tailors its curriculum to the interests and talents of its students. Although a basic curriculum is required of everyone, teachers work with students to develop individual and small group projects that encourage in-depth study of each student's special interests. Spark recently received favorable publicity in local newspapers for its efforts to match teaching methods with its pupils' individual learning styles. Spark does not have a theater club and is just beginning to develop a sports program that does not include softball.

Hughes and Michaels are both applicants for a job as a math teacher in a public high school. Write an argument for hiring either Hughes or Michaels based on the following criteria:

- The high school is trying to upgrade its math program, primarily through the use of computers.
- The high school is searching for a teacher who can develop a math program that effectively combines the curriculum with a work-study project with the local business community.

Hughes maintained a high grade point average throughout her undergraduate and graduate education. She attended a local university for her bachelor's degree in math and moved on to a prestigious program at a large university for her master's degree in education. In addition to her work as a teaching assistant while in graduate school, she has taught at the high school level for six years. She has enjoyed a reputation as a good teacher and as an effective sponsor of various extracurricular activities in the three schools in which she has taught. She left each of her three teaching jobs to seek greater professional opportunity. In her last position, she chaired a department of five full-time math faculty. The principal or division supervisor in each of the three schools has given her a favorable reference. In the last three years, she has completed a series of courses to strengthen her knowledge of computers.

Michaels earned a bachelor's degree with honors in math education and a master's degree in economics from an internationally known research institution. Although she served as a teaching assistant in graduate school, she has never taught full time. She spent three years after graduate school as an assistant budget director of a retail store. During the past ten years, she has worked as a financial analyst in a local bank, where she also has headed the computer training program for new employees. She has received several promotions in her job at the bank, but recently has found the stress and competition increasingly dissatisfying. Two years ago Michaels volunteered to work as a tutor in a community outreach program designed to combat math anxiety. She has found the work both satisfying and exciting and has decided to change to teaching as a full-time profession.

Write an argument in support of purchasing one of the following two films for a public interest program on a local television station. Both address the growing problem of homelessness. Since costs are comparable, two other considerations should guide your decision:

- The station wants to expand and diversify its viewing audience.
- The station wants to retain its reputation for serious journalism.

No Place Like Home is an hour black-and-white documentary that explores the issue of homeless people in the modern city. This film received favorable reviews when shown in several major cities. No Place Like Home contains narrated documentary footage and brief interviews with street people of every possible description in a variety of urban settings. There are also interviews with federal and local agency officials discussing economic and social causes of homelessness. No Place Like Home is an informative, eye-opening and well-paced overview of a serious social problem.

Marilyn: Portrait of a Homeless Woman is a half-hour color movie that dramatically portrays the life of Marilyn Jenks. Named after Marilyn Monroe, she left her home in a farming community in search of big-city glamour. While in her teens, Marilyn enjoyed astonishing success in the entertainment industry, but mental instability ended her career and she spent the next twenty years living on the streets. Her recent recovery was an international news story. The film stars a well-known actress who is outspoken on the issue of homelessness. The result is a moving portrayal of the realities of homelessness.

The residents of five small rural communities will soon be voting on a proposal to form one consolidated high school. Write an argument explaining whether you would vote for the consolidation or to maintain the local schools. Two considerations should guide your decision:
- Each community must cope with the financial implications of a steadily, if slowly, increasing student population.
- Each community wants to enhance its students' chances for admission to a university.

Present costs for running each of the local schools are relatively steady and manageable for the individual communities. The small budgets, however, have kept teachers' salaries so low that, in the last three years, several of the best teachers have left for higher paying jobs. The enrollment of each school is small, and class sizes range from 15 to 20 students. All five schools offer a similar standard curriculum of math, science, language arts, and social studies and a few electives such as industrial arts and music. Each school encourages students to participate in extracurricular activities and sports. Each school has a basketball, football, and lacrosse team. A strong sense of community pride characterizes each school and promotes, among other things, a healthy rivalry among sports teams. The five schools have a good record for admission to well-respected universities in the region.

The consolidated high school requires either a new building or major renovations and additions to the largest, most centrally located of the five local schools. The consolidated school would duplicate the standard core curriculum of the five local schools, but would offer a wider range of electives, such as photography and public speaking. It would have a science center with modern lab facilities. The sports and extracurricular programs would be expanded to include tennis, soccer, and gymnastics. Sports and scholastic competition with other schools would involve considerable travel. By consolidating core classes and facilities, the new school could offer higher teacher salaries. The consolidation would, at the same time, necessitate a reduction in the number of teachers.

The town of Rockburg has received two similarly priced offers to develop the site of an old schoolhouse located on the outskirts of town. Write an argument in favor of selecting one proposal over the other. Two considerations should influence your decision:
- Rockburg is trying to preserve its small town character.
- Rockburg is committed to attracting jobs and dollars to alleviate the economic slump the town has been experiencing the past few years.

Chemco, Inc. a manufacturer of chemical solvents, proposes to raze the old schoolhouse building and construct a small factory. It would employ 75 residents with an annual payroll of $2 million. Chemco proposes to design an attractive building that fits in with the local architecture. A similar Chemco plant in Mexico recently had a serious fire that damaged surrounding property. Also, the chemical process used by Chemco produces an unpleasant odor. Chemco has agreed to install sophisticated fire prevention equipment and claims to have a new method of removing the offensive gas from the plant's emissions.

Tracol Restaurants proposes to restore the existing school building and open a gourmet restaurant along with several specialty shops. Tracol Restaurants are popular throughout nearby states, and this would be the first one in the area. The restaurant and shops would employ about 25 people with an annual payroll of $500,000. The preservation of the old building, the first school in the region, would create a historical landmark. The complex is expected to attract a large number of shoppers and visitors to the town.

CATALOG OF
LSAT Preparation Tools and

Everything on these pages can be ordered by telephone (215.968.1001) if you have a valid VISA, MasterCard, DISCOVER, or American Express credit card, or via the LSAT/LSDAS Registration Form or Publications Order Form in this book. Please allow 2-3 weeks for delivery.

The Official LSAT Prep Series

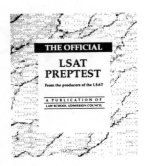

PrepTests — $6 each (plus postage and handling)

- PrepTest XI — June 1994 LSAT, (Publication Code 111)
- PrepTest XII — Oct. 1994 LSAT, (Publication Code 112)
- PrepTest XIII — Dec. 1994 LSAT, (Publication Code 113)
- PrepTest XIV — Feb. 1995 LSAT, available mid-March 1995 (Publication Code 114)
- PrepTest XV — June 1995 LSAT, available mid-July 1995 (Publication Code 115)
- PrepTest XVI — Sept. 1995 LSAT, available mid-November 1995 (Publication Code 116)
- PrepTest XVII — Dec. 1995 LSAT, available mid-January 1996 (Publication Code 117)
- PrepTest XVIII — Dec. 1992 LSAT, newly disclosed and available now (Publication Code 118)

Each PrepTest is an actual LSAT administered on the date indicated. You can practice as if you're taking an actual test by following the test-taking instructions and timing yourself. In addition to actual LSAT questions, each PrepTest contains an answer key, writing sample, and score-conversion table.

LSAT: The Official TriplePrep—Volume 1 — $14 (plus postage and handling)

Three PrepTests provide more practice than one, and buying three together in one book costs less than buying them separately. TriplePrep—Volume 1 contains PrepTests II, IV, and V, all actual LSATs. TriplePrep contains answer keys, writing samples, and score-conversion tables for all three PrepTests. (Publication Code 206)

LSAT: The Official TriplePrep—Volume 2 — $14 (plus postage and handling)

TriplePrep—Volume 2 contains PrepTests III, VI, and VII. (Publication Code 207)

LSAT: The Official TriplePrep—Volume 3 — $14 (plus postage and handling)

TriplePrep—Volume 3 contains PrepTests VIII, IX, and X. (Publication Code 208)

LSAT: The Official TriplePrep *Plus* with Explanations—$16 (plus postage and handling)

This is the only official LSAT product that contains **explanations** for all three LSAT-item types. TriplePrep *Plus* also contains 50 previously administered writing sample prompts in addition to three complete PrepTests—XI, XII, XIII. These PrepTests are also sold separately (see above). (Publication Code 209)

Legal Education Books

The Official Guide to U.S. Law Schools — $15 (plus postage and handling)

Where can you find a listing of all 177 American Bar Association (ABA)-approved law schools in the United States? Right here. This is the only law school guide that includes up-to-date admission profiles and program descriptions provided by the schools themselves. Each school describes its facilities, student body, and activities. Each profile also contains admission requirements and facts about tuition and financial aid. (Publication Code 001)

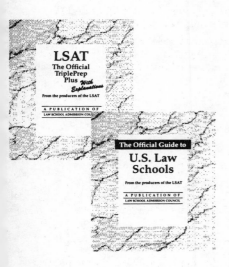

The Whole Law School Package

TriplePrep *Plus* <u>and</u> The Official Guide to U.S. Law Schools (1996 Edition) — $28 (plus postage and handling)

With this one package you can prepare for the LSAT and find the most accurate and up-to-date information about all 177 ABA-approved law schools. Save money by buying the two books together. (Publication Code 210)

So You Want to be a Lawyer: A Practical Guide — $11 (plus postage and handling)

How do you choose a law school, and how do you get a law school to choose you? This book contains answers to all your questions on how to apply and how to make your application stand out amid the competition. Learn what a law school admission committee considers from an insider's point of view. This book can save you time and money by showing you how to identify what you *should* be looking for in a law school, and which ones may be looking for someone like you. Match your qualifications with the law school that is best for you. It's easy to do using *So You Want to be a Lawyer: A Practical Guide.* (Publication Code 002)

Thinking About Law School: A Minority Guide — No Charge

This publication advises minority applicants about the legal profession and the requirements for admission to law school. This book includes profiles of successful minority lawyers, as well as statistics on law school admission for various minority groups. (Publication Code 004)

Financial Aid for Law School: A Preliminary Guide — No Charge

This brochure will help you to get started on your quest for financial aid. (Publication Code 003)

Postage and handling table is located on the Publications Order Form or the LSAT/LSDAS Registration Form.

Law Services Publications Order Form

Please do not duplicate your order on this form if you ordered publications on the LSAT/LSDAS Registration Form.
Publication prices do not include postage and handling, which must be added before totalling your order. See table below.

Publication Code

001 The Official Guide to U.S. Law Schools (1996 Edition)

order: _____ copies at $15 ea. = $ _____

002 So You Want to be a Lawyer: A Practical Guide

order: _____ copies at $11 ea. = $ _____

111 The Official LSAT PrepTest XI (June 1994 LSAT)

order: _____ copies at $6 ea. = $ _____

112 The Official LSAT PrepTest XII (Oct. 1994 LSAT)

order: _____ copies at $6 ea. = $ _____

113 The Official LSAT PrepTest XIII (Dec. 1994 LSAT)

order: _____ copies at $6 ea. = $ _____

114 The Official LSAT PrepTest XIV (Feb. 1995 LSAT)

order: _____ copies at $6 ea. = $ _____

115 The Official LSAT PrepTest XV
(June 1995 LSAT; available mid-July 1995)

order: _____ copies at $6 ea. = $ _____

116 The Official LSAT PrepTest XVI
(Sept. 1995 LSAT; available mid-Nov. 1995)

order: _____ copies at $6 ea. = $ _____

117 The Official LSAT PrepTest XVII
(Dec. 1995 LSAT; available mid-Jan. 1996)

order: _____ copies at $6 ea. = $ _____

113 The Official LSAT PrepTest XVIII
(Dec. 1992 LSAT; previously undisclosed, available now)

order: _____ copies at $6 ea. = $ _____

Publication Code

206 LSAT: The Official TriplePrep—Volume 1
(contains PrepTests II, IV, and V)

order: _____ copies at $6 ea. = $ _____

207 LSAT: The Official TriplePrep—Volume 2
(contains PrepTests III, VI, and VII)

order: _____ copies at $14 ea. = $ _____

208 LSAT: The Official TriplePrep—Volume 3
(contains PrepTests VIII, IX, and X)

order: _____ copies at $14 ea. = $ _____

209 LSAT: The Official TriplePrep *Plus* (contains PrepTests XI, XII, and XIII, plus explanations and extra writing samples)

order: _____ copies at $16 ea. = $ _____

210 The Whole Law School Package: TriplePrep *Plus*
and The Official Guide to U.S. Law Schools (1996 Edition)

order: _____ copies at $28 ea. = $ _____

003 Financial Aid for Law School: A Preliminary Guide
check here to order [ ] **No Charge**

004 Thinking About Law School: A Minority Guide
check here to order [ ] **No Charge**

000 LSAT/LSDAS Registration and Information Book
check here to order [ ] **No Charge**

Publications Fees $ _____

Postage & Handling (see table below)+ $ _____

Publications Subtotal= $ _____

PA residents must add 6% sales tax
to the Publications Subtotal **Tax+** $ _____

Total (U.S. Dollars)= $ _____

Postage & Handling	
If your subtotal is:	Add:
$ 6.00 - $12.00	$2.50
$12.01 - $28.00	$3.50
$28.01 - $48.00	$5.00
$48.01 or more	$7.00

Be sure to complete other side.

Law Services Publications Order Form

Name Last

First (Given)   **M.I.**

Mailing Address (Be sure to include apartment number, if applicable.)

Mailing Address-continued

City

State/Prov.   **Zip/Postal Code**

Social Security/Social Insurance Number

This number is used for identification purposes only. It ensures accurate and timely processing of your order and facilitates record retrieval.

Date of Birth—Month/Day/Year

Telephone Number During the Day

Mail to: Law Services
              Box 2400
              Newtown, PA 18940-0977

Remittance—Do not send cash.

Note: Incorrect payments may delay the processing of your order.

If you have a fee waiver for the TriplePrep *Plus*, be sure to include it with this form.

☐ Enclosed is my check or money order in U.S. dollars made payable to Law Services for

           $ _____
                       U. S. Dollars

or charge this amount to my   VISA ☐   MasterCard ☐

                              DISCOVER ☐   American Express ☐

                              (check one)

Account #

Month   Year   Signature
Expiration Date

Note: If you have a VISA, MasterCard, DISCOVER, or American Express credit card, you may also call in your order to 215.968.1001 (refer to the publication code for each publication).

Please allow 2 to 3 weeks for delivery.
Fees are subject to change.
All publication sales are final.

For Law Services use only

K